Organizations at the Intersections of Place

Relationships, Principles, and Dimensions of Place Building

EDITED BY: DAVID F. THOMAS / JAMES H. BANNING

Organizations
at the
Intersections
of Place

David Thomas & James Banning© 2017

Email: David@placebuilding.net

Website: www.placebuilding.net

All rights reserved. No part of this publication may be reproduced, stored in a retrieval system, or transmitted in any form or by any means—electronic, mechanical, photocopy, recording, or any other without the prior permission of the author.

ISBN-13: 978-0-9977353-5-2

ISBN-10: 0-9977353-5-X

Library of Congress Control Number: 2017944225

Printed in the United States of America

Cover Designer: Dawood Suleman, Fort Collins, CO

Typesetter: Michelle Kenny, Windsor, CO

PLACE IS MORE THAN A LOCATION FOR AN ORGANIZATION OR COMMUNITY, BUT, RATHER PLACE IS THE SEAM OF CONNECTEDNESS AND INTERSECTIONS BETWEEN AN ORGANIZATION AND ITS COMMUNITY.

WE EXPLORE THE MANY FORMS OF THIS CONNECTING AND INTERSECTING SEAM—PLACE.

TABLE OF CONTENTS

PART ONE: INTRODUCTION

Acknowledgements _____ xi

An Introductory Note _____ xiii

Chapter 1

Editor's Introduction: Organizational Place Building _____ 1
D. F. Thomas & J. H. Banning

    Organizational Place Building _____ 1

    Organizational Place: Connections and Intersections ___ 9

Introduction to the Readings _____ 10

PART TWO: READINGS

Chapter 2

Organizations as Place Builders _____ 21
D. F. Thomas & J. E. Cross

    Social Role of Organizations _____ 23

    Social Construction of Places _____ 27

    Realms of Place _____ 28

    Organizations as Place Builders _____ 30

    Four Types of Place Builders _____ 36

    Discussion and Conclusion _____ 50

    New Directions for Research _____ 54

Chapter 3

Understanding the Link between Organizational Behavior and Community Sense of Place _____ 65
D. F. Thomas, D. Gaede, R. Jurin, and Connelly

- Literature Review: Conceptual Basis for Exploring Establishment of Sense of Place _____ 66
- Methodology _____ 69
- Data Collection _____ 70
- Data Analysis _____ 72
- Findings _____ 73
- Summary: Networks as a Modeled Concept _____ 77
- Development of the Place Based Network Model _____ 78
- Implications for Community Development _____ 82

Chapter 4

Transformational Place Building: A Mixed Methods Exploration of Small Business. _____ 91
D. F. Thomas, J. Gould, J. Gaede, & R. Jurin

- Four Types of Place Builders _____ 94
- Methods _____ 97
- Implications and Recommendations for Future Research _____ 109

Chapter 5

Place Building and Mission Statements: A match or misfit? _____ 119
D. F. Thomas & J. H. Banning

- Introduction _____ 120
- Mission Statements _____ 121
- Place Building Theory _____ 122

Principles of Place Building: A Descriptive, Prescriptive And Evaluative _____ 128

Mission Statements and Place Building: A Conceptual
Perspective _____ 129
    Mission Statements and Place Building: An Empirical
    Investigation _____ 130
    Findings_____ 131
    Discussion and Implications_____ 133

Chapter 6

The Organizational Place Building Inventory: An Instrument
for Assessing and Facilitating Place-Based Corporate Social
Responsibility_____ 155
D. F. Thomas, M. Kimball, & D. Suhr
    Introduction _____ 158
    Place Building Theory _____ 160
    Method _____ 167
    Results and Discussion _____ 170
    Conclusion _____ 175

Chapter 7

Fostering Local Futures: Place Building Theory and the Living
Heritage Paradigm _____ 191
M. Kimball, R. Brunswig, S. McBeth & D. F. Thomas
    The Living Heritage Paradigm_____ 192
    Place Building Theory _____ 197
    Living Heritage Place Building: Three Examples _____ 205
    Conclusions _____ 215

Chapter 8

Enhancing student organizations as agents for community
development and civic engagement_____ 229
L. Kuk, J. H. Banning, & D. E. Thomas
    Background for Importance of Model _____ 231

      The Application of the Student Organization Place/Agent Typology _____ 236

      Summary and Future Considerations _____ 244

Chapter 9

Place-Building Theory: A Framework for Assessing and Advancing Community Engagement in Higher Education _____ 249
M. Kimball & D. F. Thomas

      Place Building Theory _____ 251

      Place Building Lines of Inquiry _____ 258

      Place Building and Institutional Social Responsibility _____ 261

      A University Example _____ 262

      Community-Engaged Place Building Research in the Curriculum: Implications and Prospects _____ 265

PART THREE: FUTURE

Chapter 10

Future of Organizational Place Building: Conceptual and Research Potential _____ 275
D. F. Thomas & J. H. Banning

      Expansion of Applications _____ 275

      Organizational Place Building: Levels of Application _____ 276

      Placelessness and Inauthenticity _____ 277

      Symbols/Artifacts and Organizations _____ 278

      A Taxonomy for Organizational Place Building: A Visual for Connections and Intersections _____ 280

      How to Use the Taxonomy for Place Building _____ 281

      Illustrations: The Taxonomy for Place Building _____ 282

About the Editors _____ 293

ACKNOWLEDGMENTS

We wish to acknowledge the encouragement and support of Pam and Melissa Thomas and Sue Banning. Their support lessened the struggles of writing this book. We also want to thank the many authors and journals that gave their permission to use their work in support of this project. Their ideas and writings not only made this effort possible, but enriched the manuscript. This project also acknowledges the importance as well as the rewards of academic colleagueship. Over the past months, we significantly supported the "bottom-line" of local coffee shops and cafes. Indeed, we found "places" for our efforts.

Finally, this book would not have been possible without the support and guidance of Andrea Sims, Ph.D., owner/publisher of TerraCotta Publishing.

AN INTRODUCTORY NOTE

David Seamon and Jacob Sowers's chapter titled "Place and Placelessness (2008), found in Edward Relph's book titled *Key Texts in Human Geography* (edited by P. Hubbard, R. Kitchen, and G. Vallentine, London: Sage, pp. 43-51) make the following statement in regard to the exploration of the Cane River by architect V. Frank Chaffin:

"Cane River is not an edge that separates its two banks, but rather, a seam that gathers the two sides together as one community and one place."

We take this notion of the river and rephrase it to capture the intent of this book:

"Place is not a location for an organization or community, but, rather place is the seam of connectedness and intersections between an organization and its community." We explore the many forms of this connecting and intersecting seam – place.

David F. Thomas & James H. Banning

1

EDITORS' INTRODUCTION

To loosely borrow from Livingston (1992, p. 7) and substitute the word *place* for *geography*, we begin our efforts in this book with the following: Place "has meant different things to different people at different times and in different places." It is beyond the scope of our efforts in this book to fully capture all the differences implied by Livingston's observation. Other complexities also exist. As noted by McClay (2014, p. 2), "Place as a concept is highly abstract, but places in particular are concrete, palpable, and intimately meaningful. Place is experienced by all in everyday life, but it is also a rich interdisciplinary concept." As Cresswell (2004 p. 1) stated: "Place ... is both simple (and that is part of its appeal) and complicated." Each place is different, but as Manzo and Devine-Wright (2014) have pointed out, the concept of place is a key interdisciplinary concept that connects many academic and applied fields—geography, human geography, ecological, and environmental psychology. In addition to the academic study of place, place has moved to application (Scannell & Gifford, 2010) in the fields of business, architecture, interior design, and landscape architecture just to name the more prominent ones. As a result of the interdisciplinary academic use and its multiple uses in the applied fields, a whole array of confusing and often conflicting definitions have emerged (Cresswell, 2015).

Cresswell (2004, 2015) notes that place can be understood as a location, as space with meaning, as similar to landscape, and perhaps a concept much like home. Seamon (2014) gives emphasis to the "dynamism" of place and offers a discussion of place processes: place interaction, place release, place realization, place creation, and place intensification. Central to the movement of the concept of place to the application arena has been the concept of place attachment (Altman & Low, 1992). Place attachment underscores the emotional/psychological bonding to an environment, not unlike Tuan's (1974) "topophilia"—the love of land. Associated with the concept of place attachment are the notions of place dependence and place identity. Place dependency refers to the strength of a person's association with a particular environment, and place identity notes the role the environment plays in one's self-identity (Proshansky, 1978). These concepts contribute to the understanding of the more popular notion of "sense of place" which denotes the general positive attachment/bonding for a geographical space. Sense of place with its ecological foundation of persons in relationship to the environment has been applied to numerous settings, particularly the campuses of higher education (Bott, Banning, Wells, Haas, & Lakey, 2006). The application of place concepts to specific environments brings into focus the role of design and asks the question: How can a positive connection between person and place (sense of place) be enhanced by design? Dober (1992) offers two concepts important to the design of places: place-making and place-marking. Place-making refers to the designing of the overall structure of an environment. For example, on campus this would include the "positioning and arrangement of campus uses and pedestrian and vehicular routes, the location of buildings and functional open space ... the definition of edges, and the interface between campus and environs" (p. 4). The overall design produced by the place-making is refered to by Dober as "an institutional metaphor" (p. 4). Place-marking, for Dober, focuses on designing an environment using elements of landmarks, materials, styles, and landscape to produce a uniqueness of place. The foregoing highlights the process of design in relation to place focusing on the physical attributes. This designing element serves as foundational to the key concept of this manuscript—the connections and intersections of organizational elements—*organizational place building*.

We have noted the concept of place referring to both locale and meaning, and in addition the concepts of place dynamics, place attachment, place dependency, place identity, sense of place, place-making, and place-marking as introductory to organizational place building—the central core of the book. The complexity of the approaches to and the use of the concept of place, along with many application concepts, make this all-encompassing framework difficult and overwhelming. However, Kuk, Banning, and Amey, (2008) use Wittgenstein's notion of family to deal with such complexity. They cite Willis (2007) who suggests that Wingenstein's approach does not focus on trying to bring complexity into a unified or simplified framework, but instead uses the concept of family resemblances or the notion of family characteristics. The family characteristics within the above complexity of place can be seen as the *importance of place in location and meaning* and *meaning is made or designed, not found*. These characteristics underscore the conclusion of the many scholars of place that "place does matter" (McClay & McAllister, 2015) and that it is a powerful influence in shaping our individual everyday and organizational activities (Gallagher, 1993). To join the "place family," we present in this manuscript the concept of *organizational place building*.

Organizational Place Building

Thomas added to this rich family history of place by introducing the concept of organizational place building in his dissertation work (Thomas, 2004). Place building as a concept is alluded to by sociologists, geographers, and other social scientists interested in matters such as enterprise movement, community and systems sustainability (Schneider, Brief, and Guzzo, 1996), sustainable development, and enterprise attributes of communities (Hudson, 2001; Schoenberger, 1997; Sagoff, 1996; Wright, 1994; Jacobs, 1984). As noted earlier, *place* is defined as both geographical and social and is organized around the meanings individuals and groups give to a place in its setting (Rodman, 1992). Places take on the meaning of events that occur there, and their descriptions are fused with human goals, values, and intentions. These "shared meanings" are held in common by the collective, are historically generated, and tend to be durable (Alvesson & Berg, 1991). Geographers refer to place as "context" explaining how social relations attach to space and place and only secondarily to people (Staeheli, 2007). Place is therefore described in this sense as a setting for social action. A university with its power can impact a given place in ways that influence social action, often on its own terms and seeking a certain outcome. As Entrikin (2000, p. 6) states: "Place shares meanings or interpretive frames of events for different actions, and second it provides resources for action." Thus, place as a platform can mediate between individuals, social groups, and broader political structure (Thomas and Cross, 2007).

Two Place Perspectives

An organization's *agent perspective* distinguishes two distinct viewpoints held by organizations, which encompass not only how organizations conceptualize themselves in relationship to place, but also the meaning they give to place, which then influences their goals, contributions to place, and all variety of their behavior. It is possible to distinguish two types of agent perspectives: one perspective conceptualizes organizations and their success as *interdependent* with the well-being of place and another that conceptualizes organizations and their success as *independent* of place (Thomas, 2004; Thomas & Cross, 2007).

Organizations with the *interdependent* perspective view themselves as members of a community and recognize that organizations and places are mutually dependent on each other. Interdependent organizations consider themselves responsible for the well-being of place, view their success as intimately tied with the greater well-being of the place, and actively seek a variety of opportunities to invest and contribute to the multiple aspects of place. In contrast, organizations with an *independent* perspective view themselves merely as occupants of place and economic agents, rather than integral members of place. Organizations that see themselves as independent agents focus their activities on satisfying internal goals while viewing the realms of place as resources to satisfy their needs. Their primary responsibility is to their shareholders, not the places in which they do business. They consider generating jobs and tax revenues as their primary, if not their only, contribution to place. Independent organizations are not committed to the well-being of place and will only maintain the relationship as long as it benefits their shareholders (Thomas, 2004; Thomas & Cross, 2007).

Three Place Building Principles

As organizations make place building commitments to the future, we see three possible place building principles; descriptive, evaluative, and prescriptive. These are typically reflected in the organization's business model, especially in its strategic intentions, and are illustrative of its mission statement. The descriptive principle is described in terms of how the organization value(s) place which is informative rather than normative, i.e., place building is discussed as expressing the quality, kind, or condition (or strategy employed) of place building in each of the five place dimensions.

The evaluative principle reveals how an organization determines the significance, worth, or condition of a place and how that organization assesses or estimates the quality or condition of a place relative to its role. The prescriptive principle specifies its intentions toward the wider community: how it will use resources and engage in activities that impact the community and what social and ethical responsibilities it acknowledges and strives to meet.

Four Types of Place Builders

Thomas, (2004) and Thomas and Cross, (2007), using a grounded theory approach (Glaser & Strauss, 1967) derived place building mode. Place building theory explains how an organization values place on five place dimensions: nature; social relationships; material environment; ethics; and economic relationships. How the organization values place, in turn, suggests its type and its strategies for building place.

Nature includes the natural—as opposed to man-made—elements, forces, and spaces, such as the landscape, earth, geography, and natural resources. How does an organization relate and contribute to nature and the environment?

Social Relationships includes the full spectrum of interactions between an organization's employees and stakeholders and among and between other organizations. How is certain space treated that reflects the culture and values of the organization?

Material Environment includes man-made buildings, roads, and other structures, such as the office building an organization occupies and how that space is treated, including interior office spaces. This also reflects the value placed on the building's architecture, landscaping, and historical construction (if any).

Ethics is the realm that describes the organization's business practices and its implicit and explicit contract with the community that seeks to establish itself as legitimate. How are an organization's practices modeled in its industry, its culture and all stakeholders?

Economic Relationships are described in terms of the organization's level of investment in the fiscal well-being of the community. For example, how does the organization attract skilled labor to the community? How does it seek to improve the economic viability of the community? How does the organization create new opportunities for economic growth?

Within the context of the two-agent perspectives described above, the OPB model includes four distinct *place agent identities*: transformational, contributive, contingent, and exploitive. *Place agent identities* reveal how organizations conceptualize themselves as social actors, or agents, in relation to the places in which they are located and do business. The four types of place building organizations differ in how they conceptualize themselves as agents, the value they assign to the dimensions of place, their corporate culture, and their strategies and behaviors. *Transformational* organizations conceptualize themselves as change agents acting to improve the lives of individuals and groups in a place. *Contributive* organizations conceptualize themselves as investors and contributors to the well-being of places in which they operate. *Contingent* organizations view themselves simply as participants in places and *exploitive* organizations view themselves as independent agents with little to no obligations to the places in which they operate (Thomas, 2004; Thomas & Cross, 2007; Thomas, Gaede, Jurin & O'Connell, 2010).

Each of the four types of organizations (*transformational, contributive, contingent,* and *exploitive*) creates a mission statement which demonstrates different levels of commitment to place well-being and fiscal success. Organizations with the same agent perspective but different agent identities develop similar but not identical missions and strategies, which include similar commitments to place well-being and/or fiscal success. Organizations with an interdependent perspective strive for a relatively equal balance between place well-being and their own fiscal success, whereas those organizations with an independent agent identity put much more emphasis and weight on fiscal success with little concern for place well-being. The place building model can illustrate the minor differences between types of place building organizations that share the same agent perspective, but distinct differences between organizations with different place agent identities (Thomas, 2004; Thomas & Cross, 2007).

Transformational Organizations

Transformational organizations view themselves as critical agents with a mission and focus on improving life and creating positive change for both the organization and the place (Thomas, 2004; Thomas & Cross, 2007). The transformational organizational culture is highly focused on team learning, collaboration, openness to change, and building partnerships. They view themselves as *interdependent* members of a place, rather than *independent* members, and their success contributes to advantage beyond that of the organization (Thomas, 2004).

Transformational place builders demonstrate an *integrative* strategy that focuses on building a shared vision with the community and holding itself accountable to the community for the quality of its contribution to place. These behaviors are not solely for a public relations advantage but an effort to surpass community business trends and regulations, perhaps even at a cost to the organization (Thomas & Cross, 2008). These strategies include initiating new policies and business practices for protecting the natural environment, neighborhoods, cultural heritage, local economy, and other local resources (Thomas & Cross, 2007).

Contributive Organizations

Contributive organizations view themselves as being a contributing member of a network of business people and community leaders who share a common ideology. Their identity as a local contributor is affirmed by engaging with local organizations, fundraising, and by philanthropy that builds place (Schneider, Brief, & Guzzo, 1996; Chaskin, Brown, Venkatesh & Vidal, 2001). In contrast to transformational organizations that view themselves as responsible for the well-being of place, a contributive organization views itself as a contributor to the well-being of place. The organizational culture is focused on "investing in its community" and conforming to local norms and values (Thomas, 2004).

Contributive organizations value place first for its social relationships and second for its economic opportunities and potential for business growth. The natural world may simply be the geographic location of their business. These organizations need a place that needs them, where they can simultaneously prosper and give back. They practice an *integrative* strategy that cultivates their role as a key contributor in their community through the network of organizations that facilitate social and philanthropic activity (Thomas, 2004; Thomas & Cross, 2007).

Contingent Organizations

Contingent organizations view themselves as disassociated and autonomous agents. They narrowly define correct corporate behavior as "corporate social responsibility" with obeying existing laws, regulations, and ethical codes, yet they make a concerted effort to act accordingly. Rather than viewing themselves as interdependent with place (transformational), or key members of place (contributive), they view themselves as control agents. The contingent organization practices a *separatist* strategy that centers on a plan that distinguishes the organization in terms of its economic power. Contingent organizations value place for what it provides for the company, such as workers for its labor force. They practice philanthropy only as a method for advancing their own causes, not out of any intrinsic commitment to place, and their principle contribution is their economic contribution and adherence to laws and regulations (Thomas & Cross, 2007).

Exploitive Organizations

Exploitive organizations view themselves as occupants of place and are more isolated from the values of the community. They are active users of the economic, cultural, social, and political resources, valuing place as a commodity that they utilize to their greatest economic benefit (Sagoff, 1996; Rodman, 1992; Entrikin, 2000). They largely plan and organize to control space in which short term financial progress and cost effectiveness trump local needs (Thomas 2004), and their preference is to be granted the rights and legal protections typically afforded only to individual citizens (Vogel, 2005).

The exploitive firm's mission to maximize profit determines their organizational philosophy, and it is usually practiced by deliberately targeting certain places for the potential to extract resources without accountability for the risks posed to the local population. While these organizations may employ locals and deal with local suppliers, they practice a *separatist* strategy in that they are not invested in ways that contribute to a sense of place. Exploitive organizations are likely to leave a place once they have determined they don't fit or the return is not as lucrative as originally anticipated (Thomas & Cross, 2007).

Each of the four types stands out from the others in their perspectives on place and the consequences of their actions. Transformational organizations orchestrate their contributions in ways that transform themselves and place. As agents of change, they are distinguished from other organizations in that they view place in a holistic manner in which all three realms are interactive and interdependent. Consequently, the business practices of transformational organizations contribute to place well-being through learning and teaching in partnership with clients (Thomas, 2004; Thomas & Cross, 2007).

Organizational Place: Connections and Intersections

The foregoing discussion of organizational place building introduced the conceptual framework for understanding the connections and intersections between and among organizations and communities. The concepts of interdependent and independent perspectives, three principles of place building, four types of place builders, and the five place dimensions provide the conceptual framework needed to explore the complexities of the connections and intersections of organizational place. Place building is an intentional activity that takes place where the organization meets its various stakeholders: community, customers, suppliers and employees. Much in the same way a river's tributaries form a network of contributors, each of which carve or shape a certain perspective of the places they occupy. The intersection of these contributors, creates new avenues or approaches to how they will explore, understand, and implement organizational place building. It's the interaction at the junctions or intersections that drive the organization's place building strategies and results. (See Figure 1 in Chapter 10: A Taxonomy for Place Building.) Place building is a dynamic process. New connections may form over time while some existing connections disappear. The interactions create opportunity for organizations to influence each other and, therefore, may modify agent perspectives over time, creating a dynamic and evolving commitment to place.

For example, organizations with the interdependent perspective (transformational and contributive organizations) view themselves as members of a community and recognize that they influence the very definition of the place in which they reside. These organizations acknowledge a shared responsibility for the well-being of place and, therefore, view their success as intimately connected and intersected with place. They actively seek a variety of opportunities to invest in and contribute to the multiple aspects of building place. In contrast, organizations with an independent perspective view themselves merely as occupants of place rather than integral members of it. These organizations see themselves as independent agents and focus their activities on satisfying internal goals while viewing place as simply a resource pool to satisfy their needs.

Organizations decide how they will enter the intersections and, thus, how they will interact. In so doing, we find the point at which they enter and interact at certain intersections, be they social networks, environmental, or economic, as indication of their likely contributions to the place they occupy. The readings we have chosen for this manuscript illustrate the complexity of connections and intersections of organizational place building using the conceptual framework outline in this chapter.

Introduction to the Readings

In Chapter 2, we present the 2007 article by Thomas and Cross titled "Organizations as Place Builders" from the *Journal of Behavioral and Applied Management*. They argue that the role of organizations as agents in the construction of place has been overlooked in the management and organization's literature. Using concepts from sociology, cultural geography, and management, they develop a typology that illustrates how organizations contribute to the social construction of place. This typology presents an analytic scheme for examining the place building characteristics of organizations and a basis for developing theories on the interdependence between communities and organizations.

In Chapter 3, we provide the 2008 article authored by Thomas, Gaede, Jurin, and Connelly titled, "Understanding the link between organizations and construction of community sense of place: The place based network model" from the *Journal of Community Development*. The authors raise and then respond to the question: What are the dynamics that affect the link between organizations (both business and non-profit) and their capacity to help develop a "sense of place" in communities? Based on a grounded-theory qualitative study, researchers investigated the critical variables whose nexus of interactions influence organizational establishment of

Standard Operating Procedures (SOP). The article will advance a model that illustrates this dynamic through the Place Based Network (PBN) model. The PBN is a foundation for an interpretation of how community sense of place is socially constructed and it recognizes the role organizations play in developing intentions and the meanings organizations may create in their community.

Chapter 4 presents the work of Thomas, Gould, Gaede, and Jurin's 2011 article titled, "Transformational Place Building: A Mixed Method Exploration of Small Businesses" from the *Journal of Enterprising Communities*. The purpose of this study was to explore the nature of transformational business practices using the construct of organizational place building (OPB). Place building refers to behaviors indicative of organizations that value a sense of place and their roles and responsibilities in the community. Members from the Chamber of Commerce of three cities in Northern Colorado participated in two phases of research. In the qualitative phase, ten interviews and three focus groups were conducted to explore specific transformative business behaviors. For the quantitative phase, 107 Northern Colorado business owners completed an online measure indexing these transformational behaviors. A median split was conducted to compare differences in organizational characteristics between the high and low scores of transformational behavior. Findings indicated that specific behaviors were identified by sample participants and that these behaviors were most evident in larger, well established businesses.

Chapter 5 presents a 2014 article titled, "Place Building and Mission Statements: A Match or Misfit?" authored by Thomas and Banning from the *Journal of Contemporary Issues in Business Research*. The purpose of this study was to investigate possible relationships between organizational Mission Statements (MS) and Place Building (PB). The basic questions addressed in the study were: 1) Do corporate MS contain a linkage to their possible place building strategies? and 2) Do the linkages suggest a match, a misfit, or is the linkage missing? Place building focuses on how an organization values the dimensions of place: nature, social relationships, material environment, ethics, and economic relationships in relation to the places in which they are located. The authors examined the MS from 41 businesses selected among a group of fortune 500 firms to determine if place building attributes were evident. Qualitative document analysis was employed to investigate the possible linkage between mission statements and the concepts of the place building model. The findings of the study suggest that corporate mission statements most often fail to address the strategies associated with organizational place building. These findings raise important questions for discussion regarding the future of organizations and their relationship to place building in the community: How is corporate space used in the community, what is the condition of the space, and what is the impact of organizational place on the community resources. The study concludes that the strategy of addressing place/community relations within corporate mission statements can provide a useful way forward in addressing the foregoing questions.

The purpose of the 2016 article in Chapter 6 is to present the justification for and efficacy of the Organizational Place Building Inventory (OPEl) by discussing the Organizational Place Building Theory (OPBT) and the presentation of a professional services firm (PSF) case study. The article was authored by Thomas, Kimball, and Suhr and titled, "The Organizational Place Inventory: An Instrument for Assessing and Facilitating Place-Based Corporate Social Responsibility." It was published originally in the *Journal of Corporate Citizenship*. Although the literature provides several methods for measuring corporate social activities, the authors do not include corporate social responsibility from a place perspective, that is, one that recognizes, values, and integrates the meanings individuals and groups give to a place in terms of its geographic and social contexts. This perspective focuses on how place can and should play an important role in the strategic relationships organizations have with their communities, their clients, and their employees. Organizational Place Building serves as both a mirror and a lens through which organizations can (1) locate themselves on a continuum of values and strategies with regard to place (i.e., their relations to its social, natural, material, economic and ethical dimensions); (2) develop strategies for how they might stay where they are or get where they would rather be. The OPEl is an objective instrument designed to assess an organization's values and strategies along five dimensions or latent constructs of place building: ethical, social, natural, built environment and economic. The article discusses the significance of the OPEl's scores with respect to four place building profiles: exploitive, contingent, contributive, and transformational. It concludes by offering a three-phase process in which the OBPI may be incorporated into participatory research.

Chapter 7 is the first in a series of three readings that have an educational focus. The first article was authored by Kimball, Brunswig, McBeth, and Thomas in 2013 and titled, "Fostering Local Futures: Place Building Theory and the Living Heritage Paradigm" published in *The Applied Anthropologist*. In contrast to essentialist and static notions of heritage, encapsulated here as the Good Old Days (GOD) and Saving the Past for the Future (SPF), the living heritage paradigm offers an alternative model that sees heritage as a social construct evolving in response to its changing relations with extant communities of people. Place building theory (PBT), an applied and explanatory theory arising from research on place-based corporate social responsibility, offers tools and perspectives to operationalize living heritage research and to reveal and unpack place-keeper (investment in place identity) and place-user (investment in place utility) identities and roles. Using three examples from our Colorado heritage research programs, the authors present three different approaches to PBT living heritage research: evaluative, integrative, and restorative. The authors conclude with a summary discussion of PBT's broader relevance to living heritage research and offer suggestions for future applications.

In Chapter 8, Kuk, Banning, and Thomas present their 2010 article titled, "Enhancing Student Organizations as Agents for Community Development and Civic Engagement." It was originally published in *The Journal of Student Affairs*. The concept of community has become an important component of the learning process on most college campuses. However, campus-based student organizations have not been effectively integrated into these initiatives. This article presents a new typology to develop student organizations as agents for community development, civic engagement, and organizational development on college campuses. This typology presents a way of conceptualizing student organizations as agents that can promote student learning and civic engagement, and enhance relationships with the greater community in which they exist. The authors utilized a focus group approach to explore the application of this new typology to student affairs practitioners' work with student organizations as the first step in the application of this model.

In Chapter 9, we present the Kimball and Thomas 2012 article titled, "Place-Building Perceptions: A New Model for Catalyzing Change in University-Community Relations and Student Civic Development," published in the *Michigan Journal of Community Service Learning*. In this reading, place building theory explains how an organization values place on five dimensions: nature, social relationships, material environment, ethics, and economic relationships. How the organization values place, in turn, suggests its type, its strategies for building place, and recommendations for how it might move in a desired direction between the ends of a place building continuum that includes four types: exploitive, contingent, contributive, and transformational organizations. This paper introduces place building theory, how it has been applied to business organizations, and a new application, the university. To explicate this new direction, the authors present a service learning case study in which the first author delivered an applied anthropology course that engaged students as both voluntary research subjects and researchers. Participants used the place building methodology to discover perceptions of the university's place building role held by a small sample of faculty members and representatives of community-based organizations. The results from the project illustrate the application of the place-building framework to a university as a descriptive, prescriptive, and evaluative tool. The authors conclude with implications and prospects for community-engaged place building.

Finally, in Chapter 10, we speculate on the future of the organizational place building work. Particularly, we note its potential expansion to organizational segments beyond those presented in the readings, the promise of applying the typology of organizational building to different levels of the organization—from the organization's place in the community, sub-units within the organization to the larger organizational entity, and to the individual's relationship to the organization. The specific topics of placelessness and authenticity, and symbols and organizational artifacts are also addressed. In conclusion, we present a taxonomy that deepens the concept of organizational place building and the notions of connections and intersections which can give guidance to organizational sustainability and cooperate responsibility.

References:

Altman, I. & Low, S. M. (Eds.). (1992). *Place attachment. Human behavior and environment: Advances inTheory and Research* (Vol. 12). New York: Plenum.

Alverson, M., & Berg, P. O. (1991). *Corporate culture and organizational symbolism: An overview.* New York: W. de Gruyter.

Bott, S. E., Banning, J. H., Wells, M., Hass, G., & Lakey, J. (2006). A sense of place: A framework & Its application to campus ecology. *College Services, 6*(5), 42-47.

Chaskin, R. J., Brown, P., Venkatesh, s., and Vidal, a. (2001) *Building community Capacity.* New York: Aldine de Gruyter

Cresswell, T. (2004). *Place: A short introduction.* Oxford, UK: Blackwell Publishing.

Cresswell, T. (2015). *Place: An introduction.* West Sussex, UK: Wiley Blackwell.

Dober, R. P. (1992). *Campus design.* New York. John Wiley & Sons.

Entrikin, J. N. (2000). *The betweeness of place: Towards geography of modernity.* New York: Routledge.

Gallagher, W. (1993). *The power of place: Hour our surroundings shape our thoughts, emotions, andactions.* New York: Poseidon Press.

Glaser, B. and Strauss, A. (1967). *The discovery of grounded theory: strategies for qualitative research.* New York: Aldine de Gruyter.

Hudson, R. (2001). *Producing places.* New York: The Guildford Press.

Jacobs, J. (1984). *Cities and the wealth of a nations.* New York: Random House.

Kuk, L., Banning, J. H., & Amey, M. J. (2010). *Positioning student affairs for sustainable change: Achievingorganizational effectiveness through multiple perspectives.* Sterling, VA: Stylus Publishing.

Livingston, D. (1992). *The geographical tradition.* Oxford, UK: Blackwell.

Manzo, L. C., & Devine-Wright, P. (Eds.). (2014). *Place attachment: Advances in theory, methods, andapplications.* New York: Routledge.

McClay, W. M. (2014). Why place matters. In W. M. McClay & T. V. McAllister (Eds.). *Why place matters: Geography, identity, and civic life in modern America (pp.1-9).* New York: Encounter Books.

Proshansky, H. M. (1978). The city and self-identity. *Environment and Behavior, 10*, 147-169.

Rodman, M. (1992). Empowering place: Multilocality and multivocality. *American Anthropologist, New series, 94*(3), 640-656.

Sagoff, M. (1996). Values and preferences. *Ethics, 2*, 19-54.

Scannell, L., & Gifford, R. (2010). Defining place attachment: A tripartite organizing framework. *Journalof Environmental Psychology, 30*, 1-10.

Schneider, B., Brief, A. P., & Guzzo, R. A. (1996). Creating a climate and culture for sustainable organizational change. *Organizational Dynamics.* Spring: 7- 18.

Schoenberger, E. (1997). *The cultural crisis of the firm.* Cambridge: Blackwell.

Seamon, D. (2014). Place attachment and phenomenology. In L. C. Manzo & P. Devine-Wright, (Eds.). *Place attachment: Advances in theory, methods, and applications* (pp. 11-22). New York: Routledge.

Staeheli, L. A. (2007). Place. In J. Agnenew, K. Mitchell, & G. Toal (Eds.), *A companion to Political Geography* (pp.157-169). New York: Blackwell publishing.

Thomas, D. F. (2004). Toward an understanding of organizations place building in communities.(Doctoral Dissertation). Retrieved from ProQuest Dissertation and Thesis Global database. (UMI No.3173093)

Thomas, D. F. & Cross, J. (2007). Organizations as place builders. *Journal of Behavioral and Applied management, 9*(1), 33-61.

Thomas, D. F., Gaede, D., Jurin, R. R., & Connolly, L. S. (2008). Understanding the link between business organizations and construction of community sense of place: The place based network. *Journal of the Community Development Society, 39*(3), 33-45.

Tuan, Y. (1974). *Topophilia: A study of environmental perception, attitudes, and values*. Englewood, CA: Prentice-Hall.

Vogel, D. (2005). *The market for value: The potential and limits of corporate social responsibility*. Brookings Institution Press: Washington D.C.

Vogel, D. (2005). The low value of virtue. *Harvard Business Review*, June: 26.

Willis, J. W. (2007*). Foundations of qualitative research: Interpretative and critical approaches*. Thousand Oaks, CA: Sage Publications.

Wittgenstein, L. 2001). *Philosophical investigations* (G.E.M. Anscombe, Trans.). Oxford, UK: BlackwellPublishers, Ltd.

Wright, S. (Ed.). *Anthropology of organizations*. New York: Routledge.

2

ORGANIZATIONS AS PLACE BUILDERS

David F. Thomas
University of Northern Colorado

Jennifer E. Cross
Colorado State University

ABSTRACT

We argue that the role of organizations as agents in the construction of place has been overlooked in the management and organizations literature. Using concepts from sociology, cultural geography, and management, we developed a typology that illustrates how organizations contribute to the social construction of place. This typology presents an analytic scheme for examining the place-building characteristics of organizations and a basis for developing theories on the interdependence between places and organizations.

Organizations as Place Builders

In the past two decades, the concept of place has garnered increasing attention across many disciplines. Since place has become a widely used concept, scholars have become increasingly sensitive to the ways it is utilized in research. Over the past decade, sociologists have pointed out the need for researchers to make explicit their assumptions about place, to be more place-sensitive, and to treat place as agents in social phenomena (Agnew, 1993; Gieryn, 2000; Werlen, 1993). They argue that sociology has too often treated place in reductionistic ways, as a simple independent variable or backdrop to social action, rather than intertwined with other social processes (Gans, 2002; Gieryn, 2000).

This critique of social science applies also to management and organizations literature, where place is typically considered the backdrop for organizational practices, treated in reductionistic ways, or simply ignored. In the management literature, place has been traditionally limited to the study of organizational climate and employee commitment or productivity in a given space, such as a building or work place environment (Denison, 1996; Ouchi and Wilkins, 1985; Guion, 1973; and Jams and Jones, 1974; Guzzo, R.A., 1996). Instead of being informed by the growing literature on place, use of the concept in the organization's literature has not advanced beyond considerations of organizational climate, attachment, and affiliation (Hudson, 2001; Sagoff, 1996; Schoenberger, 1997; Wright, 1994).

Herbert Gans has recently argued that the current challenge for social scientists who study space and place is to examine the causal relationships between space and society without reifying space or simply confirming the obvious fact that society exists in space (2002: 329). He contends that researchers should be focusing their efforts on the ways in which individuals and collectivities turn natural space in social space and shape its uses. In this article, we take up this challenge by examining how organizations, a particular type of collective, shape places through the full range of their values and behaviors. In so doing, we propose a new definition of corporate social responsibility (CSR), one that defines corporations as agents, whose actions, values, behaviors, and strategies contribute in myriad ways to the social construction of places. This nascent view of CSR emerges from an interdisciplinary outlook that broadens CSR to includethe complete array of a corporation's actions.

CSR is defined in numerous ways with some definitions being narrower than others. In its most basic definition, CSR is associated with a narrow scope of activities that may benefit communities, but are intended primarily to protect or enhance highly visible brands or reputations (Vogel, 2005). CSR has often been simplistically defined as a synonym for philanthropy (Kotler & Lee, 2005; McClenahen, 2005). A more comprehensive definition of CSR argues that social responsibilities must be integrated into all aspects of business and is marked by a commitment to improve community well-being through business practices and corporate resources (Kotler and Lee, 2005). Another definition of CSR suggests that it includes the act of making long-term commitments to social issues, initiatives, and forming strategic alliances (Smith, 1994). Our intention in this article is to expand the conceptual tools available for theorizing about the causal influence of organizational strategies and behaviors on the places in which they are located. Towards that end, we propose a typology of organizational orientations and strategies that differentiate the ways organizations participate in the social construction of place. Fundamentally, we believe that examining organizations as "place builders" is timely and important to both organizations and communities.

In this article we do three things: First, we review the literature on the social role of corporations and the concept of place as a social construction. Second, we propose a typology of organizational priorities and behaviors that characterize how a corporation's actions contribute to the social construction of place. We use the common definition of place—a meaningful location or site (Cresswell, 2004). Third, we examine the causal relationship between a corporation's actions and the dynamic process of place construction.

Social Role of Organizations

When the relationship between an organization and place is discussed, it is primarily addressed in terms of corporate social responsibility (CSR) and corporate citizenship. Before laying out a model for understanding how organizations act as "place builders", we review the literature on corporate social responsibility in order to discuss current conceptions of the relationships between places and corporations. Although we recognize that corporations and organizations are different in many respects and we will be using only corporations as illustrative examples, we will use the terms corporations and organizations interchangeably as our model applies to both.

CSR has blossomed into a growing scholarly literature and public discussion. Nevertheless, no single objective method has emerged which corporations and their stakeholders might use to evaluate the level or extent of a corporation's social responsibility, its intentions, and more importantly its contributions (Hopkins, 1999). Hopkins points to a list of items that might define or measure CSR; among them is profitability, tax contributions, socially responsible projects and operations, philanthropic contributions, good working conditions, support of social investments and the like. Kotler and Lee (2005) have identified philanthropy as only one of five major activities typically described as CSR. The other four are: cause promotions, cause related marketing, community volunteerism, and business practices. As we will discuss later, each of these activities is a significant piece of an organization's role as agent in place building. McClenahen has described how corporate philanthropy is capable of producing some tangible social and environmental benefits (2005); however, corporate philanthropy is only a small portion of an organization's activities.

Enterprises have noted that CSR is good for business and for each group of shareholders and the places within which they operate. Research has shown that positive contributions that grow and sustain a place are likely to have positive effects on profitability and return on investment (Vogel, 2005). Conversely, poor internal human-resource policy, cavalier downsizing, an industrial caused environmental disaster or conviction for a corporate crime are likely to have harmful effects (Hopkins, 1999; Anderson, 1989; Cooper, 2004).

More general literature on the role of organizations as agents focuses primarily on organizations as fiduciary agents with legal responsibilities to their shareholders and stakeholders. This view of organizations as fiduciary agents limits the scope of their responsibilities to economic vitality and legal mandates (May, 1983). Anderson (1989) posits that "CSR involves a legal responsibility (complying with the law), setting-

and abiding by-moral and ethical standards, and philanthropic giving" (p. 9). Further, he defines CSR as "the obligation of both businesses and society (stakeholders) to take proper legal, moral-ethical and philanthropic actions that will protect and improve the welfare of both society and business as a whole; all of this must of course be accomplished within the economic structures and capabilities of the parties involved" (p. 9).

In recent decades, policy makers and social scientists alike have critiqued liberalism for its overemphasis on individual freedom and neglect of communal responsibilities (Etzioni 1993, Hopkins 1999). Tony Blair (as cited in Hopkins, 1999) posits that:

> [L]egislation could not guarantee that a company will behave in a way conducive to trust and long-term commitment. Companies should shift their notion of their legal responsibilities to one of community partner in which each employee has a stake and where a company's responsibilities are clearly stated (p. 13).

This notion that companies ought to expand their conception of their responsibilities beyond fiscal responsibility to shareholders and basic legal responsibilities to the state parallels the communitarian argument that individuals and groups both act as agents influencing society, and thus must also recognize their responsibilities to individuals, institutions, and society (Selznick 1995, Etzioni 1998). The question is not whether a company should practice socially responsible behavior, but rather *how deeply* a company should become involved and invested in the places in which they operate. As Cooper states, "organizations more generally should be held accountable to the society within which they operate" (2004, 62). It is time to look beyond the landscape of CSR as a legal responsibility and philanthropic duty to a new horizon that views the corporation as an agent that *invests* its resources in its community as place and not as control in or over its community.

This expanded conception of CSR fits with recent work by scholars who have expanded the literature to examine the interactions between organizations and places (Black and Hartell, 2004; Newell, 2005;

Langtry, 1994). Any useful framework to guide CSR practices and philanthropy must address the specific interactions between a business and the social conditions in which the organization operates. It is not enough to say an organization is doing well because one or more of their philanthropic acts has resulted in tangible results. To this end, we have seen the emergence of a number of management models that help businesses find new ways to respond to the unforeseen challenges and demands of a society in transition (Jonker and de Witte, 2006).

The triple bottom line typology has gained wide-spread recognition as a valuable tool in helping organizations position CSR into their regular operations (Savitz and Weber, 2006). Other models like the Integrated Management model (Jonker and Witte, 2006) provide a generic approach to linking all organizational aspects of CSR. The Molecule model (Folkerts and Weijers, 2006) is designed to help firms integrate the concept of sustainable development into their strategies and operations for societal and corporate development.

The Global Compact Performance model (Fussler and van der Vegt, 2004) provides efficient and effective strategies for making operational changes in order to improve a firm's CSR. These models are evidence that organizations are exploring new tools to help them integrate CSR in their strategies and daily operations. Our typology mirrors the intentions of these models in that we propose that all the activities of the organization contribute to the building of place. What we are proposing is a comprehensive examination of a corporation's actions and their influence on the places in which they are situated.

The intention of this article is to take the literature on place and apply that knowledge to organizations, in order to offer an external view of the consequences of organizational behavior. We are not making any suggestions about what organizations should be doing (injunctive norms), rather we examine what they are doing (descriptive norms) and categorize those from an external rather than an internal frame. We are not concerned here with the intentions or motivations of the organizations, per se, but rather we are concerned with their stated priorities and the consequences of their actions in relationship to places.

Social Construction of Places

Studies of *place* begin by distinguishing between *space* and *place*. *Space* is made up of the natural and man-made material world, and is transformed into *place* when imbued with meaning through individual, group, or cultural processes (Altman & Low, 1992; Cresswell, 2004). As Tuan (1977) states, "space becomes place when it is endowed with meaning. And in so doing a commitment to that place is made on both an emotional and physical level" (p. 6). Places take on the meaning of events that occur there, and their descriptions are fused with human goals, values and intentions. Place is therefore not merely a phenomenon that exists in the minds of individuals but that develops from and becomes part of everyday life and experiences. The ordinary routines of life produce places that are meaningful, sacred and special to individuals, their organizations, and their communities (Williams, 1998).

Place, then, is defined as both geographical and social, and is organized around the meanings individuals and groups give to a place in its setting (Rodman, 1992). Place is not synonymous with community, though many people use the word "community" to indicate a place, the people who live and work there, their interactions with each other, and their attachment to that place. Community is one of the most overused and vaguely defined concepts in sociology, used to mean everything from a geographic place, to a group of people with common interests, to a sense of belonging in a group (Day 2006). In this paper, use of the word community is limited to referencing ideas expressed by others about their conceptions of social responsibility when it connotes a geographical place including the people and social relationships that occur within that place.

Two premises underlie the assertion that place is a social construction. First, individuals are agents in the world, free to make meaning from their environment in ways that will contribute to the construction of place. Entrikin (2000) sees our ability to "socially construct" places as the result of our freedom to create meaning (p. 6). Finding meaning in space is both an individual and group process where humans act towards a place based on the meanings they have associated with that place; place requires human agency (Sack 1998).

Second, the meanings of a place are derived from or arise out of the interaction individuals and groups have with others in that place (Tuan, 1977). As Blumer posits, "the simple premise that human beings act toward things on the basis of the meaning of things is much too simple" (1969, p. 10), suggesting that there is more to consider when identifying how place creates meaning. The meaning of place for a group or individual rises out of the ways in which people act toward each other with regard to that place (Blumer, 1969). The notion that places evolve from the interaction rather than simply geography, is described as early as 1925 by Carl Sauer in *The Morphology of Landscape*, and in a variety of more contemporary writings (Gustafson 2005, Sack 1997, Zelinsky 1992). For example, a place could be defined as a tourist attraction, a sacred religious site, a natural wonder, or a wilderness site and each of these definitions of place suggest different interactions between people and the place as well as between individuals and groups within that place. The actions of individuals in a place simultaneously shape place and are guided by the meanings they form through interaction with individuals, groups, and organizations in that place.

Realms of Place

Researchers agree that *place* is a multi-dimensional concept including the natural world, the built environment, social relationships, economic relationships, patterns of interaction, as well as socially constructed meanings about each dimension; however, the models they offer for helping us to understand these dimensions vary. Geographer Robert Sack identifies the dimensions of place as including nature (synonymous with space), social relations (the economy, political institutions, families, etc.) and meaning (perceptions and theories of the other two realms) (1997, p. 28). Per Gustafson (2005) found that

Organizations as Place Builders

the meanings associated with places revolve around three primary themes: self, others, and the environment, which includes both the built environment and the natural world (p. 10).

Drawing on these two models of place, we have diagrammed the three realms of place that are particularly relevant to our discussion here, the material environment, the natural environment, and social relations (see Figure 1). Layered over the top of these three realms is meaning. Our model is similar to the model proposed by Sack, with the addition of one realm, the material environment. *Nature* includes the natural—as opposed to man-made—elements, forces, and spaces. These include the rocks and trees, hills and valleys, wind and rain, climate and gravity[1].

Social Relations is the realm of human interaction, which includes the full spectrum of interactions between people whether between strangers, family members, or co-workers. Interactions form the building blocks of this realm. This realm includes not only the interactions between individuals and groups but also includes the social context of those interactions as well as lasting patterns of interaction such as family dynamics, inter-agency collaboration, and group conflicts.

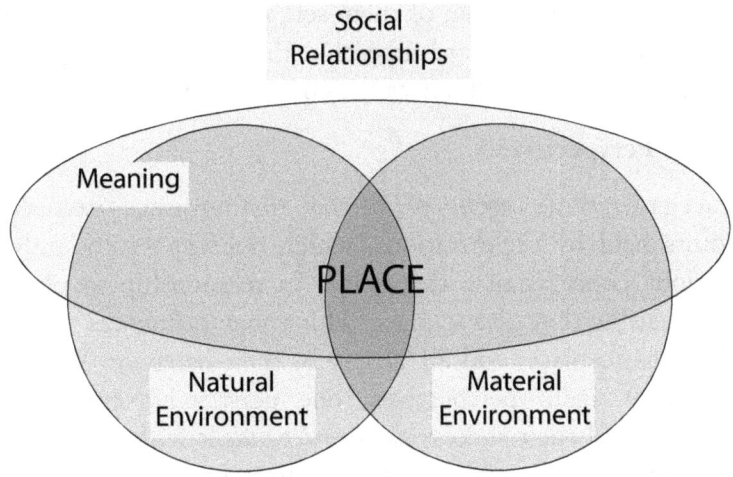

Figure 1. Realms of Place

The *Material Environment* includes both the economy as well as the built environment—man-made buildings, roads, and other structures. Whereas, Sack (1997) defines economic relationships as being part of the social relations realm, we see the economy as conceptually distinct from other social relations and patterns of interaction. Especially because we are interested in the economic activities of corporations, adding the material environment as a distinct realm allows us to discuss the relationship between aspects of the material environment and the other realms of place with greater conceptual clarity. In this article, we will focus our attention on how organizations contribute to each of the three realms—nature, social relationships, and the material environment—as well as the meanings associated with places and the relationships between realms.

Organizations as Place Builders

We posit four qualitatively different types of organizations, each of which value place in unique ways, and therefore vary in how they contribute to or detract from the social construction of place. These four types of organizations are divided into two groups based on their conception of themselves as agents, which we have named their *agent perspective*. A corporation's *agent perspective* shapes its goals and values, then determines their *corporate mission*. Taken together, an organization's conception of them self as an agent and its mission determine its actions in regards to each realm of place thereby defining how each organization influences the construction of place.

Two Place Perspectives

An organization's *agent perspective* distinguishes two distinct viewpoints held by organizations, which encompass not only how corporations conceptualize themselves in relationship to place, but also the meaning they give to place, which then influences their goals, contributions to place, and all variety of their behavior. We identify two types of agent perspectives; one perspective conceptualizes corporations and their success as *interdependent* with the well-being of place, and another which conceptualizes corporations and their

Organizations as Place Builders

success as *independent* of place (see Figure 2). Organizations with the interdependent perspective view themselves as members of a community and recognize that corporations and places are mutually dependent on each other. Interdependent organizations consider themselves responsible for the well-being of all three realms of place, view their success as intimately tied with the greater well-being of the place, and actively seek a variety of opportunities to invest and contribute to the multiple aspects of place. In contrast, organizations with an independent perspective, view themselves merely as occupants of place and economic agents, rather than integral members of place. Organizations that see themselves as independent agents focus their activities on satisfying internal goals while viewing the realms of place as resources to satisfy their needs. Their primary responsibility is to their shareholders, not the places in which they do business. They consider generating jobs and tax revenues as their primary, if not their only, contribution to place. Independent organizations are not committed to the well-being of place and will only maintain the relationship as long as it benefits their shareholders.

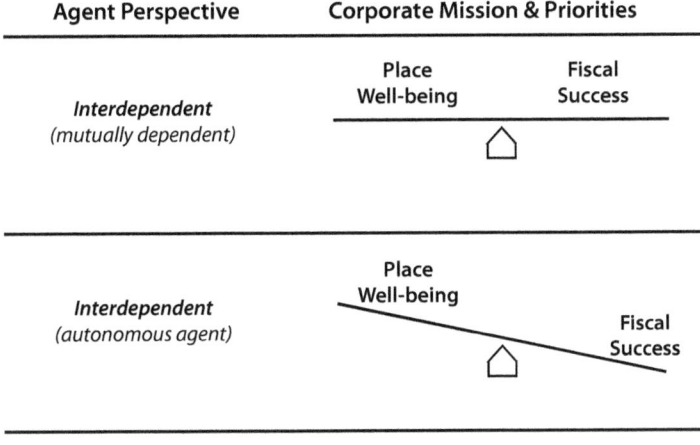

Figure 2. Two Types of Agent Perspectives

Within the two agent perspectives, we identify four distinct *place agent identities: transformational, contributive, contingent,* and *exploitative. Place agent identities* reveal how organizations conceptualize themselves as social actors—agents—in relation to the places in which they are located and do business. The four types of organizations differ in how they conceptualize themselves as agents, the value they assign to the realms of place, their corporate culture, and their strategies and behaviors. *Transformational* organizations conceptualize themselves as change agents acting to improve the lives of individuals and groups in a place. *Contributive* organizations conceptualize themselves as investors and contributors to the well-being of places in which they operate. *Contingent* organizations view themselves simply as participants in places and *exploitative* organizations view themselves as independent agents with little to no obligations to the places in which they operate.

Place agent identities are associated with particular values of place and are reflected in corporate culture as well as in their corporate behaviors and strategies (Table 1). One significant aspect of corporate culture is the value given to place. Interdependent and independent agents have distinctly different views on the value of place. Those with an interdependent perspective value places for their intrinsic worth while those with an independent perspective view places as commodities or resources to be utilized.

Table 1. Organizations as Place Builder

	Place Agent Identity	Value of Place	Cultural Characteristics	Behavior	Strategy
Transformational	change agents	cultural and environmental entity, interdependent systems	team-focused, collaboratively minded, values shared learning	invest cultural and economic resources towards the well-being of place	to orchestrate organizational and place well-being, community collaboration
Contributive	investors, contributors	social network, resource	community supporters, philanthropic/benevolent, paternalistic	give to place via fundraising, sponsorship, and leadership without a specific accounting of how it benefits the organization	to participate in achieving place goals that build social and cultural capital which are consistent with the organizational mission
Contingent	participants	social, geographic, and economic commodity	competitive, instrumental	instrumental giving to place is based on specific and identifiable benefit to organization	to participate in achieving place activities/events that satisfy an organization's investment
Exploitative	independent agents, industrycentric	social, geographic, and economic commodity	profit-oriented, manipulative, arrogant ignorance	exploit environmental, human, and cultural capital for corporate profit, limited giving (financial & volunteerism) to local organizations	to achieve organizational goals at the expense of place

As the management literature has taken up the idea of culture, it has emphasized a fairly consistent set of themes and problems. Schoenberger (1997) posits, "Corporate culture is generally viewed as a set of social conventions embracing behavioral norms, standards, customs, and the rules of the game underlying social interactions within the firm" (p. 113). On one level, organizational culture refers to values that are shared by the people in a group and tend to persist over time (Kotter and Heskett, 1992) or as a concept that refers to how the company manages problems, and practices imposed by management (Wright, 1994) that can, to some extent, improve its ability to respond to global competition.

Corporate and organizational culture is a set of commonly shared values and beliefs which influences the behavior of people, including work and business practices (Hatch, 1993) and the total way of thinking, feeling, and behaving (Kluckhohn, as cited in Geertz, 1973). These perspectives then guide an organization's strategies and behaviors in a place, thus shaping not only its own economic vitality, but also the development of place.

We agree with Smircich (1983, p. 19) who argues that "culture is a process-it cannot be fixed onto a checklist of attributes of a delineated group: that would be to treat culture as a thing". Once you adapt this root metaphor for 'organizations as culture', we leave behind the view that culture is something an organization has, in favor of the view that a culture is something an organization *is* (Smircich, 1983; Morgan, 1997). From this point of view of organization as culture, we avoid the positivistic models of culture and instead build on the deeper, more complex anthropological and social constructivist models. Culture will be most useful as a concept if it helps us better understand the hidden and complex aspects of how place is created through the meanings and interactions of multiple actors. Simply put, one cannot talk about space and its use which we believe leads to place making, if we are limited to the traditional concepts (Schein, 1992).

This dialectic nature of place making and culture is a key construct for organizational leaders in organizations of all size, but in particular to those who are responsible for guiding their organization in new arenas of global competition. Treating culture as a political and social process provides a theoretical approach for examining organizations as place builders. This approach helps avoid conceptualizing organizations as bounded units and focuses instead on organizations as cultural settings within ideological and material relationships. In other words, as Schoenberger (1997) would concur, that culture is really about "creating a way of life both in the organization and in the community in which it lives" (p. 121). We are saying that humans, through their organizations, its social interactions and relationships, actually produce culture while culture is producing them and their organization. The notion that culture is constitutive strongly supports the notion that place creates the culture in which people interact with their environment in ways that are meaningful to them and by extension to the organization.

Each of the four types of organizations (*transformational, contributive, contingent,* and *exploitative*) create corporate missions which demonstrates different levels of commitment to place well-being and fiscal success. Organizations with the same agent perspective, but different agent identities, develop similar, although, not identical missions and strategies, which includes similar commitments to place well-being and/or fiscal success. Organizations with an interdependent perspective strive for a relatively equal balance between place well-being and their own fiscal success, whereas those organizations with an independent agent identity put much more emphasis and weight on fiscal success with little concern for place well-being. Figure 3 illustrates the minor differences between organizations that share the same agent identity but distinct differences between organizations with different agent identities.

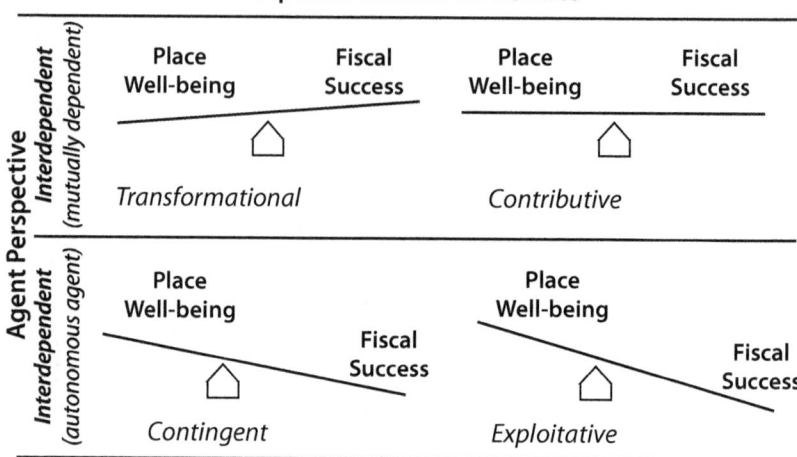

Figure 3. Four Types of Place Builders and Their Corporate Priorities

Corporations that conceptualize themselves as mutually dependent on place, develop missions which integrate and seek to balance place well-being and corporate fiscal success. These organizations utilize an integrative strategy, which focuses on fostering and incorporating its resources in ways that help improve and/or change place. In contrast, those organizations that consider themselves independent of place develop missions that emphasize corporate fiscal success over place well-being. These organizations practice a separatist strategy, which focuses on the organization's access to and use of local resources. When comparing organizations that share the same agent identity perspective, there are minor differences in the degree to which they balance place well-being with fiscal success. It is these differences that distinguish the four types of organizations, *transformational, contributive, contingent,* and *exploitative*.

Four Types of Place Builders

To develop these four types, we will describe four different companies operating in the western United States[2]. We present these companies not because they are representative of all companies in the region or nation, but because they illustrate radically different types of corporate agents: *transformational, contributive, contingent, and exploitative* (see Table 1). As such, they provide concrete cases through which to explore the range of ways in which companies intentionally and unintentionally contribute to or detract from the material, social, and natural realms of place and their symbolic meanings.

Transformational Organization

Transformational organizations are characterized by viewing themselves as a critical agent for change in the community. They hold an interdependent perspective and have corporate missions which focus on improving life and creating positive change for both the organization and the place. Their organizational cultures are highly focused on team learning, collaboration, and openness to change and building partnerships (Table 1). Members of transformational organizations have developed the skills and mind-sets that embrace their philosophy and attitudes of learning and teaching clients. These organizations value place as a cultural and environmental entity made up of unique social relationships, material relations, and natural resources and characteristics. They think of themselves as members of that place, not separate from it. Because transformational organizations see themselves as part of an interdependent system, their success contributes to the success of the place, and vice versa. They practice an *integrative* strategy that focuses on creating and orchestrating a shared vision for the community and the organization which holds itself accountable to the community for the quality and content of its contribution to place. Transformational strategies and behaviors include initiating new policies and business practices for protecting the natural environment, neighborhoods, cultural heritage, local economy, and other local resources. Often these behaviors are a cost to the firm, are ahead of industry trends and regulation, and are not intended to create a public relations advantage.

World Partners. World Partners is a mid-sized company specializing in integrated real estate services. The organization has been operating since the 1960s and employs approximately 150 people. The organization is an innovator in construction and architecture design. They combine both of these for the purpose of creating buildings that reflects the value of the community and the client, as well as transforming the construction industry. These practices have earned them regional and national recognition as a leader in advancing new technologies, safe-guarding the environment, and enhancing place.

This organization exemplifies the transformational type in several ways. First, its mission is distinguished from typical mission statements because it includes the well-being of its clients and community as well as the organization's fiscal well-being. World Partner's mission is to "significantly improve the economic vitality of our clients business and improve the lives of all that we touch to such a degree that it transforms the industry of the built environment, one project at a time". The language of this organization's mission statement is unique because it extends beyond organizational goals and specifically identifies which realm of place (the built environment) they intend to positively impact. This explicit mission to help improve the lives of others, is a bit didactic, like the corporate missions of noteworthy companies such as Cadbury, which explicitly aimed to foster self-improvement (Dellheim, 1986).

Second, this organization does more than design buildings; it partners with clients in designing buildings that meet the needs of the client, the larger place, and local stakeholders. For example, they have worked with local school districts to assess local needs and design buildings within budget and are compatible with local needs and values. By working closely with clients, they change their own business practices to best meet client needs. For example, when working with schools, they develop a design plan that meets the needs for the school and then they provide a guaranteed bid, months or years before construction will begin. This allows schools to secure community funding by improving the perception of fiscal responsibility of the school district and guaranteeing the community that the project will operate within the approved budget. This business model requires that both the client and corporation act as interdependent agents, resulting in new ways of building schools and financing bond issues.

Third, World Partners does more than provide design and construction services to its clients; it also works to teach clients to improve their own practices. World Partner's behaviors and strategies are congruent with their mission statement that values community well-being on an equal ground with corporate fiscal success. Key managers state, "we don't necessarily just do what we do because we think it is good business, we also realize that training and teaching people how to take care of the community is critical. We carry that philosophy and concern into the community via our professional and personal lives." The organization emphasizes a teaching relationship with its clients, "A lot of our clients take some of the things we do well and apply it to their own businesses. We aim to influence our clients and the community." Notice here that this corporation does not place boundaries between personal and professional values nor between corporate and community well-being.

Fourth, the firm encourages its employees to invest their personal funds in client projects to advance productivity and their connectedness and commitment to both the organization and the place[3]. Employee participation in client projects enables employees to interact with clients on a more personal level, distinguishing them as partners and agents of change. Employees describe the firm's culture as pro-learning and pro-relationship. As one employee stated, "Employees can say I own a piece of that building, thus creating a positive attachment to the organization. And that is what makes this organization an important part of the community." Whereas, traditionally, employees are able only to invest in corporate stock, this business practice allows employees to invest in both the company and the community. This mutually beneficial investment model is based on the organization's conception that the company's well-being is inseparable from the well-being of place.

Finally, World Partners demonstrates concern for the well-being of all three spheres of place, social, natural, and material. The organization encourages employees to contribute in ways that are unique and special to them. The owner states, "If an employee wants to volunteer for junior achievement which takes an hour or two during the work day, that's hard, but if their work is done then we encourage them to find ways to participate in the community." Allowing employees to contribute to local organizations during the work day results in tangible benefit to the social relations realm of place. Although, World Partner's primary intention is to transform the built environment in ways that contribute to community well-being, it also recognizes the importance of protecting the natural environment. Building designs include the use of natural landscaping, green building materials, maximizing energy efficiency, compatibility with local history and architecture (Thomas, 2004). It voluntarily monitors the impact its construction has on local ecology and turns down projects that violate their principals or may negatively impact the natural environment (Thomas, 2004). Rather than being motivated by laws and regulations to protect the natural environment, World Partners is motivated by their own desire to transform place and their industry in positive ways, as reflected in the mission statement.

Contributive Organization

Contributive organizations view themselves as a contributing member of a network of business people and community leaders who share a common ideology. Their identity as a local contributor is affirmed by engaging in local organizations, fundraising, and philanthropy that give back to place (Schneider, Brief, and Guzzo, 1996; Chaskin, Brown, Venkatesh and Vidal, 2001). In contrast to transformational organizations that view themselves as responsible for the well-being of place, a contributive organization views itself as a contributor to the well-being of place. The organizational culture is focused on "giving back" and conforming to local norms and values.

Contributive organizations value place first for its social relationships and second for economic opportunities and potential for business growth. The natural world is just the setting or geographic location of their business. These organizations need a place that needs them; part of the value of place is that it provides a niche for these organizations to simultaneously prosper and give back to place. They practice an *integrative strategy* that cultivates and promotes its role as a key player/contributor in the community. Contributive organizations value each of the three realms of place for what that realm provides for the community and the organization; nature for its natural resources that make the place unique: material environment for its community's infrastructure and access to organizations; and the social realm for the community's network of individuals and businesses that facilitate its philanthropic and social membership activities.

Corbin Company. The Corbin Company is a small electric supply company that employs 20 employees. They sell and install electric support systems to large commercial users. This company is typical of contributive organizations because of its value of "giving back" to the community. The owner of this small business states that, "the purpose of my business and any business is to simply 'make life better'. The only reason that we exist as a business is to improve life." "Making life better" is the official mission statement of this small electrical company.

This company strives to make life better for their clients and community residents in many ways. First, it provides free electrical workshops on how to bring your home up to code and reduce electrical hazards in the home. The owner of the company also conducts seminars for electricians on best practices, consults with local government officials on improving code standards, and provides workshops to other business owners on ethical business practices.

Second, when working with clients, Corbin Company strives to ensure that their installations are designed for the greatest benefit of the client, community, and environment. As part of the bid, Corbin Company provides free consulting on how to develop the most efficient design, whether or not it receives the contract. The owner of the company is more focused on providing safe, state-of-the-art products than on submitting the lowest bid. He prefers to offer only the highest quality design and service, rather than the most competitive bid. Through his business practices, he places a higher value on the client's long-term benefit than on the company's financial gain. In some cases, Corbin Company has reduced its margins in order to provide the client with the highest long-term benefit. In every bid, the owner reduces his margins in order to install products that improve efficiency and reduce environmental impacts but are more costly. This business practice is driven by the owner's commitment to "making life better", which he sees as including reducing environmental impacts, energy consumption, and the client's long-term costs.

Third, Corbin Company gives back to the community in more philanthropic avenues as well. The company regularly does pro-bono work, providing free labor (design and electric installation) for community projects including schools, low income housing, and a health clinic for low income women. The owner and employees sit on community boards (Chamber of Commerce, Hospital District), are members of philanthropic organizations (Kiwanis, Lions Club), and contribute to local community projects.

The organization emphasizes networking, conducting moral and ethical business practices, as the key to *making life better*. The organization values place for its networking or connections to others and the spirituality of those connections for the owner. The organization represents and promotes strong ethical business practices. The owner believes in teaching its employees and customers the value of living life in ways that contribute and benefit those with whom they deal. Everything the Corbin Company does from consulting with clients, to pro-bono work, to community philanthropy is driven by the owner's philosophy:

> I think you are the place that you are located as a company. That's why we have businesses to improve people's lives, to improve the customer's life. And in turn if you improve in life for people, you improve on the living environment, the city; I think it kind of goes hand in hand.

Corbin Company makes its strongest contributions to the social relationships realm of place through regular donations to philanthropic organizations and existing charitable projects. Although this company makes substantial contributions to community well-being and existing initiatives, it does not seek to improve or help those organizations grow and change. Corbin Company improves the material environment by going beyond compliance with existing codes to working with local government to improve building codes, by using the most long-lasting and energy efficient technology in their installations, and by inspecting and monitoring the compliance and performance of electrical systems across the community. Both transformational and contributive organizations share a commitment to sustainability and well-being of place.

They differ in that transformational organizations intend to be change agents while contributive organizations view themselves more as stewards, maintaining quality of life without a vision for change.

Contingent Organization

Contingent organizations view themselves as disassociated and autonomous agents. They narrowly define CSR as obeying existing laws, regulations, and ethical codes, but they make a concerted effort to act accordingly. Rather than viewing themselves as interdependent with place (transformational) or key members of place (contributive), they view themselves as control agents. They operate from a managerial point of view; the organization's culture is highly structured and values the processes or systems. The contingent organization practices a *separatist strategy* that centers on a plan that distinguishes the organization in terms of its economic power. Contingent organizations value each of the three realms of place for what that realm provides for the company; nature for its ability to attract and retain employees as well as natural resources used by the company; the material environment for the community's infrastructure; and the social realm for its labor force. They practice philanthropy only as a method for advancing their own causes, not out of any intrinsic commitment to place, and their principle contribution is their economic contribution and adherence to laws and regulations.

Benson Industry. Benson Industry is a globally recognized manufacturer with a reputation for quality products. The organization was recruited to its current location in the 1970s and currently employs over 2000. The firm prefers to be seen as the "employer of choice" and as a "good corporate citizen" which the firm views as a key strategy in advancing its image and brand. This firm exemplifies the contingent type through its inward-looking view or attitude that is geared toward protecting its brand reputation and achieving business goals. Any discussion of corporate social responsibility and local communities is secondary to its profit motives.

First, Benson Industry typifies contingent organizations because it values places for the opportunities available there. Benson chose its current location because of the accessibility to land, natural resources, and distribution networks. Local governments offered Benson tax incentives and financing for improving local infrastructure. The local community also offered a low-cost, non-unionized labor pool. Benson located where it did, not because of a desire to contribute to the local place, but because of the opportunities that the place offered. This perspective that place is a commodity, chosen for the advantages it offers the company, is characteristic of the contingent organization.

Second, this company contributes to the local place in order meet their own strategic goals. They have a "community committee", comprised of business members from the surrounding community, whose task is to identify and anticipate areas of conflict between the organization and the place in which they do business. For example, this committee is asked if there are any complaints being expressed in the local community that might impact the corporate image or any new regulations that might impact the company's business. This company regularly scans their business environment to identify threats and opportunities and then makes local investments and contributions based on their potential to reduce threats or exploit an opportunity. For example, the local county proposed to increase the mill levy and the company fought that change because it would have reduced their profit.

This company supports local non-profit organizations not because it values giving back to the community or improving the lives of others, but rather because of the societal expectation that corporations contribute to local non-profit and philanthropic organizations. Both the corporation and employees contribute to United Way every year because it meets a minimum expectation to make a contribution to the local place and because association with a reputable philanthropic organization facilitates good public relations and favorable publicity. Benson gives back to the community, not because they are invested in improving the local place, but because it is good for business. One manager stated, "We have to have that positive reputation as a solid citizen. Otherwise people aren't going to buy your products; people aren't going to come to work for you." Benson views their philanthropy and involvement as a two-way relationship. "It's not just a one-sided thing, but it's what the community needs as well as what benefits to the firm."

Third, this company identifies their own corporate social responsibility in much more limited terms than the two we have already discussed. The corporation identifies CSR as including a) obeying local, federal, and international laws, b) upholding ethical standards, c) respecting worker's rights, d) environmental responsibility, and e) philanthropy that reflects its corporate goals. Rather than intending to transform the local community or help places grow and improve quality of life, Benson intends nothing more than operating in a legal and ethical manner, and making philanthropic contributions that support its own goals.

Benson's impact on the three realms of place is governed by their primary concern with meeting corporate goals. Although Benson complies with labor laws and environmental regulations which impact all three realms of place, none of their actions are intended to have a specific benefit to any realm of place. To the degree that contingent organizations, who strive only to meet the letter of the law, are able to pollute the environment or take advantage of workers without violating environmental or labor regulations, they may have a negative impact on one or more realms of place, whereas both transformational and contributive organizations look for ways not only to minimize their environmental impact but also improve the social realm of place as well. Benson's contributions to local philanthropic organizations are designed to satisfy to most basic expectations for corporate giving at the local level. In the material realm, Benson seeks to minimize their economic contribution to wages and the local tax base. Unlike transformational and contributive organizations which may reduce their own profits in order to deliver a superior product to the client and community, contingent organizations like Benson, seek first and foremost to maximize their profit, though within strict legal and ethical bounds. Benson's corporate impact on the three realms of place is always contingent on first meeting corporate goals and avoiding risk. Their contributions to place in the three realms are limited by the strength of laws, regulations, and ethical standards.

Exploitative Organizations

Exploitative organizations view themselves as occupants of place. They are isolated with respect to the traditions and values of the community. These organizations argue for corporate citizenship where organizations are afforded the rights and legal protections typically afforded only to individual citizens (Vogel, 2005). It plans and organizes its control over place. Cost effectiveness and short term financial progress trumps any local need (Thomas, 2004). Exploitative organizations value place as a commodity where each of the three realms of place is valued for what the realm can provide for the organization. They are active users of the economic, cultural, social, and political resources, which they utilize to their greatest economic benefit (Sagoff, 1996; Rodman, 1992; Entrikin, 2000).

The exploitative firm practices a *separatist* strategy. Their mission to maximize profit determines the exploitative organizations strategy, to deliberately target certain places for the potential to extract resources without accountability or regard for the risks posed to local population. While some exploitative organizations employ locals and deal with local suppliers, in the end, these organizations are not invested in ways that contribute to place well-being. Exploitative organizations are likely to leave a place once they have determined they don't fit or the return is not as lucrative as originally anticipated.

Centro Associates. Centro Associates is a commercial and residential real estate company owned by its employees. It has been operating for over 30 years and employs over 200 sales agents. In its operating region, this agency holds about 25% of the real estate listings, and claims to participate in the largest proportion of real estate transactions of any agency. Centro Associates has branded their agency as the top real estate company in the region. Centro Associates exemplifies the exploitive type because they use their market dominance to maximize their revenues at the expense of its clients, other real estate firms, and the local housing market.

First, Centro Associates distinguishes itself as an exploitive company through its own marketing. It consistently identifies itself as a market leader, but makes no claims about its contributions to place. This company has no mission statement or articulated vision, and makes no mention of corporate responsibility in its promotional materials. Its only value statement espouses the importance of being a market leader through alignment of individual and organizational goals. Unlike the transformational organization, World Partners, which endeavors to improve and transform the local community as it grows and learns as a company, Centro Associates has only inward-looking goals focused on financial dominance. In contrast to other real estate agencies in the region, who describe good agents as those who take seriously their fiduciary responsibility to their clients, are good listeners, true partners, and advocates (Coldwell Banker, 2006; Remax, 2006). Centro Associates describes agents as primarily transaction specialists whose responsibility is information provision. What is most telling about this agency's values and goals is the lack of any discussion of their responsibility to their clients, to the larger place, or to legal and ethical standards. Exploitive companies stand out from the other types because of their self-focused mission and values statements. When describing themselves, Centro Associates describes its agents as leaders, highly trained, and having access to the latest technology. In contrast, its competitors emphasize the responsibility of agents to represent the personal, financial, and legal interests of their clients (Coldwell Banker, 2006; Remax, 2006).

These organization-focused goals and values are apparent in the activities of Centro Associates. This company has exploited the communities in which it operates by treating the local real estate market as a commodity to be exploited for its own financial gain, with little concern or responsibility for individual clients or the overall well-being of the local housing market and economy. For example, Centro Associates employs three strategies that take advantage of the local market, clients, and neglect established ethical principles of their industry. First, it encourages its agents to pursue listings and represent buyers in the top 50th percentile of the local housing market, while discouraging working with buyers and sellers in the lower half of the market. Their listings comprise 25% of the total market, but represent less than 20% of the market below the median versus over 30% of the market above the median, and less than 10% of the market below $150,000 versus over 40% of the market over $600,000 (Multiple Listing Service, 2006). This practice serves the financial goals of individual agents and the company while neglecting property owners in the lower half of the market.

Second, Centro Associates agents are known to routinely outbid agents from other agencies when vying for listings. Evidence of this can be seen in a market analysis of local listings where properties listed by Centro Associates are consistently at top of the price range for comparable properties (Multiple Listing Service, 2006). Third, they use their market dominance to pressure buyers they represent into purchasing over-priced listings held by other Centro agents. One way they do this is by taking advantage of a tight housing market—offering home buyers "the unique chance" to make the first bid on a property listed by another agent in their company before it is officially listed and then encouraging them to offer the listing price immediately. During periods of high housing demand, this tactic was highly successful and gave the appearance of representing the buyer's interests by helping them to get a contract in a tight market. This practice represents the interests of both agents and the company by maximizing their commission and reducing the time on the market, but neglects the financial and other interests of the buyer (Leavitt & Dubner, 2005). Combined, these three strategies allowed Centro Associates to increase and maintain their market dominance and maximize company profits. These practices are exploitive because they neglect whole segments of the market, rely on unethical business practices, undercut competitors, and are a disservice to the financial interests of clients, other homebuyers, and the industry. Centro Associates' webpage has no mention or discussion of social responsibility. The "community involvement" page on Centro Associates' website includes only a list of philanthropic organizations to which it has made contributions. A careful look at this listing reveals that their donations are targeted to groups and organizations that include likely high-end clients, arts councils and symphony orchestras, and those who can assist them or favor their business in some way. Notably, they do not list low-income service organizations, such as Habitat for Humanity, as regular beneficiaries.

Comparison of Four Types of Place Builders

Each of the four types stands out from the others in their perspectives on place and the consequences of their actions. Transformational organizations orchestrate their contributions in ways that transform themselves and place. As agents of change, they are distinguished from other organizations in that they view place in a holistic manner in which all three realms are interactive and interdependent. Consequently, the business practices of transformational organizations contribute to place well-being through learning and teaching in partnership with clients. The other organization that operates from an interdependent perspective, contributive, also engages in business practices that benefit the community, however in a slightly different manner from transformational types. The contributive organizations' foci are on satisfying their need to "give back". They are not motivated to change themselves or place, but rather to fit in as an advocate and participant in worthwhile community activities. As a result, contributive organizations add to the community capacity to address local concerns by being persistent contributors.

In contrast to the interdependent agents, the organizations with an independent perspective engage in business practices that restrict their contributions to place well-being because priority is made to fiscal success. The contingent organization contributes primarily in manners that garner some return or benefit to the organization. Unlike the transformational and contributive organizations, the contingent organization respects local laws, regulations, and ethical codes without pro-actively investing it resources or assets. The degree to which their business practices enhance or damage place is determined by the nature and scope of laws, ethical codes, and regulations to which they comply. In comparison, exploitative organizations are more than indifferent to the impact of their actions; they may go so far as to intentionally create harm and avoid responsibility for their actions. The exploitative organization has little regard for place and views the realms as resources or commodities (Logan & Molotch, 1983; Cross, 2001). They are absentee organizations in the sense that while they may occupy a place, they are not engaged or invested in place. Additionally, these are the organizations that are the greatest threat to the well-being of all three realms of place.

Discussion and Conclusion

The relationship between place and organizations is important for understanding the role and social responsibilities of an organization within its community (Kemmis, 1990). Bio-regionalists like Gary Snyder (1995) suggest that organizations, as well as all other agents, should consider their responsibility to the well being of the environment and the people that live in a place. Snyder perceived the organization as located in a place in which it either adds or detracts from the "great landscape." Geographer Robert Sack (1997) argues similarly that all actions in place have a moral aspect:

> The geographic also extends the realm of the moral. Almost all abstract moral precepts focus on our relations to other human beings. But geography draws attention to the fact that this in an incomplete conception of our responsibilities. Real actions, awareness, and moral concerns in place and space inevitably draw nature into the picture. This is because real actions and real places themselves are integrations of nature and culture (or, more precisely, of nature, social relations, and meaning). When we construct cities, schools, factories, and streets we are removing many facts of nature while retaining and controlling others... Constructing and maintaining any place require decisions about whether particular natural or cultural elements should exist here rather than there, or exist at all. Each and every decision we make about places to live, work, and visit engages us in this calculus, balancing our interest in nature and culture. Place helps make us aware that moral concern is not bounded by the neat conventions of academic disciplines and, in particular, that the social world is not divorced from the natural, but intimately linked to it at every geographic scale, from home to world. This role of place increases our understanding of these virtues and of our moral role as geographical agents (p. 22).

If bio-regionalists and others are right about place, its construction, and the role of agents, then advancing the notion of organizations as place building agents takes on new significance regarding the strategic value of organizations to the communities or places. Not only do social and physical scientists mistakenly consider their subject matter as though it is not only placeless but also spaceless (Agnew, 1993; Sack, 1997). The same is true of corporations; many of them conceptualize their activities as being placeless and spaceless. Only those organizations who conceptualize themselves as belonging to a particular place develop an organizational culture which understands that their responsibilities expand beyond the placeless and spaceless financial interests of the shareholders.

The typology we have presented here illustrates how one type of organization, the corporation, contributes to the social construction of place through its mission, priorities, value of place, and subsequent behaviors. Although our illustrative examples and narrative describe corporations, the four types of agents might also be applied to other types of organizations including governmental agencies and not-for-profit organizations. While the basic mission of governments and most non-profits is typically defined as service to a geographic space or shared interest community rather than financial profit, this does not preclude them from adopting practices that exploit or endanger one or more realms of place. In addition to expanding the conception of CSR, the typology we have presented might also be used to examine the social responsibility and comprehensive impact of any organization on the place in which it operates.

Implications for Corporations & Communities

The traditional model of CSR is limited in scope and influence. In contrast, we have argued for a more expansive perspective which examines not only a corporation's philanthropic actions and their compliance to laws and regulations but which also examines their place values, their mission, and the potential of their business practices to enhance or diminish place well-being. We have described four types of organizations, each of which influences the social construction of place in unique ways. Keeping these four types in mind, we ask, "what are the implications for place and organizations if CSR is measured by how corporations conceptualize themselves and act as agents in the construction of places?" If an organization examines where they fit in the typology, then our model provides a framework for considering first, whether conceptualizing themselves as an interdependent or independent agent is serving their true goals. Second, the model (Figure 2) might provoke an organization to examine the balance between their commitments to place well-being and fiscal success.

The model we have proposed also offers a new framework for thinking about what types of organizations communities are attracting and recruiting. For cities, towns, and other groups working to attract organizations, this typology offers a new model for considering the role of an organization as an agent and assessing its behavior and strategies in building place. Second, the model (Figure 2) might provoke municipalities and/or chambers of commerce to examine whether the firms they are attracting share their commitments to place well-being and economic development. Governing bodies should consider whether the incentives they offer produce not just the desired return, but attract a partner that can help them build and transform their place in ways aligned with current community goals. The governing boards of cities, counties, business districts, and chambers of commerce might ask, "Do these organizations have the values and vision for expanding our community's capacity while creating a competitive advantage to the organization?" We have provided a typology that can be useful in assessing the best fitting organization. While its one thing to attract the best fitting firm; it's another to build a sustainable partnership. Perhaps cities, counties, and business districts should also ask, "What are the costs of attracting, and retaining the wrong organization." The benefits of attracting organizations that help build the economic well-being of place are obvious, but assessing the degree to which a corporation might make minimal contributions to the three realms of place or engage in behaviors that are destructive versus constructive (exploit local labor, pollute the natural environment, value profits over long-term sustainability, etc.) should be considered in balance with economic contributions. The typology we present here provides a starting point for examining the breadth of an organizations priorities and the degree to which their regular business practices are likely to contribute to or detract from the three realms of place. Identifying and attracting organizations that will make tangible contributions and consider the impact of their actions on all three realms of place will provide places with legacies that last long after the initial economic benefits have been realized.

New Directions for Research

The typology we presented is a step in the direction of building a coherent theory of how organizations construct place and poses new questions about the role of corporations in relation to places. We have shown that corporate identities, missions, and practices are all tied to how corporations influence the well-being of place. Future work is needed to create a viable device or instrument to measure and validate the typology we have proposed. If a tool were developed to accurately type organizations, then researchers could examine other questions, including: What predictors could we use to identify these organizations? What specific strategies and behaviors are associated with each type? Taking up Gan's call to examine the causal relationships between organizations and place elicits a variety of new questions posed by the application of our typology: What are the advantages of a corporation acting as one type versus another? Is size of company or industry associated with greater success as one kind of agent versus another? Does acting as one type of agent versus another create a competitive advantage? Are the types of agents associated with size of corporation, industry, region, profitability, and products/services? Can organizations be more efficient and effective when they know how to define place and their role in the community? Finally, can these types provide new insights and the basis of a metric for defining and measuring CSR, as both a predictor and dependent variable?

Further, a theoretical understanding of how place is constructed can advance the field of community management and economic development by advancing a new way of thinking about what types of firms that are likely to advance the community's interests, solve collective problems and improve or maintain the well-being of community (Chaskin, Brown, Venkatesh, and Vidal, 2001). A theoretical understanding of how organizations contribute to the construction of place would benefit from the work of economists, geographers, sociologists as well as management theorists. Perhaps even more important is the contribution various social scientists might contribute to improving the economic, environmental, and social well-being of places through a more sophisticated examination of the relationship between place well-being and organizational missions, strategies, and practices. This examination of relationships is critical as it helps identify best fitting organizations and provides a new model for how communities can assess and even predict an organization's contribution. This kind of examination goes beyond the typical economic assessment that counties, municipalities, chambers of commerce and other governing bodies typically employ, which focus on primary jobs and building industry clusters.

References

Agnew, J. (1993). Representing Space: Space, Scale and Culture in Social Science. In J. Duncan & D. Ley (Eds.), *Place/Culture/Representation* (pp. 251-271). New York: Routledge.

Agnew, J. A. (1987). *Place and politics.* Boston: Allen & Unwin.

Altman, I., & Low, S. (1992). (Eds.). *Place Attachment* (Vol. 12). New York and London: Plenum Press.

Alvesson, Mats. (1990). On the popularity of organizational culture. *Acts Sociologica*, 33, 1:31-49.

Alvesson, Mats and Berg, Per Olof. (1992). *Corporate culture and organizational symbolism: An overview.* Walter de Gruyter: New York.

Anderson, J. W. (1989). *Corporate social responsibility: Guidelines for top management* Quorum Books: New York.

Black, L. D. & Hartel, C.E.J. (2004). The five capabilities of socially responsible companies. *Journal of Public Affairs*, 4(2): 125-144.

Blumer, H. (1969). *Symbolic interactionism: Perspective and method.* Los Angles: University of California Press.

Buttimer, A., & Seamon, D. (1980). (Eds.). *Human experience of space and place.* New York: Martins.

Butz, D., & Eyles, J. (1997). Reconceptualizing Sense of Place: Social Relations, Ideology and Ecology. *Geografiska Annaler, Series B, Human Geography*, 79: 1-25.

Chaskin, R. J., Brown, P., Venkatesh, S. & Vidal, A. (2001). *Building community Capacity.* New York: Aldine de Gruyter.

Coldwell Banker website. Retrieved August 23, 2006, from http://coldwellbanker.feedroom.com.

Cooper, S. (2004). *Corporate social performance: A stakeholder approach.* Burlington, VT.

Cresswell, T. (2004). *Place: a short introduction*. Malden, MA: Blackewell Publishing.

Cross, J. E. (2001). *Disruptions in community attachment: The social-psychological impacts of rapid economic & demographic change.* Paper presented at the 11th Headwater's Conference, Gunnison, CO.

Dellheim, C. (1986). Business in time: The historian and corporate culture. *The Public Historian,* 8: 9-22.

Denison, D. R. (1996). What is the difference between organizational culture and organizational climate? A native's point of view on a decade of paradigm wars. *The Academy of Management Review*, 21: 619-65.

Dennis, L. H., & Herring, L. (1999). Corporate relocation takes its toll on society. Workforce. 78(2):121-132.

Entrikin, J. N. 2000. *The betweeness of place: Towards geography of modernity.* New York: Routledge.

Etzioni, Amitai. (1993). *The Spirit of Community: rights, responsibilities, and the communitarian agenda.* New York: Crown Publishers.

Etzioni, Amitai. (1998). "The responsive communitarian platform: Rights and responsibilites". In Etzioni, A. (Ed.), *The Essential Communitarian Reader* (p. xxv- xxxix). New York: Rowman & Littlefield Publishers, Inc.

Folkerts, H., & Weijers, R. (2004). *De winst zit in de opbremgst, naar een duurzame ontwikkeling,* in: Mastering Strategy, Het Finacncieele Dagblad.

Fussler, C. A. Cramer & van de Vegt, S. (2004). *Raising the bar, creating value with the United Nations Global Compact.* Sheffield: Greenleaf Publishing.

Gans, H. J. (2002). The sociology of space: a use-centered view. *City and Community,* 1(4): 329-339.

Geertz, C. (1973). *The interpretation of cultures.* New York: Basic Books. Geertz, C. (1983). *Local knowledge.* New York: Basic Books.

Gieryn, T. F. (2000). A Space for Place in Sociology. *Annu. Rev. Social.,* 26:463-496.

Guion, R. (1973). A note on organizational climate. *Organizational behavior and human performance* 9:120-125.

Gustafson, P. 2005. Meanings of Place: Everyday Experience and Theoretical Conceptualizations. *Journal of Environmental Psychology,* 21, 5-16.

Hatch, M. J. (1993). The dynamics of organizational culture. *The academy of management review,* 18(4):657-693.

Hamad, G. (1974). Strategy as revolution. *Harvard business review,* July: 24-30. Hopkins, M. 1999. *The planetary bargain: corporate social responsibility comes of age.* St. Martins press: New York.

Hudson, R. (2001). *Producing places.* New York: The Guilford Press.

James, L., & Jones, A. (1974). Organizational climate: A review of theory and research. *Psychology Bulletin,* 18: 1096-1112.

Jonker, J., & de Witte, M. (2006). *Management Models for Corporate Social Responsibility.* (Eds.). Berlin: Springer.

Kaufman, H. F. (1959). Toward an interactional conception of community. *Social Forces,* 38(1): 8-17.

Kemmis, D. (1990). *Community and the politics of place.* Norman, OK.: University of Oklahoma Press.

Kotler, P. & Lee, N. (2005). *Corporate social responsibility: Doing the most good for your company and your cause.* Hoboken, N.J.: Wiley.

Kotter, J. P. & Heskett, J. L. (1992). *Corporate culture and performance.* New York: The Free Press.

Langtry, B. (1994). Stakeholders and the moral responsibilities of business. *Business Ethics Quarterly,* 4 (4): 431-441.

Levitt, S. D. & Dubner, S. J. (2005). *Freakonomics: A Rogue Economist Explores the Hidden Side of Everything.* New York: Harper Collins Publishers.

Logan, J. R. & Molotch, H. L. (1983). *Urban Fortunes: The Political Economy of Place.* Berkeley, CA: University of California Press.

May, L. (1983). Vicarious agency and corporate responsibility. *Philosophical Studies,* 43: 69-82.

McClenahen, J. (2005). Defining social responsibility. *Manufacturing and Society, March:* 64-66.

Morgan, G. (1997). *Images of organization.* (2nd Ed) Thousand Oaks: Sage.

Multiple Listing Service website. Retrieved August 23, 2006, from http://www.mls.com. http://www.remax.com/residential/real_estate_101/buying_a_home/index.aspx;

Newell, P. (2005). Citizenship, accountability and community: The limits of the agenda. *International Affairs,* 81 (3): 541-537.

Ouchi, W. G., & Wilkins, A. L. (1985). Organizational culture. *Annual Review of Sociology,* 11: 457-483.

RE/MAX website. Retrieved August 23, 2006, from http://www.remax.com/residential/real_estate_101/buying_a_home/index.aspx;

Rodman, M. (1992). Empowering place: Multilocality and multivocality. *American Anthropologist, New series,* 94(3): 640-656.

Sack, R. (1997). *Homo Geographicus*. Baltimore, MD: The Johns Hopkins University Press.

Sack, R. D. (1988). The consumer's world: Place as context. *Annals of the Association of American Geographers*, 78(4): 642-664.

Sagoff, M. (1996). Values and preferences. *Ethics*, 2: 301-316.

Sauer, C. (1925). *The morphology of landscape*. Berkeley: University of California Publications in Geography, 2:19-54.

Savitz, A. W., & Weber, K. (2006). *The triple bottom line: How today's best run companies are achieving economic, social, and environmental success-and you can too*. San Francisco: Jossey-Bass.

Schneider, B., Brief, A. P., & Guzzo, R. A. (1996). Creating a climate and culture for sustainable organizational change. *Organizational Dynamics*. Spring: 7-18.

Schein, E. H. (1992). *Organizational culture and leadership*. San Francisco: Jossey-Bass.

Schoenberger, E. (1997). *The cultural crisis of the firm*. Cambridge: Blackwell.

Selznick, P. (1995). Thinking about community: Ten theses. *Society*, 32: 33-37.

Senge, P. (1990). *The fifth discipline: The art and practice of the learning organization*. New York: Currency Doubleday.

Smircich, L. (1983). Concepts of culture and organizational analysis. *Administrative Science Quarterly*, 28(3):339-54

Smith, C. (1994). The new corporate philanthropy. *Harvard Business Review*, 72, 3.

Snyder, G. (1995). *A place in space: Ethics, aesthetics, and watersheds*. Washington D.C.: Publishers Group West.

Thomas, D. F. (2004). *Toward an understanding of organization place building in communities.* Unpublished doctoral dissertation, Colorado State University, Fort Collins, Co.

Tuan, Yi-Fu. (1977). *Space and place: The perspective of experience.* Minneapolis: University of Minnesota Press.

Vogel, D. (2005). *The market for value: The potential and limits of corporate social responsibility.* Brookings Institution Press: Washington D.C.

Vogel, D. (2005). The low value of virtue. *Harvard Business Review,* June: 26. Weick, K.E. (1995). Sensemaking in organizations. Thousand Oaks: Sage. Werlen, B. (1993). Society, Action, and Space: An Alternative Human Geography. London: Routledge.

Williams, R. (1989). *Resources of Hope: Culture, democracy, socialism.* New York: Verso Publishers.

Wright, S. (1994). (Eds.). *Anthropology of organizations.* New York: Routledge. Zelinsky, W. (1992). *Cultural geography of the United States.* Englewood Cliffs, NJ: Prentice Hall.

NOTES

1. We recognize that the natural world has been altered to varying degrees by human activity; however, we maintain that nature as a realm of place is distinct from the built environment and other man-made aspects of space.

2. Data for these company profiles were collected by the first author for his doctoral dissertation. Respondents were informed of the basic goals of the research, and each signed consent forms guaranteeing their confidentiality. Interviews of company employees were approved by company managers and in some cases, corporate headquarters. Names of companies and other details have been changed to ensure the anonymity of respondent.

3. This practice raises both legal and ethical concerns, and the authors have heard conflicting viewpoints on the matter from employees. However, World Partners continues to believe that investing in projects enhances the value of those projects.

Published with permission from: Thomas, D. F. & Cross, J. E. (2007). Organizations as place builders. *Journal of Behavioral and Applied Management, 9*(1), 33-61.

3

UNDERSTANDING THE LINK BETWEEN BUSINESS ORGANIZATIONS AND CONSTRUCTION OF COMMUNITY SENSE OF PLACE:
THE PLACE BASED NETWORK MODEL

David F. Thomas, Diane Gaede, Richard R. Jurin, and Laura S. Connolly

What are the dynamics that affect the link between organizations (both business and non-profit) atid their capacity to help develop 'sense of place' in communities? Based on a grounded-theory qualitative study researchers investigated the critical variables whose nexus of interactions influence organizational establishment of SOP. This paper will advance a model that illustrates this dynamic through the Place Based Network (PBN) model. The PBN is a foundation for an interpretation of how community sense of place is socially constructed, and it recognizes the role organizations play in developing intentions and the meanings organizations may create in their community.

Keywords: organizations, sense of place, community resources, networks, community relationships

Successful business organizations behave in ways that are consistent with their culture, history and strategic intentions. Communities likewise operate in ways that are consistent with their own vision and stakeholder wishes. Communities desire to recruit or import business organizations that will satisfy valued economic and social requirements, and which portray the desirable characteristics of the community (Kemmis.1990: Wright, 2002). It is in the best interests of a community to develop an appealing 'sense of place' in order to attract successful business organizations that want to locate there and contribute to community growth and development. The authors propose that in order for business organizations to succeed in communities - beyond market considerations - a cultural dimension that embraces 'sense of place' becomes a critical component of establishing and sustaining a viable business organization and community partnership. This paper focuses on both the business organization as a cultural agent in the coconstruction of a sense of place, and the community as a partner in this effort. This focus on community development in a place-building context helps position community development as a collaborative between the business organization and its community. To explore this collaborative relationship, a qualitative study was conducted on how business organizations in northern Colorado defined and practiced place building activities.

Literature Review: Conceptual Basis for Exploring Establishment of Sense of Place

'Place building' as a concept is alluded to by sociologists and geographers who are interested in matters such as enterprise movement, community and systems sustainability (sustainable development), and enterprise attributes of communities (Hudson, 2001; Schoenberger, 1997; Sagoff, 1996: Wright, 1994; Jacobs, 1984). What is the role of business organizations in the construction of sense of place in their community? In approaching the question of how business organizations relate to their communities, different geographers and sociologists have explored different dimensions of human activity in geographic settings. Cultural geographers concern themselves with the notion of sense of place: humanistic geographers focus on locale variables; and social geographers examine the relationship between space and society. These are important dimensions to understanding a business organization's view of their relationship to communities. This understanding contributes to community policy formation and evaluation, and the intention to attract and retain business organizations. However, at this time a summative view of what each strand of inquiry contributes to the business organization and its community relationship is missing (Agnew, 1987; Thomas & Cross, 2007).

Business organizations can be more efficient and effective when they know how to help define 'sense of place.' By incorporating this knowledge, business organizations make better decisions regarding the location of their business, their activities, and their behavior in the community. Community partnerships that encourage the business organization's ability and willingness to create a sustainable fit can result in the creation of a "sense of place" for the business organization within the community (Anderson & Gale. 1992). This has the characteristic of creating sustainable development where place is improved and made better, but not necessarily grown as in urban sprawl.

Likewise when communities understand the value of attracting and retaining a business organization with the right cultural, economic, and social 'fit', they improve their chances for long term economic viability' and achieve an acceptable balance between social ethics, environment, and economic growth (commonly called the Triple Bottom Line). This is also true for business organizations that operate or behave in ways that build local relationships - that are an intrinsic part of both the community and the business organization's culture.

Sometimes business organizations and their communities can find themselves at odds on local issues ranging from economic to cultural and social initiatives and goals (Kemmis, 1990). Most of these issues revolve around space and its use. Business organization/community struggles can be at the center of 'cultural wars' that can result in disruptive relationships, and can occur when an business organizations values conflict with the values of the larger community in which it resides (Mitchell, 2002). Therefore, achieving maximum cultural congruence with their community is important to business organizations (Sauer, 1925; Williams, 1989).

Business organizations can have a positive influence in how conflicts over culture, spatial, and social issues are resolved. In such scenarios the business organization's culture and its strategic intentions give important insights into the business organization's capabilities and capacity to match the community's desired goals for attracting and retaining the 'best fit' business organizations.

The notion that places evolve from human interaction rather than simply geography is described as early as 1925 by Carl Sauer in The Morphology-of Landscape, and in a variety of more contemporary writings (Sack, 1997; Zelinsky, 1992). Relph (1976, pg. 47) posted "place as the focus of meanings or intention, either culturally or individually defined in knowing that a certain place is where one belongs". "Other meanings of a place are derived from or arise out of the interaction individuals and groups have with others in that place" (Tuan, 1977), or the ways in which people act toward each other with regard to that place (Blumer, 1969).

For example Santa Fe, New Mexico, could be defined as an urban business environment, a tourist destination, a cultural arts district, or an historic 'old town' and each of these definitions of place suggest different interactions between people and the place as well as within the place. The actions of individuals in a place simultaneously shape place and are guided by the meanings they form through interaction with individuals, groups, and business organizations in that place.

A theoretical framework that embraces the dynamics associated with creating sense of place involves "webs of significance" that describe a network of relationships. The notion of "webs of significance" causes examination of a community; its history', social rules and patterns of participation and community building, and the role (interplay) a business organization has in the community. The proximity of a business organization operating within a web of relationships constructed from a community's activity allows the business organization to identify the elements to be addressed in creating a sense of place (Felkins, 2002; Geertz, 1973; Bridger and Alter, 2006).

Methodology

Qualitative research in this particular study sought depth rather than breadth. Indepth and intimate information was collected from the owners of twelve small business organizations in Northern Colorado. A variety of small business organizations were examined and information was gathered about their relationships in their community and their role in the construction of community sense of place.

Business Organization Selection Criteria

A group of business organizations were purposively selected from the total population of over 500 small business organizations identified from the Northern Colorado Economic Council and the Chamber of Commerce directories. From this data twelve business organizations were selected that satisfied the criterion listed below.

Criterion One. The business organization must have been in business in the community for at least five years.

Criterion Two. The organization had a history of contributing to the community.

Criterion Three. The organization had less than 500 employees.

Criterion Four. The organization was locally owned and operated.

Criterion Five. The organization had annual revenues exceeding $1 million in sales.

This study plan ensured that business organizations selected would help build theory regarding how a business organization constructs a sense of place, as well as provide varying conditions for examining and making the emerging concepts more conceptually dense.

Participant Selection Criteria

Consultation with four recognized business leaders in the community regarding the applicability and understandability of the interview questions prior to the first set of interviews was a key benefit in selecting a final set of questions (Thomas, 2004). The business leaders in this case were two presidents of the top five small business employers in the region, the Chief Executive Officer of the Regional Economic Development Council and Vice President of the region's largest non-profit organization. An empathic stance was employed in the interview process, which sought to understand without judgment (neutrality) by showing openness, sensitivity, respect, and responsiveness to the interviewee about their business organization's culture and processes (Strauss and Corbin. 1998).

Individual business owners were contacted in each of the business organizations to determine if that organization had an interest in participating. The business owners were determined to be the first and best contact, since that individual is in a position to describe the business organization's strategies and culture as well as the relationship of the business organization to the community. Second, he/she has the authority to endorse the research and encourage participation. And third, the owner can identify those individuals within the business organization that may be able to provide important data on how the business organization works and interacts in its community. The participants interviewed were chosen to help form the 'grounded' theory. (Grounded theory, a mode of inductive analysis, can be thought of as a theory that is derived from or "grounded" in everyday experiences (Glaser and Strauss, 1967)).

Data Collection

The four data collection instruments employed were: (a) observations (including attending company meetings and functions), (b) interviews (ranging from semi-structured to open-ended), and (c) documents (ranging from private to public) that detail organization policies and procedures relating to community activities. One-on-one interviews were conducted using a recording procedure. An interview protocol was designed to guide a number of semi-structured questions with ample space between questions to write responses and interviewer comments. The protocol of questions (see Appendix A) was intended to guide the interview conversation.

Each owner was interviewed in their business office for approximately an hour or more and information was gathered about their relationships in their community and their role in the construction of community sense of place. Data collected from interviews were transcribed from tape recordings to a document for the purposes of analysis and interpretation. Data usually are collected until no further new information is found. This process is termed saturation and signals the end of data collection (Strauss and Corbin, 1998).

Data collected from the twelve interviews were transcribed into documents for discovering and coding. A cross-case analysis was employed to enhance generalizability and deepen understanding and provide an explanation of how business organizations build sense of place. The intention of the in-depth interviews was to discover how humans and their groups construct meaning in their place, and the process by which a business organization constructs place in its community.

In addition to interviewing, other data were collected and analyzed that added thick description and validated or added to interview data. Observations of the business organizations activities in the community gave insights to its culture and intentions. Documents and records, such as a business' annual plan, marketing programs, customer service policy documents and press releases in local newspapers were collected for their value as a stable source of information, in the sense that they may accurately reflect the policies and procedures related to how a business organization deals with its community and issues related to space (Lincoln & Guba, 1985).

Cultural artifacts provided alternative insights into the ways in which people and their business organizations contribute to the construction of a sense of place. The study of material culture is thus of importance to this research as it offered a way to explore the multiple variations that may be present in a business organization. Artifacts studied included the business organization's visible symbols and tangible evidence that supported or undermined what it preached which included web sites, promotional materials and articles in local newspapers regarding their business activities.

The summary of the twelve cases revealed four major categories of business organization, place perspectives, contribution, and community from the data in each case.

Data Analysis

For data analysis, *inductive coding* was employed whereby codes were "induced" from the text and information collected moved from the more literal to the more abstract. Open code "names" were examined through the process of *constant comparative analysis* to produce a more analytic or abstract category that held a group of the open codes together (axial codes). The axial codes formed the major categories that built the conceptual framework that denoted the relationships between and among categories (Creswell, 1998; Patton, 2002; Strauss and Corbin, 1998). The final code or summary is referred to as the "selective code" or the "core category," and at this point moves from data analy sis to concept and theory development (Miles and Huberman, 1994).

Many variables surfaced through the interviews which explored the complex and holistic picture of how a business organization constructs place. The information gathered from the research was examined to discover practices or behaviors, forms of business organizational structure, and/or ways of thinking or interpreting how place is constructed by a business organization. Examining multiple business organizations pinned down the specific conditions under which a finding would occur and helped form the more general categories of how those conditions may be related. However, it is crucial to understand the dynamics of each particular case before proceeding to cross-case explanation (Miles and Huberman, 1994). Although a general idea about the properties of constructing sense of place are presented, such variables usually become clear when real case data have been explored in some depth.

Each of the twelve cases were stacked in a meta-matrix display (see Table 1) which further condensed the data permitting systematic comparison. The matrix allowed for what Miles and Huberman (1994) refer to as "interactive synthesis" in which each case is first described, then a cross-case narrative highlighting categories is provided, followed by a summary or "general condensation" of what has been discovered (p. 176). This synthesizing approach allows for an analysis of the parts in a way that does not obscure the wholes and compares whole cases as configurations of parts. A meta-matrix display was selected as the best method for determining how cases share similar characteristics, and to give a general idea about the properties of major categories.

Findings

As the matrix indicates, business organizations value place from an economic, geographic, and social perspective.

Table 1. Meta-matrix display: Shared business organization and community characteristics

Organization	How the organization values place	How the culture of the organization influences its ability to build place	How the organization interacts with the community
Org A	Economic and Geographic	Protecting Brand	Political
Org B	Social Network	Improving Life	Partnerships
Org C	Social Network	Shared learning Advocating change and growth	Partnerships Influencing investment

74 Organizations at the Intersections of Place

Organization	How the organization values place	How the culture of the organization influences its ability to build place	How the organization interacts with the community
Org D	Social Network	Improving life and serving others	Partnerships Social Obligation
Org E	Economic and Geographic	Advocating change and growth	Partnerships Influencing investment
Org F	Social Network Geographic	Geographic Improving life	Partnerships Guardian
Org G	Physical building Social Network	Shared learning Protecting Brand	Relationships Employment activities
Org H	Social Network Geographic	Geographic Improving life	Partnerships Guardian
Org I	Economic and Social Network	Advocating change and growth Improving life	Partnerships Influencing investment
Org J	Economic and Geographic	Advocating change and growth	Partnerships Influencing investment
Org K	Economic and Social Network	Advocating change and growth Improving life	Partnerships Influencing investment
Org L	Economic and Social Network	Advocating change and growth Improving life	Partnerships Influencing investment

An *economic perspective* is the view or attitude that governs how a business organization acts towards the local economy. An economic perspective is grounded in the business organization's needs and strategies to view place as affording certain resources in the environment and community that advantage the business organization.

For example, organization A values place as a central point for distributing its products and access to a favorable labor pool. Organization E favors the area's population growth as a source of new business. Organization H views the area's potential for attracting new employers and a growing labor pool as key ingredients. In each case these business organizations view the economy of the area as favorable to their short and long term goals.

Geographic perspectives is the view or attitude toward the physical or environmental aspects of the community from which the business organization draws certain benefits such as environmental beauty, quality of life, and certain physical attributes that favor the organization's place of business. Both business organizations C and F value place for its environmental beauty and history. Business organizations E and G value place for their business' physical structure or building as reflecting their cultural and social position in the community.

Social network is the web of relationships in which the business organization finds itself both a contributor and influencer. This is where a business organization contributes and gains from the interaction among other business organizations, and can create a sense of attachment and belonging or "fitting in" with the larger community. As one interviewee from organization B stated, "The purpose of all business is to simply make life better." He added. "The only reason that we exist as a business is to improve life." The business organization's internal policies and procedures direct employees to behave in specific ways in dealing with customers and others in the community, and are consistent with their stated goals.

Organization C considered the network of learning business organizations, created out of their own design and culture, as a principle aspect of the social network. Organization E considered the people who share and learn through highly collaborative and ethical business practices a key aspect of the value of a social network. Business organization A focuses on the reach of the social network in a community as a way to build its reputation.

In every case, the business organization's culture influenced its ability to build a sense of place as defined by improving life for its employees and the general community, and acting as an advocate for change and shared learning. In addition, business organizations considered their image and reputation as a key to building their influence and ability to construct place.

Improving life is a strategy of serving others in the community, that fits both the business organization and community values. In some cases, some organizations (B and F) would accept a short term financial loss in favor of long term gain for the community and their business. In addition, ethical business practices and financial contributions to certain causes were considered essential aspects of a business organization's strategy and contribution.

As advocates for change, business *organizations define their place or role in the* community as an advocate for change and growth. In the case of organization H, their mission is to advocate for businesses and to create community competitive advantages. Organization F views their role as both an advocate for change and guardian of what they call "the community's cultural treasury".

Protecting reputation and brand is a major concern among all business organizations studied. Each organization managed its brand protection strategy in ways unique to its situation and culture. In the case of organizations C, D, F, and G, their family legacy and name, and the owner's personal reputation directed their investment decisions. Conversely, organization A was solely focused on protecting its image and brand by controlling or comanaging its relationships.

Shared learning is the act of promoting and teaching others the value of "mutual investment" that can help transform a community.

For example, organization D shared its expertise with institutions in finding ways to reduce the causes of health problems and proactively build new programs for the community. Similarly, business organization E shared its expertise in design and construction as a way to build an ecologically sustainable environment. Business organization B likewise used its expertise to help its clients save operational costs.

These business organizations acted out a strategy unique to their organization that can be further explained and coded as *"cultivating"* or *"authoring"* their place in the community. In essence, a business organization constructs sense of place out of a specific intention or strategy. Although each business organization's strategy varies, each employs a specific strategy unique to its culture and perceived place and role in the community.

How Business Organizations Interact with the Community in Constructing Sense of Place

Some business organizations interacted with their community through such categories as; *influencing investment, partnerships, and building relationships* that serve the business and community needs. *Influencing investment* in certain projects supports a business organization's principles such as its social obligation to give back to the community which also acts to build it's legitimacy. *Partnering or building partnerships* is an activity where a business organization creates alliances and associations intended to achieve a common set of goals. In all cases the business organizations shared local knowledge about the community and how their practices and activities were an appropriate fit for the community and the business organization (Thomas, 2004).

Summary: Networks as a Modeled Concept

Business organizations are integral to the social and cultural networks necessary to sustain community success. Additionally, when business organizations operate in a manner that is consistent with a community's values and culture, it sets the stage for facilitating a network of relationships that can lead to building a "sense of place". Therefore, examining sense of place as a social construct that influences interaction among networks and relationships produces a sense of place supportive for business and community success.

Viewing the interface between a business organization and a community can offer an understanding of how to deconstruct the creation of sense of place. This dynamic can be viewed as a "Place Based Network Model" (PBN Model). A model such as the PBN serves as a lens to view how sense of place is socially constructed from a business organization and community vantage point (Light and Smith, 1998).

Development of the Place Based Network Model

The Place Based Network (PBN) is a framework for exploring the "pushes" and "pulls" that exist between a community and its business organizations as they execute a strategy that creates a sense of place in a community. Its three dimensions of: (1) cultural congruence, (2) community social order perspective, and (3) environmental knowledge, create a context for understanding the influences or components in a business organization's sense of place creation strategy.

The PBN model illustrates how the three dimensions intersect to construct sense of place, and assumes the presence of an outer realm of pressures pushing (external factors) or pulling (internal factors) these dimensions in different or similar directions based on the business organization's culture and behavior (see Figure 1) and its relationship with its community. In establishing a community sense of place a business organization is guided by three strategies. First, the business organization must evolve its business strategy to be congruent or aligned with the culture of the community and the business organization (cultural congruence). Second, a business organization must interpret the mix of social factors that make up the characteristics of the community and their influence in the community (community social order perspective). Finally, a business organization must acquire certain knowledge of what resources the environment affords or offers (environmental knowledge) that can help guide the business organization's contributions.

Understanding the Link Between Business Organizations and 79
Construction of Community Sense of Place

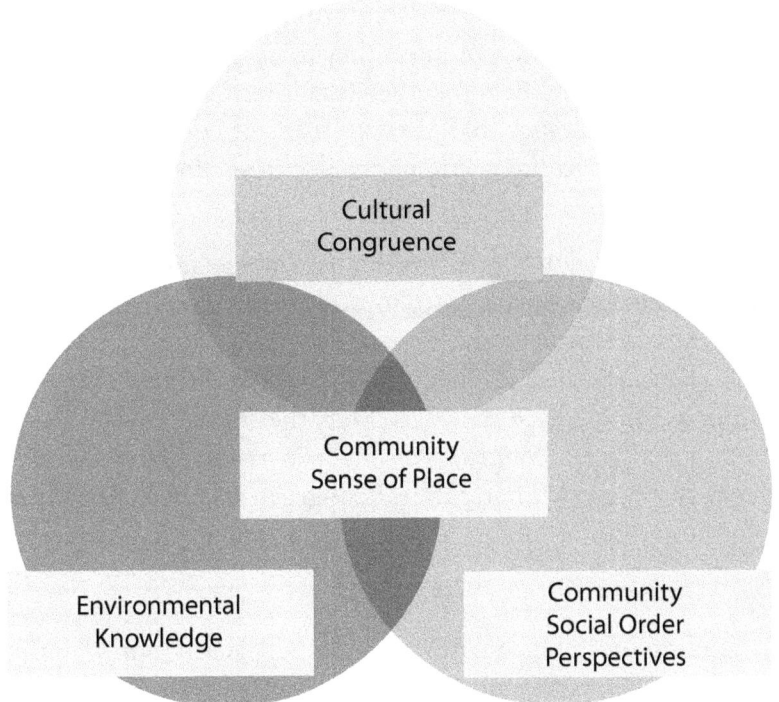

Figure 1. Place Based Network Model (PBN)

Cultural Congruence

Certain things in groups are shared or held in common, and these cultural components are variously described as traditions, rituals, and commonly shared values and beliefs influencing the behavior of people. Sense of place is constructed in part out of shared meanings and values that orient the business organization to behave in ways that build relationships and support decisions regarding use of space that are in the interests of both the community and the business organization (Schein, 1992). 'Culture' has become the property of a 'group' (both conceptualized as bounded and unitary), which 'persists over time' in the sense of being unchanging, and is 'shared' in the sense that there is consensus and no ambiguity (Wright. 1994). When business organizations and communities share a common set of intentions regarding the distribution of the community's resources (labor, small business support, quality of life) they have effectively negotiated settlements that group them together as cultural "compadres" who are seeking similar outcomes that are congruent or consistent with their cultures, and produce favorable physical settings for all stakeholders (Hardesty, 1974).

Sense of place is largely defined by the diverse and authentic view individuals and their business organizations bring to given space. For example an examination of the history of Santa Fe, New Mexico reveals that the traditions and architecture of the community that created its unique sense of place emerged from the mutually advantageous agreements (cultural congruence) made between the three ethnic groups in that region. That cultural congruence continues to survive today.

Community Social Order Perspectives

To understand and establish sense of place from a business organizational vantage requires a set of perspectives that build on environmental cognition - how the business organization understands the social order and social characteristics of a community. These perspectives should incorporate insights into the temporal, monetary, sentimental, and ideological orders of a community.

The temporal order of a community refers to how the community is geared to its own time scale, pace, and rhythm. Monetary order refers to where and how money and finance mediate relationships between people. A resort community may embrace tax revenues, and the strategies to increase them, as their principal activity and concern. Sentimental order is the emotional tone of the people who live and visit the community. Conflict can occur when development and growth initiatives strike against what people cherish or view as the "heart and soul" of a community. The same applies to the ideological order, which represents the fundamental assumptions and values people have about how the community actually works and is governed (Moore & Golledge, 1976).

Variations in community social order perspectives are important to understand because they can inform and influence business organizational strategies that might otherwise generate conflict around the use of community resources. This is particularly true in the case of Wal-mart, a corporation that continues to struggle with local jurisdictions regarding the impact of their super stores on traffic congestion and loss of small businesses in the areas they inhabit. Community social order perspectives prepare an business organization to understand in greater detail the manner in which individuals and the community interact with one another, and what frames their issues relative to the use of space and other natural resources (Light & Smith, 1998).

Environmental Knowing

The third dimension, environmental knowing, is divided into two areas: resource affordances and effectivities. Each of these describes how the business organization and community utilize the human and natural resources presented to them in their environment.

Affordances are what the environment offers, what it provides or furnishes in the way of resources to the community and to its business organizations. To a business organization it means those natural (gas and oil, wood, water) and human (paid labor, volunteer) resources that are accessible and provide unique opportunities to the business organization that create advantage in the market place and help sustain the community. Affordances imply the complimentarity of the community and the environment's resources and the complimentarity of the business organization and individual human and social capital (Hardesty, 1974).

Complimentarity establishes the business organization and its community as partners or "compadres" in their efforts to create a "distinctive" way of life. It is the social relationships developed between business organizations and the community, to which people are attracted and attached, and out of which grows a sense of belonging, that is central to how sense of place is constructed. The relationship between people and the environment is two-way, and to a large extent business organizations and communities can and do decide how to live within certain limits of nature and community. Therefore, the environment presents people with a variety of options or alternatives from which they can chose to satisfy their needs. Options chosen (affordances) are largely due to the influence of human culture. The capacity to act on these options are called *effectivities* (Altman & Low. 1992: Jones & Eyles, 1977).

While affordances are properties of the real environment as directly perceived by the business organization and the community (such as social capital and natural resources) the reciprocal term 'effectivity' denotes the action capabilities of the business organization, i.e. what it is practically equipped to do. Thus the range of affordances of a resource will be constrained by the effectivities of the business organization and the community.

Business organizations engage their community through the strategies implicit in the PBN Model and build 'webs' of influence that link or connect the business organization with community stakeholders in ways that protect the environment, help build social capital, and work to sustain the community's economic, social, and cultural vitality (Dear & Flusty, 2002).

Implications for Community Development

The concept of sense of place is easier to grasp when we think of ourselves as agents always "in place." much as we are always "in culture." For this reason our relations to place and culture become elements in the construction of our individual and collective identities, and are reflected in how we market and manage a community's resources (Entrikin, 2000). How business organizations are 'situated' in a community may impact their contribution to their own business organization and to the community.

The Place Based Network model provides a basis for discussion of how sense of place can be socially constructed through the interaction and affiliation of a business organization *in* a community. Businesses and non-profit business organizations have missions and visions regarding their business organization's primary function and clientele, but they also act and behave in ways that cause them to mesh well or fit in well with a community, or to be at odds with the community where they reside. The model does not necessarily offer a complete framework for the description of all experiences and strategies, nor is it intended that these dimensions or categories are absolute. Rather, it is a foundation for an interpretation of how sense of place is socially constructed, and it recognizes the role business organizations play in their community. Within the context of the PBN a new definition of sense of place emerges: Sense of place is created out of a social network of ideas, concepts, and meanings about the community and environment that are embedded in the community's culture, as expressed by their activities: symbolic, language, rituals, and everyday living.

The PBN theoretical framework is grounded in three notions: first, that sense of place is an interactive process between the business organization and its community: second, that the business organization and the community are intrinsically linked as partners in how sense of place is culturally defined; and third, that environmental knowledge of how the business organization integrates environmental resources and thus operates in a community is a key component that completes the weaving together of all three.

The twelve business organizational 'cases'. through their responses to the interview questions, validated the importance of the business organization's culture in the construction of place, participation in a social network and the importance of symbols in the construction of meaning. The 'place based model' can benefit business organizations and their communities by providing a well defined set of concepts that can direct their strategies for constructing sense of place in their community and identify ing communities that best fit or match their culture and strategic imperatives. Further, a theoretical understanding of how sense of place is constructed on a community level can advance the field of community development by advancing a new way of thinking about how business organizations contribute to their community.

References

Agnew, J. A. (1987). *Place and Politics.* Boston: Allen & Unwin

Altman, I. & Low, S.M. (Eds.). (1992). Place attachment. New York: Plenum. Donaldson, T & Dunfee, T. W. (1999). *Ties that hind: A social contracts approach to business ethics* Boston: Harvard Business School Press.

Blumer, H. (1969). *Symbolic interactionism: Perspective and method.* Los Angles: University of California Press.

Bridger, J. & Alter. T. R. (2006). Place, community development, and social capital. *Journal of the Community Development Society.* 37. 5-20.

Chaskin, R. J., Brown, P., Ventaketsh, S., and Vidal, A. (2001). Building community capacity. New York: Aldine de Gruyter.

Creswell, J. W. (1998). *Qualitative inquiry and research design: Choosing among five traditions.* Thousand Oaks. CA: Sage.

Dear, M. J. & Flusty, S. (Eds.) (2002). *The spaces of postmodernity: Readings in human geography.* Oxford: Blackwell Publishers, p 74.

Entrikin, J. N. (2000). *The betweeness of place: Towards geography of modernity.* New York: Routledge.

Felkins, P. K. (2002). *Community at work: Creating and celebrating community in business organizational life.* Cresskill, N.J.: Hampton.

Geertz, C. (1973). *The interpretation of cultures.* New York: Basic Books.

Glaser, B. & Strauss. A. (1967). *The discovery of grounded theory: Strategies for qualitative research.* New York: Aldine de Gruyter.

Hardestv, D.L. (1974). The niche concept: Suggestions for its use in human ecology. *Human 'Ecology.*, 3. 71-85.

Hudson, R. (2001). *Producing places.* New York: The Guilford Press

Jacobs, J. (1984). *Cities and the wealth of nations.* New York: Random House.

Jones, E. & Eyles, J. (1977). *Introduction to social geography.* Oxford: Oxford University.

Kemmis, D. (1990). *Community and the politics of place.* Norman, OK: University of Oklahoma Press.

Light, A. & Smith, J. M. (Eds.) (1998). *Philosophy and geography III: Philosophies of Place.* New York: Rowman & Littlefield.

Massey, D. & Jess. P. (1995). *A place in the world? Places, cultures and globalization.* New York: Oxford Press.

Mitchell, D. (2002). *Cultural geography: A critical introduction.* Maiden. MA: Blackwell.

Moore, G. T.. & Golledge. R. G. (Eds.).(1976). *Environmental Knowing: Theories, research, and methods.* Stroudsburg, PA: Dowden. Hutchinson & Ross.

Patton, M. Q. (2002). *Qualitative research and evaluation methods.* Thousand Oaks. CA: Sage.

Relph, E. (1976). *Place andplacelessness.* London: Pion Ltd. Sack, R. (1997). *Homo Geographicus* Baltimore, MD: The Johns Hopkins University Press.

Sagoff, M. (1996). Values and preferences. *Ethics.* 2. 301-316.

Sauer, C. (1925). *The morphology of landscape.* Berkeley: University of California Publications in Geography. 2, 19-54.

Schein, E. H. (1992). *Organizational culture and leadership.* San Francisco: Jossey-Bass.

Schoenberger, E. (1997). *The cultural crisis of the firm.* Cambridge: Blackwell.

Stokowski, P. A. (2002). Languages of place and discourses of power: Constructing new senses of place. *Journal of Leisure Research.* 34. 368-382.

Strauss, A., & Corbin, J. (1998). *Basics of qualitative research: Techniques and procedures for developing grounded theory.* Thousand Oaks, CA: Sage.

Thomas, D. F. & Cross, J. (2007). Organizations as place builders. *Journal of Behavioral and Applied Management.* Sept. 2007.

Thomas, D. F. (2004). *Toward an understanding of organization place building in communities.* Unpublished doctoral dissertation. Colorado State University, Fort Collins, Co.

Tuan, Yi-Fu. (1974). *Topophilia: a study of environmental perception, attitude, and values.* Englewood Cliffs, NJ: Prentice Hall.

Williams, R. (1989) *Resources of Hope: Culture, democracy, socialism.* New York: Verso Publishers.

Wright, S. (Eds.). (1994). *Anthropology of organizations.* New York: Routledge.

Zelinsky, W. (1992). *Cultural geography of the United States.* Englewood Cliffs, NJ: Prentice Hall.

Appendix A

Semi-Structured Interview Questions and Protocol

Organizational issues and opinion questions

1. How long have you lived in the community? How long have you been with the firm?

2. What do believe are the challenges facing the business organization and the community today and in the next 5-10 years?

3. How would you describe the community: its culture, business climate?

4. What are the organizations priorities and challenges in dealing with the community?

5. What in your opinion are the key assets and resources available for the organization in the community ?

6. How are these assets or resources utilized?

7. What is the impact of this usage?

8. What have been the positive changes in the community over the last 3 years?

9. What have been the negative changes?

10. How would you describe the organizations relationship with the community?

11. What have been the challenges in that relationship?

12. How would you define the organizations relationship?

Cultural setting and Social Setting

13. In what ways does the business organization reflect the community's spirit of the people? Its history, future and values?

- Where are the majority of employees hired? Locally? Out of town?

- In what ways is the organization's culture reflected in the community? How is it celebrated in the community?
- In what ways does the organization contribute to the community's stated economic, political and social viability?

Published with permission from: David F. Thomas, Diane Gaede, Richard R. Jurin & Laura S. Connolly (2008). Understanding the Link Between Business Organizations and Construction of Community Sense of Place: The Place Based Network Model, Community Development, 39(3), 33-45, DOI: 10.1080/15575330809489667

4

TRANSFORMATIONAL PLACE BUILDING: A MIXED METHOD OF EXPLORATION OF SMALL BUSINESSES

David F. Thomas
Monfort College of Business, University of Northern Colorado, Greeley, Colorado, USA

James M. Gould and Diane b. Gaede
School of Human Sciences, University of Northern Colorado, Greeley, Colorado, USA, and

Richard R. Jurin
Biology/Environmental Studies, University of Northern Colorado, Greeley, Colorado, USA

ABSTRACT

Purpose – The purpose of this paper is to explore the nature of transformational business practices using the construct of organizational place building. The objective is to develop a more expansive model of place building that examines and the potential of their business practices on place.

Design/methodology/approach – This project employed a mixed method research focusing on collecting, analyzing, and mixing both quantitative and qualitative data in a single study or series of studies. Members from the chamber of commerce of three cities in Northern Colorado participated in two phases of research.

Findings – The mixed method approach captured key themes that provided a discernible structure to the place building construct, and revealed that businesses build place in a variety of ways each according to their own culture and business model.

Research limitations/implications – The traditional model of corporate social responsibility while important, is limited in scope and influence. In contrast, we have argued for a more expansive perspective which examines how transformational organizations value place and the potential of their business practices to enhance or diminish community well-being.

Social implications – The paper presents a step in the direction of building a coherent theory of how organizations build place and poses new questions about the role of organizations in relation to places.

Originality/value – A theoretical understanding of how organizations contribute to the construction of place would benefit from the work of economists, geographers, sociologists as well as management theorists.

Keywords United States of America, Organizational culture, Small enterprises, Social responsibility, Place building, Small business

Paper type Research paper

"Place building" as a concept is alluded to by sociologists, geographers, and other social scientists interested in matters such as enterprise movement, community and systems sustainability (Schneider *et al.*, 1996), sustainable development, and enterprise attributes of communities (Hudson, 2001; Schoenberger, 1997; Sagoff, 1996; Wright, 1994; Jacobs, 1984). In the past 30 years the concept of place has received examination from scholars in a variety of disciplines. Sense of place, community development, corporate culture, and organization behavior has been researched by sociologists (Gans, 2002; Gieryn, 2000), geographers (Agnew, 1987; Buttimer and Seamon, 1980; Entrikin, 2000; Werlen, 1993), anthropologists (Geertz, 1983; Wright, 1994) environmentalists (Gustafson, 2005;

Snyder, 1995), and business researchers (Delheim, 1986; Hatch, 1993; Thomas *et al.*, 2008).

Place is defined as both geographical, and social, and is organized around the meanings individuals and groups give to a place in its setting (Rodman, 1992). Places take on the meaning of events that occur there, and their descriptions are fused with human goals, values and intentions. These "shared meanings" are held in common by the collective, and are historically generated and tend to be durable (Alvesson and Berg, 1991). Therefore, place is not merely a phenomenon that exists in the minds of individuals but also a construct that develops from and becomes part of everyday life and experiences. The ordinary routines of life produce places that are meaningful, sacred, and special to individuals, their organizations, and their communities (Williams, 1989). Sense of place is a complex phenomenon, derived from a wide range of coinciding factors and experiences. And studying place building through a mixed method approach helps preserve both the complexity and sense of pace (through quantitative methods and perspectives), and the broader-based formulations from qualitatively examined understandings (Ardoin, 2009).

Additionally, research involving business organizations and social responsibility has traditionally focused on multinational corporations (Jamali *et al.*, 2009) and their peculiarities in ethical behavior and decision making. However, a growing body of literature has addressed corporate social responsibility (CSR) models as applied to small- and medium-sized enterprises (SMEs) with mixed results. For Burton and Goldsby (2009), social responsibility concerns differed between large corporations and small business owners in that SMEs not only focused on different responsibility "domains" but that focus, if well placed, has a clear effect on the organization's behavior and success. Furthermore, Crane (2009) indicated that entrepreneurs are more likely to perceive certain practices as unethical relative to corporate managers. Houghton and Simon (2009) also indicated that employees of smaller, younger organizations selected more compromised ethical choices than employees of larger, older organizations. Given these differences and fallacies, Fassin (2008) argued that a specific approach, that is a departure from CSR models, would be necessary for SMEs. Thus, the authors intend to build upon a small business model that contributes to a sense of place and attachment for communities and the businesses within them.

While some social responsibility models (Vogel, 2005) capture the importance of businesses and communities acting in ways that seek mutual advantages, the place building approach goes further by placing businesses as responsible agents that build and protect a community's sense of place (Thomas, 2004). The focus on place, rather than on social relations exclusively, serves to broaden conceptions of how business behavior can contribute to a community's overall quality of life. Therefore, the place building approach can be viewed as both a strategy and behavior in that business organizations are agents that shape places through the full range of their values and behaviors. Thomas and Cross (2007) postulated that place building occurs within four types of organizations (transformational, contributive, contingent, and exploitative) that vary in how they contribute to, or detract from, the social construction of a place in communities. These four qualitatively different types of organizations vary in how they contribute to, or detract from, the social construction of place (Thomas, 2004).

Four types of place builders

Transformational organizations

Transformational organizations view themselves as critical agents with a mission and focus on improving life and creating positive change for both the organization and the place (Thomas, 2004; Thomas and Cross, 2007). The transformational organizational culture is highly focused on team learning, collaboration, openness to change, and building partnerships. They view themselves as interdependent members of a place, rather than independent members, and their success contributes to advantage beyond that of the organization (Thomas, 2004).

Transformational place builders demonstrate an integrative strategy that focuses on building a shared vision with the community and holding itself accountable to the community for the quality of its contribution to place. These behaviors are not solely for public relations advantage but an effort to surpass community business trends and regulations, perhaps even at a cost to the organization (Thomas and Cross, 2008). These strategies include initiating new policies and business practices for protecting the natural environment, neighborhoods, cultural heritage, local economy, and other local resources (Thomas and Cross, 2007; Thomas et al., 2008).

Contributive organizations

Contributive organizations view themselves as being a contributing member of a network of business people and community leaders who share a common ideology. Their identity as a local contributor is affirmed by engaging with local organizations, fundraising, and by philanthropy that builds place (Schneider et al., 1996; Chaskin et al., 2001). In contrast to transformational organizations that view themselves as responsible fore the well-being of place, a contributive organization views itself as a contributor to the well-being of place. The organizational culture is focused on "giving back" and conforming to local norms and values (Thomas, 2004).

Contributive organizations value place first for its social relationships and second for its economic opportunities and potential for business growth. The natural world may simply be the geographic location of their business. These organizations need a place that needs them, where they can simultaneously prosper and give back. They practice an integrative strategy that cultivates their role as a key contributor in their community, through the network of organizations that facilitate social and philanthropic activity (Thomas, 2004; Thomas and Cross, 2008).

Contingent organizations

Contingent organizations view themselves as disassociated and autonomous agents. They narrowly define correct corporate behavior as "CSR" with obeying existing laws, regulations, and ethical codes, yet they make a concerted effort to act accordingly. Rather than viewing themselves as interdependent with place (transformational), or key members of place (contributive), they view themselves as control agents. They operate from a managerial point of view; the organization's culture is highly structured and values the processes or systems (Thomas, 2004). The contingent organization practices a separatist strategy that centers on a plan that distinguishes the organization in terms of its economic power. Contingent organizations value place for what that it provides for the company, such as workers for its labor force. They practice philanthropy only as a method for advancing their own causes, not out of any intrinsic commitment to place, and their principle contribution is their economic contribution and adherence to laws and regulations (Thomas and Cross, 2008).

Exploitive organizations

Exploitative organizations view themselves as occupants of place and are more isolated from the values of the community. They are active users of the economic, cultural, social, and political resources (valuing place as a commodity) which they utilize to their greatest economic benefit (Sagoff, 1996; Rodman, 1992; Entrikin, 2000). They largely plan and organize to control space in which short-term financial progress and cost effectiveness trump local needs (Thomas, 2004), and their preference is to be afforded the rights and legal protections typically afforded only to individual citizens (Vogel, 2005).

The exploitive firm's mission to maximize profit determines their organizational philosophy, and it is usually practiced by deliberately targeting certain places for the potential to extract resources without accountability for the risks posed to the local population. While these organizations may employ locals and deal with local suppliers, they practice a separatist strategy in that they are not invested in ways that contribute to a sense of place. Exploitive organizations are likely to leave a place once they have determined they do not fit or the return is not as lucrative as originally anticipated (Thomas and Cross, 2007).

Each of the four types stands out from the others in their perspectives on place and the consequences of their actions. Transformational organizations orchestrate their contributions in ways that transform themselves and place. As agents of change, they are distinguished from other organizations in that they view place in a holistic manner in which all three realms are interactive and interdependent. Consequently, the business practices of transformational organizations contribute to place well-being through learning and teaching in partnership with clients. The other organization that operates from an interdependent perspective, contributive, also engages in business practices that benefit the community, however, in a slightly different manner from transformational types (Thomas, 2004; Thomas and Cross, 2008).

Given the breadth and variation of business behaviors that exist in each of these four types, findings derived from the individual interviews and focus groups were used to compile an inventory of behaviors that are considered within the four-organizational typology construct to be of the "transformational" type. Research concentrated on studying those transformational business practices that most contribute to building and maintaining a positive sense of place in a community.

The first research question asked was:

RQ1. What specific practices are considered transformational among business owners? (This was addressed by the phase one qualitative component).

The second research question investigated was:

RQ2. What differences in business characteristics exist between those scoring high and those scoring low across quantifications of transformational behaviors? (This was addressed in the phase two quantitative component).

Methods

Mixed method research focuses on collecting, analyzing, and mixing both quantitative and qualitative data in a single study or series of studies. Its central premise is that the use of quantitative and qualitative approaches in combination provides better understanding of research problems than either approach alone (Creswell and Plano Clark, 2008). In general, researchers are encouraged to collect data using multiple strategies and approaches so that the resulting mixture is of complementary strengths and non-overlapping weaknesses (Johnson and Turner, 2003). The central advantage for this research project is the promise mixed method offers for both practioneers (business in this study) and researchers (Johnson and Onwuegbuzie, 2004). Therefore, a two-phase mixed method of qualitative and quantitative approaches was utilized to address the two research questions.

Phase 1. Qualitative

Qualitative research is descriptive and well suited to the study of place building because it involves discovery on how humans and their groups construct meaning in their place, and the process by which an organization constructs place in its community. The new information gathered from this research effort may reflect new practices or behaviors, new forms of organizational structure, and/or new ways of thinking or interpreting how an organization builds place.

Sampling and procedure. A combination or mixed purposeful sampling strategy assisted in selecting small businesses for this study. These businesses were likely to possess the local knowledge of the key environmental, social and economic issues that impact the community and their business. Individual interview and focus group respondents were business owners selected from the Northern Colorado communities of Fort Collins, Loveland, and Greeley. This region of Colorado boasts several industries – health, finance, real estate, agriculture, etc. and enjoys the influence of three large state universities, close proximity to the Rocky Mountains, and a nearby thriving Denver metropolitan area. A sample of individual business owners was purposively selected from the membership directory of the chambers of commerce (COC), with the consent of their directors, in each of the three cities.

Individual and focus group interviews. For the focus group interviews, a convenience sample of 30 small business owners were contacted that had been in their respective communities for at least five years, were recognized as business owners with a record of community activity, and were members of their COC. A total of 17 respondents from Fort Collins, Loveland, and Greeley agreed to attend one of three focus group meetings conducted by researchers and run by an independent facilitator in each of the cities.

The individual and focus group interviews were recorded, and respondents were asked to reflect on a series of nine semi-structured, open-ended questions (Table I). A modicum of time was spent defining the terms of place building and the four typologies, and interviewees were asked to give their thoughts and opinions. This action engaged the interviewees in a conversation that elicited genuine and relevant responses (Patton, 1990) and assured the interviewee's understanding of the typology, its validity, its value and applications. The investigators assumed the roles of observer and took note of common themes, interaction dynamics, and individual responses.

The lead author was the principal investigator in this research. During the interviews he assumed the role of observer and took note of the interaction dynamics and respondent responses. These notes were compiled and shared with the other authors to assure coding process was both rigors in terms of the examination and discernment of extant themes. In addition, the collaboration assured that the place building content domains and place constructs were germane and connected to the research. The semi-structured nature of the interview was intended to identify and analyze patterns, including unanticipated influences, related to explaining and exploring how organizations values place. Second, and to identify plausible relationships shaping transformational behavior.

1. How do you define and practice social responsibility?
2. How is a small business' contribution different from a large corporation's?

3. Facilitator presents and explains the OPB typology (exploitative, contingent, contributive, and transformational), and asks respondents: do these types of business exist? If so, do you agree with the characteristics of each type? Can you add to these types?

4. What specific practices are considered in each type? Where does a small business start on the typology? For example, where would you initially place a small business, and how do you think it would evolve or move between the types? If so, what factors and practices drive an organization across, or move them through the types?

5. What are the barriers to organizational movement or maturation across each type? Describe the movement in your own terms

6. What influence does each type have in the community? On the environment? Social networking and interaction? In other words, does a type negotiate its way through the community differently and how so in each case?

7. In what ways do organizations interact with other organizations in their community?

8. To what extent are organizations and communities mutually dependent and independent of each other?

9. Is it possible to categorize organizations based on their contributions and how they interact in a community?

Data analysis. Data collected from the individual interviews and focus groups were transcribed from tape recordings for analysis of common categories and creation of codes, or themes. The semi-structured nature of the interview was intended to identify and analyze patterns related to explaining and exploring how organizations value place and contribute to their community through their organizational behavior.

Prior to creating the codes, each manuscript was read three times, and researchers then employed the process of constant comparative analysis (Glaser and Strauss, 1967). The analysis began with dividing the interview text into small units (phrases, sentences, and paragraphs), and these discrete units generated 15 level-one codes. The next analytical process generated five second-level codes: "personal obligations to community", "common values and principles", "teaching and mentoring", "care taking", and "ethical behavior". Further analysis led to a third and final level of codes: "custodial duty", "shared ideology", and "social contract" (see Table II for coding categorizations). This comprehensive coding process created an integrated qualitative schema for understanding how organizations value place and interact in their community.

Results. Coding was interpreted from respondent narratives (individual and focus group interviews) by the lead author. Transcripts were shared with one other author to control for bias and to discuss any differences or disagreement. The initial coding generated 15 level one codes. The next coding process generated five-second level codes: personal obligations to community, common values and principles, teaching and mentoring, care taking, and ethical behavior (Table II). This in turn finally produced three constructs or themes in the third level: custodial duty, shared ideology, and social contract and ethics. This comprehensive coding process created an integrated qualitative schema for understanding how organizations value place and interact in their community.

The first- and second-level codes grouped together reflected the broader perspectives of how small businesses value place and community. These codes indicated three constructs or themes at a third level: custodial duty, shared ideology, and social contract and ethics – plausible relationships shaping transformational behavior. Each of these themes was woven into how respondents described "building place".

Custodial duty. Custodial duty emerged from the data based on the interpretation of the respondents' commitment to place in its community. From an economic point of view the respondents indicated that businesses should "give what they can" and that "giving back goes beyond one's business requirements". In other words, "the giving back

Table II. Cross-case coding for describing and comparing OPB

First-level codes	Second-level codes	Third-level codes themes
II – giving back and sharing their wealth and skills	*Personal obligation to community* Obligation to contribute	Custodial duty
II – giving back to satisfy owners emotional attachment to the community	*Personal obligation to community* Obligation to family and employees to contribute as "pay-back"	
II – guardianship of community history and culture	*Care taking* Ethical duty to community	
FG – advising business owners on ethical practices	*Ethical behavior and care taking* Ethics and duty	
FG – mentoring employees to grow the business through community contributions	*Teaching and mentoring* Teaching and mentoring employees as good citizens	
FG – taking care of the community	*Common values and principles* Obligation to preserve business' legacy and future place	
II – association and alliance with like minded business owners	*Personal obligation to community* Connection with those of common philosophy	Shared ideology
FG – protect and safe keep the acknowledge norms and values of the	*Care taking* Responsibility to the community	

business community as key to "fitting in"	Opportunity to share and create network of common practices	
FG – business connections valued to build business and fit in	Common values and principles Connectedness to others	
II – coaching and mentoring employees to contribute to the community	Teaching and mentoring	Social contract
II – guide and advise new business owners on successful business tactics	Ethical behavior Responsibility to operate in an ethical manner	
II – protect the environment and nature	Ethical behavior Obligation to adopt new business standards and practices	
II – obligations to community extend beyond businesses financial needs	Ethical behavior Ethical standards and requirements as part of company mission	
FG – personal commitment to represent the business in an ethical manner	Ethical behavior Obligation and ethical duty	

Note: II – individual interview categorical data, FG – focus group categorical data needs to be a step beyond what you would have to do or need to do". Businesses can achieve this by encouraging employees to be a part of the community. Respondents also agreed that a business owner must believe in what he/she is supporting. This belief transcends any monetary benefit derived from the support. Thus, the owner views himself as a "custodian" in the sense that they perceive themselves as a care taker of the community.

Employee participation in community "giving back" begins with the owner and the business, and owners see themselves as care takers of both employees and their community. One respondent stated, "Getting employees involved is important to me personally. Employees are real assets that can impact my business and the community". Another respondent stated, "Looking after the employee's well being makes for a healthier community". The owner of a manufacturing firm stated that "How people are treated is key to taking care of the community". This connectivity to place through employee is echoed by others: "Social responsibility at the business level is tied to what I think of as 'doing right'. So in taking care of our people are we doing the right thing? Yes we are".

This "custodial duty" also encompasses a concern for community well-being by reflecting the respondent's philosophy and strategy to commit its resources to protect or guard place. An owner of a small manufacturing plant stated, "I think that businesses are citizens [...] it is our duty to protect and advocate for employees, community and [the] environment". Another respondent stated:

"If you care about the community, you want to make it a better place [...] businesses must 'seed' the community with ideas from people who have healthy concepts that serve the entire community. You need to invest in Northern Colorado, whatever it might be."

Shared ideology. This theme of a shared ideology resonated throughout the interviews and served to motivate a respondent's actions and strengthened their bond to each other. As one respondent stated:

"The one thing I think that kind of ties us together are our individual actions and beliefs [...] and I think that social responsibility is collaborating, partnering with people for the common good, working together to achieve something in which we all see value."

This sense of connectedness strengthens the network that exists. Respondents indicated that their ideology drives their business strategy. This shared ideology may be unique to small businesses in that they are influenced by their interactions, reputation, and connectedness to each other and the community.

Social contract. The respondents indicated that they share a responsibility to create mutually favorable agreements and relationships between themselves and their community. Respondents view their relationship with employees as the focal point of their contract with their community. One respondent stated:

"I would probably say the employee is our greatest asset. By looking after the employee and creating a good working environment you look after their well being which produces a healthier community."

Respondents generally agreed that caring for the community has a positive impact on their company. But they agreed this is not "why you do it". More significant is the view that respondents are "compelled to act and contribute". As stated by one respondent, "If nobody did it (contributed/protected the community) we'd deteriorate a lot more than we are". This loosely tied relationship among businesses and between each other frames how they relate to and value each other.

The critical aspect to the respondent's social contract is their shared or common commitment to place. Another respondent stated:

I think getting employees involved in their community makes them feel better. They learn about their job and its impact on the community, and in the end everyone wins. It is my job to get employees involved in their community.

All of the respondents agreed that engaging employees and aligning their mission and values with how they lead and motivate employees is a key to their personal and business success:

> "Besides the tax dollars and money that we pump into the community [...] you want it to be a community that your great grand children would want to live in."

Respondents agreed that the place building typology was an appropriate conceptual approach for describing their own business practices and impact, and how other businesses behaved as well. Many stated that their ethics and business practices served to remind them of their specific support to the community. "I pride myself on honest, hard work, and on giving back to the community. I support where I can with time or money in the community". The majority of respondents viewed themselves as transformational types and spoke passionately about their role as "co-creating place" both in their own firm and in the larger community.

Phase II. Quantitative

For the quantitative phase, first- and second-level codes derived from the interviews and focus groups were used to compile an index of behaviors that were identified as "transformational" practices. In order to quantify these behaviors, the codes were crafted into 14 Likert items composing a transformational index (TI) that reflected the third level qualitative themes of custodial duty, shared ideology, and social contract. With this quantification of transformational behaviors the researchers endeavored to explore differences in organizational characteristics between those businesses scoring high and those scoring low across the TI. For example, owners were asked to rate their business on contributions made to the community in areas related to the environment, quality of life, fiscal well-being, and ethical leadership.

Table III. Transformational index items

1. My organization works to create positive change for the community
2. My organization's mission includes the fiscal well-being of the community
3. My organization takes a leadership role in attracting skilled labor to the community
4. My organization holds itself accountable for the quality of its contribution to the community
5. My organization helps clients improve their business practices
6. My organization collaborates with other organizations to improve the community's quality of life
7. My organization helps build a more ethical business place
8. My organization's success contributes to the success of the community
9. My organization's employees are expected to contribute to local non-profit and philanthropic organizations
10. My organization is respected for its contributions to the natural environment
11. My organization is respected for its contributions to the economy
12. My organization is a member of a network of business people who share common business ethics
13. My organization values cooperative efforts to increase its influence in the community
14. My organization provides services or products to maintain the quality of life within the community

Note: Six-point Likert scale response: strongly disagree to strongly agree

Sampling and procedure. With consent from the directors of the COC in Greeley, Loveland, and Fort Collins, an online questionnaire link was disseminated to their members by electronic newsletter, and by posting the link on their home page. In all, 107 Northern Colorado businesses completed the questionnaire, and analysis yielded the following convenience sample characteristics: average sales volume = $11,393,059.05, average number of employees = 60, average number of years in their respective community = 24, average number of years in business = 27, and average annual contributions to non-profit and philanthropic organizations = $102,117.10. The mode for industry type in this sample was the service industry (n = 51).

Data analysis. In order to establish two meaningful groups for data analysis a median split of the TI scores was conducted, and a series of t-tests were performed to find significant differences in the five variables of sales volume, number of employees in the organization, years in the community, years in the business and annual contributions. Each Likert-type item represented in the TI utilized a six-point response scale ("strongly agree", "agree", "somewhat agree", "somewhat disagree", "disagree", and "strongly disagree"). Thus, the goal of the analysis was to focus on the differences between organizations with polarized (high and low) TI scores. T-tests were conducted on the external variables related to sales volume, number of employees in the organization, years in the community, years in the business and annual contributions.

Results. The 14 items composing the TI were tested using SPSS (version 15.0). The TI items were combined to form a single index (Cronback's = 0.84) ranging from a high of 84 to a low of 14 possible points. A median split was conducted to establish the two groups: businesses with low (range = 47-68) TI scores (n = 54) and businesses (n = 53) scoring high (range = 69-84) on the TI. Analysis revealed significant differences ($p \leq 0.05$) between high and low TI scores among four of the five external variables tested (see Table IV for *t*-test results). The differences in sales volume and number of employees indicated that business size may be a factor contributing to an organization's ability to transform place. Analysis also revealed that length of years in the community and length of years in business may also be significant factors in transformational place building.

Conclusions

The mixed method approach of capturing various sources and types of data proved worthwhile in achieving the aims of this study and in expanding the understanding of organizational place building (OPB), particularly in transformative place building. The three themes found in level three qualitative coding provide a discernable structure to the place building construct, and reveal that businesses build place in a variety of ways each according to their own culture and business model. As one respondent indicated, "I think that social responsibility is collaborating, partnering with people for the common good, working together to achieve something that we all see value in". This supports previous work (Smith, 1994) that found that over half of a company's employees say loyalty to their employers is strengthened when they are involved in company philanthropic programs.

By revealing various forms of transformational behavior from the interviews and discussions, the index was useful in identifying characteristics of transformational businesses. The results seem to signify that organizations with a relatively large sales volume, number of employees, and being established in the community are important determinants of transformational organizational behavior and annual giving. It would appear that as businesses begin to grow and establish themselves in both their industry and community so grows their capacity for place building through transformational action. A business's capacity for transformational place building action may be a function of its financial health as well as the owner's ideology and status in the community.

Implications and recommendations for future research

A number of interviewees and focus group participants indicated a new understanding of how a business mission may be attuned to its economic growth, its community and surrounding environment, its culture, and its meaningful contribution to that community. With this new approach of viewing organizations and their communities as co-creators of place, both entities can build sustainable competitive advantages while improving quality of life. Research findings seem to indicate that an owner's understanding of transformational place building, not simply social responsibility, may prove useful in decision-making processes regarding their positive community involvement and their place within it. The coding of interviews and focus groups provided clarity in understanding how organizations themselves value place and how they build place might be built with a well-informed business model and ethical framework.

Future research incorporating multiple methods and validated measures may be able to address such questions as: what specific practices contribute to transformational behavior for competitive advantage? Would these behaviors vary by industry or location? What factors explain the evolution of organizations along the continuum of transformative place building action? What is the relationship between transformational place building and profitability? What are the specific financial and economic impacts of transformational action in communities? Perhaps continued explorations may yield a well-defined framework useful for identifying best fits between businesses and communities and their respective plans for development. Further, an understanding of how place is constructed on an organizational level can advance the field of management with a new way of thinking about organizations as critical agents in the construction of place in their community.

TABLE IV. Mean comparisons of TI scores

Measure	Low transformational		High transformational		t	df	p-value
	Mean	SD	Mean	SD			
Sales volume	$3,238,281	6,816,353	$19,068,144	44,760,000	-1.98	64	0.05
Annual contributions	$20,129	47,234	$189,073	705,629	-1.4	66	0.16
Number of employees	19	29.75	100	216.86	-2.5	91	0.01
Years in community	18	16.89	30	30.61	-2.4	95	0.02
Years in business	18.7	20.38	36.18	37.48	-2.9	94	0.01

References

Agnew, J. A. (1987), *Place and Politics*, Allen & Unwin, Boston, MA.

Alvesson, M. and Berg, P. O. (1991), *Corporate Culture and Organizational Symbolism*, Walter de Gruyter, New York, NY.

Ardoin, N. M. (2009), "Sense of place and environmental behavior at an ecoregional scale", unpublished doctoral dissertation, Yale University, New Haven, CT.

Burton, B. and Goldsby, M. (2009), "Corporate social responsibility orientation, goals and behavior: a study of small business owners", *Business & Society*, Vol. 48 No. 1, pp. 88-104.

Buttimer, A. and Seamon, D. (1980), *Huma Experience of Space and Place*, Martins, New York, NY.

Chaskin, R. J., Brown, P., Venkatesh, S. and Vidal, A. (2001), *Building Community Capacity*, Aldine de Gruyter, New York, NY.

Crane, F. G. (2009), "Ethics, entrepreneurs and corporate managers: a Canadian study", *Journal of Small Business and Entrepreneurship*, Vol. 22 No. 3, pp. 267-76.

Creswell, J. W. and Plano Clark, C. L. (2008), *Designing and Conducting Mixed Method Research*, Sage, Thousand Oaks, CA.

Delheim, C. (1986), "Business in time: the historian and corporate culture", *The Public Historian*, Vol. 8, pp. 9-22.

Entrikin, J. N. (2000), *The Betweenness of Place: Towards Geography of Modernity*, Routledge, New York, NY.

Fassin, Y. (2008), "SMEs and the fallacy of formalizing CSR", *Business Ethics*, Vol. 17 No. 4, pp. 364-78.

Gans, H. J. (2002), "The sociology of space: a use-centered view", *City and Community*, Vol. 1 No. 4, pp. 329-39.

Geertz, C. (1983), *Local Knowledge*, Basic Books, New York, NY.

Gieryn, T. F. (2000), "A space for place in sociology", *Annual Review of Sociology*, Vol. 26, pp. 463-96.

Glaser, B. and Strauss, A.L. (1967), *The Discovery of Grounded Theory: Strategies for Qualitative Research*, Aldine de Gruyter, New York, NY.

Gustafson, P. (2005), "Meanings of place: everyday experience and theoretical conceptualizations", *Journal of Environmental Psychology*, Vol. 21, pp. 5-16.

Hatch, M. (1993), "The dynamics of organizational culture", *The Academy of Management Review*, Vol. 18 No. 4, pp. 657-93.

Houghton, S. M. and Simon, M. (2009), "Ethical compliance behavior in small and young firms: the role of employee identification with the firm", *New England Journal of Entrepreneurship*, Vol. 12 No. 2, pp. 15-26.

Hudson, R. (2001), *Producing Places*, The Guilford Press, New York, NY.

Jacobs, J. (1984), *Cities and the Wealth of Nations*, Random House, New York, NY.

Jamali, D., Zanhour, M. and Keshishian, T. (2009), "Peculiar strengths and relational attributes of SMEs in the context of CSR", *Journal of Business Ethics*, Vol. 87 No. 3, pp. 355-77.

Johnson, R. and Onwuegbuzi, A. (2004), "Mixed methods research: a research paradigm whose time has come", *Educational Researcher*, Vol. 33 No. 7, pp. 14-26.

Johnson, R. and Turner, L. (2003), "Data collection strategies in mixed method research", in Tashakkori, A. and Teddlie, C. (Eds), *Handbook of Mixed Methods in Social and Behavioral Research*, Sage, Thousand Oaks, CA.

Patton, M. Q. (1990), *Qualitative Research and Evaluation Methods*, Sage, Thousand Oaks, CA.

Rodman, M. (1992), "Empowering place: multilocality and multivocality", *America Anthropologist, New Series*, Vol. 94 No. 3, pp. 640-56.

Sagoff, M. (1996), "Values and preferences", *Ethics*, Vol. 2, pp. 301-16.

Schneider, B., Brief, A. P. and Guzzo, R. A. (1996), "Creating a climate and culture for sustainable organizational change", *Organizational Dynamics*, Vol. 24, pp. 7-18.

Schoenberger, E. (1997), *the Cultural Crisis of the Firm*, Blackwell, Cambridge.

Smith, C. (1994), "The new corporate philanthropy", *Harvard Business Review*, Vol. 72, p. 3.

Snyder, G. (1995), *A Place in Space: Ethics, Aesthetics, and Watersheds*, Publishers Group West, Washington, DC.

Thomas, D. F. (2004), "Toward an understanding of organization place building in communities", unpublished doctoral dissertation, Colorado State University, Fort Collins, CO.

Thomas, D. F. and Cross, J. (2007), "Organizations as place builders", *Journal of Behavioral and Applied Management*, Vol. 9 No. 1, pp. 33-61.

Thomas, D. F., Gaede, D., Jurin, R. R. and Connolly, L. S. (2008), "Understanding the link between business organizations and construction of community sense of place: the place based network model", *Journal of the Community Development Society*, Vol. 39 No. 3, pp. 33-45.

Vogel, D. (2005), "The low value of virtue", *Harvard Business Review*, Vol. 83 No. 6, p. 26.

Werlen, B. (1993), *Society, Action, and Space: An Alternateive Human Geography*, Routledge, London.

Williams, R. (1989), *Resources of Hope: Culture, Democracy, Socialism*, Verso, New York, NY.

Wright, S. (1994), *Anthropology of Organizations*, Routledge, New York, NY.

Further reading

Miles, M. B. and Huberman, A. M. (Eds) (1994), *Qualitative Data Analysis*, Sage, Thousand Oaks, CA.

About the authors

Dr. David F. Thomas is responsible for program development of UNC's Entrepreneurship program. This innovative program concentrates on the applied aspects of entrepreneurship, with an emphasis on supporting student start up opportunities and collaboration with the Northern Colorado business community. Dr. Thomas received his Ph.D. from Colorado State University. He has held various senior level positions in the travel and tourism industry. In addition, he has managed corporate start-up enterprises and small business turn around operations. UNC has recognized his contributions to students and faculty as both Advisor of the Year and Professor of the Year in the Monfort College of Business. His research has produced a new model for describing and evaluating and how an organization contributes to their communities. His models have been instrumental in helping community's recruit and retain best fitting firms. Dr. Thomas serves as a Board Member on the Rocky Mountain Initiative Institute and is actively involved in community development initiatives in Northern Colorado. David F. Thomas is the corresponding author and can be contacted at: david.thomas@unco.edu.

James M. Gould has developed specialization in the implementation and management of commercial recreation services and public sector programs and events. His teaching involves event leadership, administration and law, research and evaluation, and experiential learning. His research agenda includes the construction and development of psychometric instruments in leisure behavior, environmental ethics, natural resource management, special event tourism, and Olympic development. His interests also include outdoor recreation, adventure special events, documentaries, and philosophy.

Dr. Diane B. Gaede is an Associate Professor of Recreation, Tourism, and Hospitality in the School of Human Services at the University of Northern Colorado. She received her doctorate in Recreation Resources from Colorado State University. She teaches several undergraduate major curriculum courses, and her research interests include: commercial recreation, international and eco-tourism, and recreation, tourism, and hospitality survey research.

Richard R. Jurin worked as a Biochemist Researcher for over 20 years before going back to graduate school and gaining a PhD in Environmental Communication/Education/Interpretation with Adult-Community Focus, at The Ohio State University (OSU) in 1995. He taught for three years as a Graduate Teaching Associate and one year as Research Associate in Community Development within the Extension Service while doing his doctorate and then five more years as an Instructor at OSU in Environmental Communication, Education, Interpretation, and Management and since 2000, at University of Northern Colorado in School of Biology, and Head of Environmental Studies Program. Research interests include: worldviews as barriers to sustainability; sustainable development; media literacy; perceptions of wilderness; business leadership for sustainability; sustainability in tourism and interpretation, and interpretations of visual media perceptions during non-formal and informal educational settings.

5

PLACE BUILDING AND MISSION STATEMENTS:
A MATCH OR MISFIT?

David F. Thomas
Monfort College of Business, University of Northern Colorado,
Greeley, Colorado, USA

James H. Banning
School of Education, Colorado State University, United States

ABSTRACT

The purpose of this study was to investigate possible relationships between organizational Mission Statements (MS) and Place Building (PB). The basic question addressed in the study was do corporate MS statements contain a linkage to their possible place building strategies. Do the linkages suggest a match, a misfit, or is the linkage missing? Place building focuses on how an organization values the dimensions of place: nature, social relationships, material environment, ethics, and economic relationships in relation to the places in which they are located. We examined the MS from 41 businesses selected among a group of fortune 500 firms to determine if place building attributes were evident. Qualitative document analysis was employed to investigate the possible linkage between mission statements and the concepts of the place building model. The findings of the study suggest that corporate mission statements most often fail to address the strategies associated with organizational place building.

These findings raise important questions for discussion regarding the future of organizations and their relationship to place building in the community: how is corporate space used in the community, what is the condition of the space, and what is the impact of organizational place on the community resources. The study concludes that the strategy of addressing place/community relations within corporate mission statements can provide a useful way forward in addressing the foregoing questions.

Keywords: Place; Mission Statements; Place Building; Qualitative Research; Corporate Social Responsibility

INTRODUCTION

Corporate mission statements are ubiquitous, but their relationship to organizational practices, and specifically to place and Corporate Social Responsibility (CSR) remains a source of limited research. There is a plethora of research and volumes of texts on how to write a successful mission statement. Yet, there is limited research on the application of Mission Statements (MS) to ongoing operations and a lacuna of evidence on the relationship between MS and a firm's ongoing operation. MS remain a prominent keystone to describing how a business will operate, its nature and purposes. The mission statement came into popular usage in the early 70's with the explosion of business books that popularized the design and critical need for MS. Tom Peters in his book in search of excellence and Drucker's work all kick started MS as a mandatory recital for any serious business plan. Even investors and the casual observers found the articulation of a MS an indication of a serious enterprise. MS gained increased popularity again in the 2000's with the advent of the "evaluator pitch" – that 30 second prose that capsulized the entire business concept. Business models, a favorite of the dot.com error in the late ninety's, all include MS as a key part of the strategic asset components. It seemed that without a MS the fledging techno-enterprise and software startup all regaled the MS as the legitimizing characters of their play (Sheaffer, Landau, Drori, 2008).

Perhaps the reason for limited research in this area is due to the difficulty in sorting through the multiple factors or variables that impact a firm's performance or a valid method for evaluating the relationships between MS and firm performances. Clearly, this is a rich area of future research we intend to pursue. However, for the purposes of this paper we selected a number of firms among America's top corporations to compare their MS to a set of place building principles.

After presenting a broad background to the concepts of mission statements and place building theory, the current study engages in a conceptual perspective of the relationship between the two and then concludes with an empirical investigation of the relationship between the two concepts within a selected number of United States' top corporations.

MISSION STATEMENTS

MS is a broadly defined statement of purpose that specifies, "Who the organization is and what it does" (Levin, 2000, p. 93). As such, mission statements (henceforth MS) aim at providing organizations with a strategic direction and a unique sense of enduring purpose. Consequently, a MS focuses on describing preferable business domains and potential value to stakeholders aiming at distinguishing an organization from others of its type (Bart, 2001).

Mission statements serve as common corporate reporting tool. Their long-term use by corporations has been characterized by significant change, however, especially in the format and delivery of these statements (Williams, 2008) often found an organizations' web sites, annual reports, various promotional material. An effective MS is inclusive in nature, embodying shared beliefs, organizational values and an indication as to its aspired future (Sheaffer, Landau and Israel, 2009). A MS also indicates how the organization will achieve its future objectives (Ireland & Hitt, 1992; Vandijck, & Desmidt, 2007) and we add to that, how the organization views its role in the community, industry and market place.

A MS facilitates performance by guiding resource allocation and it provides ground rules for a detailed and concrete action plan (Bart and Baetz, 1998; Bart, 1997). When the MS is aligned with intrinsic place building values and strategic planning, the ensuing place building strategies become deliberate and proactive, allowing the organization to generate its own MS is not merely a portrayal of the future to be, but it actively, if imperceptibly, encourages organization members to help attain future goals (Thomas and Cross, 2007).

Moreover, through its clear sense of direction, a MS nurtures and promotes an adaptive and innovative organizational culture, enabling the formation of an effective strategic planning process, augmenting organizational effectiveness, sustaining entrepreneurial spirit, guiding and directing HR activities and functional responsibilities (Cetro & Peter, 1992; Larwood, Falbe, Kreiger, & Miesing, 1995).

In sum, a MS defines the enduring basic tenets of the organization's modus operandi as well as its values, norms and behavior. A well-articulated MS is expected to simplify and actively interpret the general organizational vision and provide a concrete and accurate expression of this vision (Sheaffer, Landau & Drori, 2008).

PLACE-BUILDING THEORY

"Place building" as a concept is alluded to by sociologists, geographers, and other social scientists interested in matters such as enterprise movement, community and systems sustainability (Schneider, Brief, and Guzzo, 1996), sustainable development, and enterprise attributes of communities (Hudson, 2001; Schoenberger, 1997; Sagoff, 1996; Wright, 1994; Jacobs, 1984). In the past thirty years the concept of place has received examination from scholars in a variety of disciplines. Sense of place, community development, corporate culture, and organizational behavior have been researched by sociologists (Gans, 2002; Gieryn, 2000), geographers (Agnew, 1987; Buttimer and Seamon, 1980; Entrikin, 2000; Werlen, 1993), anthropologists (Geertz, 1983; Wright, 1994), environmentalists (Gustafson, 2005; Snyder, 1995), and business researchers (Delheim, 1986; Hatch, 1993; Weick, 1995; Morgan and Smircich).

Place is defined as both geographical and social and is organized around the meanings individuals and groups give to a place in its setting (Rodman, 1992). Places take on the meaning of events that occur there, and their descriptions are fused with human goals, values, and intentions. These "shared meanings" are held in common by the collective, and are historically generated and tend to be durable (Alvesson and Berg, 1991). Geographers refer to place as "context" explaining how social relations attach to space and place and only secondarily to people (Staeheli, 2007). Place is therefore described in this sense as a setting for social action. A university with its power can impact a given place in ways that influence social action, often on its own terms and seeking a certain outcome. As Entrikin (2000, p. 6) states "Place shares meanings or interpretive frames of events for different actions, and second it provides resources for action." Thus, place as a platform can mediate between individuals, social groups and broader political structure (Thomas and Cross, 2007).

Two Place Perspectives

A organization's *agent perspective* distinguishes two distinct viewpoints held by organizations, which encompass not only how organizations conceptualize themselves in relationship to place, but also the meaning they give to place, which then influences their goals, contributions to place, and all variety of their behavior. It is possible to distinguish two types of agent perspectives: one perspective conceptualizes organizations and their success as *interdependent* with the well-being of place and another that conceptualizes organizations and their success as *independent* of place (Thomas, 2004; Thomas and Cross, 2007).

Organizations with the *interdependent* perspective view themselves as members of a community and recognize that organizations and places are mutually dependent on each other. Interdependent organizations consider themselves responsible for the well-being of place, view their success as intimately tied with the greater well-being of the place, and actively seek a variety of opportunities to invest and contribute to the multiple aspects of place. In contrast, organizations with an *independent* perspective view themselves merely as occupants of place and economic agents, rather than integral members of place. Organizations that see themselves as independent agents focus their activities on satisfying internal goals while viewing the realms of place as resources to satisfy their needs. Their primary responsibility is to their shareholders, not the places in which they do business. They consider generating jobs and tax revenues as their primary, if not their only, contribution to place. Independent organizations are not committed to the well-being of place and will only maintain the relationship as long as it benefits their shareholders (Thomas, 2004; Thomas and Cross, 2007).

Four Types of Place Builders

Thomas, (2004) and Thomas and Cross, (2007) using a grounded theory approach (Glaser and Strauss, 1967) derived the place-building model. Place-building theory explains how an organization values place and on five place dimensions: nature; social relationships; material environment; ethics; and economic relationships. *Nature* includes the natural—as opposed to man-made. Such as the landscape, earth, geography and natural resources. How does an organization relate and contribute to nature and the environment? *Social Relationships* includes the full spectrum of interactions between an organization's employees and stakeholders and among and between other organizations. How is certain space treated that reflects the culture, strategies and values of the organization?

Material Environment includes man-made buildings, roads, and other structures such as the office building an organization occupies and how that space is treated. This includes interior office spaces. This also reflects the value placed on the buildings architecture, landscaping and historical construction (if any). *Ethics* is the realm that describes the organization's business practices and its implicit and explicit contract with the community that seeks to establish itself as legitimate. How are an organization's practices modeled in its industry, its culture and all stakeholders? *Economic relationships* are described in terms of the organizations' level of investment in the fiscal well-being of the community. For example, how does the organization attract skilled labor to the community? How does it seek to improve the economic viability of the community? How does the organization create new opportunities for economic growth? How the organization values place in each of these dimensions suggests its type, and its strategies for building place. The Organizational Place Building (OPB) Model is a complex theoretical statement that has been subjected to both quantitative modeling and continuous empirical testing.

Within the context of the two agent perspectives described above, the OPB model includes four distinct *place agent identities*: transformational, contributive, contingent, and exploitive. *Place agent identities* reveal how organizations conceptualize themselves as social actors – agents – in relation to the places in which they are located and do business. The four types of place building organizations differ in how they conceptualize themselves as agents, the value they assign to the dimensions of place, their corporate culture, and their strategies and behaviors. *Transformational* organizations conceptualize themselves as change agents acting to improve the lives of individuals and groups in a place. *Contributive* organizations conceptualize themselves as investors and contributors to the well-being of places in which they operate. *Contingent* organizations view themselves simply as participants in places and *exploitive* organizations view themselves as independent agents with little to no obligations to the places in which they operate (Thomas, 2004; Thomas and Cross, 2007; Thomas, Gaede, Jurin and O'Connell, 2010).

Each of the four types of organizations, i.e. *transformational, contributive, contingent,* and *exploitive* create a mission statement which demonstrate different levels of commitment to place well-being and fiscal success. Organizations with the same agent perspective, but different agent identities, develop similar although not identical missions and strategies, which include similar commitments to place well-being and/or fiscal success. Organizations with an interdependent perspective strive for a relatively equal balance between place well-being and their own fiscal success, whereas those organizations with an independent agent identity put much more emphasis and weight on fiscal success with little concern for place well-being. The place building model illustrates the minor differences between types of place building organizations that share the same agent perspective, but distinct differences between organizations with different place agent identities (Thomas, 2004; Thomas and Cross, 2007).

Transformational organizations. Transformational organizations view themselves as critical agents with a mission and focus on improving life and creating positive change for both the organization and the place (Thomas, 2004; Thomas & Cross, 2007). The transformational organizational culture is highly focused on team learning, collaboration, openness to change, and building partnerships. They view themselves as *interdependent* members of a place, rather than independent members, and their success contributes to advantage beyond that of the organization (Thomas, 2004).

Transformational place builders demonstrate an *integrative* strategy that focuses on building a shared vision with the community and holding itself accountable to the community for the quality of its contribution to place. These behaviors are not solely for public relations advantage but an effort to surpass community business trends and regulations, perhaps even at a cost to the organization (Thomas & Cross, 2008). These strategies include initiating new policies and business practices for protecting the natural environment, neighborhoods, cultural heritage, local economy, and other local resources (Thomas & Cross, 2007).

Contributive organizations. Contributive organizations view themselves as being a contributing member of a network of business people and community leaders who share a common ideology. Their identity as a local contributor is affirmed by engaging with local organizations, fundraising, and by philanthropy that builds place (Schneider, Brief, and Guzzo, 1996; Chaskin, Brown, Venkatesh & Vidal, 2001). In contrast to transformational organizations that view themselves as responsible for the well-being of place, a contributive organization views itself as a contributor to the well-being of place.

The organizational culture is focused on "investing in its community" and conforming to local norms and values (Thomas, 2004).

Contributive organizations value place first for its social relationships and second for its economic opportunities and potential for business growth. The natural world may simply be the geographic location of their business. These organizations need a place that needs them, where they can simultaneously prosper and give back. They practice an *integrative* strategy that cultivates their role as a key contributor in their community, through the network of organizations that facilitate social and philanthropic activity (Thomas, 2004; Thomas and Cross, 2007).

Contingent organizations. Contingent organizations view themselves as disassociated and autonomous agents. They narrowly define correct corporate behavior as "corporate social responsibility" with obeying existing laws, regulations, and ethical codes, yet they make a concerted effort to act accordingly. Rather than viewing themselves as interdependent with place (transformational), or key members of place (contributive), they view themselves as control agents. The contingent organization practices a *separatist strategy* that centers on a plan that distinguishes the organization in terms of its economic power. Contingent organizations value place for what it provides for the company, such as workers for its labor force. They practice philanthropy only as a method for advancing their own causes, not out of any intrinsic commitment to place and their principle contribution is their economic contribution and adherence to laws and regulations (Thomas and Cross, 2007).

Exploitive organizations. Exploitive organizations view themselves as occupants of place and are more isolated from the values of the community. They are active users of the economic, cultural, social, and political resources, valuing place as a commodity that they utilize to their greatest economic benefit (Sagoff, 1996; Rodman, 1992; Entrikin, 2000). They largely plan and organize to control space in which short term financial progress and cost effectiveness trump local needs (Thomas, 2004) and their preference is to be granted the rights and legal protections typically afforded only to individual citizens (Vogel, 2005).

The exploitive firm's mission to maximize profit determines their organizational philosophy, and it is usually practiced by deliberately targeting certain places for the potential to extract resources without accountability for the risks posed to the local population. While these organizations may employ locals and deal with local suppliers, they practice a *separatist* strategy in that they are not invested in ways that contribute to a sense of place. Exploitive organizations are likely to leave a place once they have determined they don't fit or the return is not as lucrative as originally anticipated (Thomas & Cross, 2007).

Each of the four types stands out from the others in their perspectives on place and the consequences of their actions. Transformational organizations orchestrate their contributions in ways that transform themselves and place. As agents of change, they are distinguished from other organizations in that they view place in a holistic manner in which all five place dimensions are interactive and interdependent. Consequently, the business practices of transformational organizations contribute to place well-being through learning and teaching in partnership with clients (Thomas, 2004; Thomas and Cross, 2007).

PRINCIPLES OF PLACE BUILDING: A DESCRIPTIVE, PRESCRIPTIVE AND EVALUATIVE

Principles of place building are evident in every organization. The degree by which these principles are incorporated in the business model and the MS can help identify the type of place builder. The first principle is *descriptive* (see Appendix B) in the sense of strategies that reveal how an organization values or de-values place (Thomas, 2004; Thomas & Cross, 2007; Kimball and Thomas, 2012). The organization's valuation of place informs how the organization *designates the use of space* in ways that ascribe meaning and reflect the organization's culture.

Second principles of *evaluative* (see Appendix C) in the sense of revealing how an organization *determines the significance, worth or condition of a place*, and how that organization assesses or estimates the quality or condition of a place relative to its role. Each organization determines the significance of place across five place dimensions. This can be apparent in terms of the words and intentions of its MS.

The third principle of *prescriptive* (see Appendix D) specifies, generally through its mission statement, its *intentions toward the wider community*: how it will *use resources and engage in activities that impact the community*, and what social and ethical responsibilities it acknowledges and strives to meet. These three principles are the codes or the norms of place building that we contend are evident in an organization's business model and can serve to direct the organizations duties and responsibilities to place and community.

The three place building principles (evaluative, descriptive and prescriptive) explain the tentative framework for incorporating PB in the organization's MS. The principles can also direct or guide an organization that seeks legitimacy in its community. Finally, these principles reconfigure Corporate Social Responsibility (CSR) as an *integrated strategy* in which both the organization transitions from stakeholders to "place holders". This transition in strategy and intentions are intimately connected to a new paradigm—a place building paradigm. Although this place-building framework typically has been applied to business organizations, it seems equally applicable to other types of organizations such as institutions of higher education, small businesses and non-profit groups. Next we explore the conceptual link of mission statements to place building.

MISSION STATEMENTS AND PLACE BUILDING: A CONCEPTUAL PERSPECTIVE

MS's will continue to be a significant reporting tool in identifying an organization's strategic intentions and can signal how it builds place. The MS is one of several components of an organization's business model; however, we focus on the conditional fit of the attributes of OPB that might be evident in a MS. The MS can illustrate this in the same manner a mission statement can guide all matters of a firm's strategies and activities, such as its CSR, its marketing and operational imperatives. Another way of looking at it is this: if MS are an indication of how the firm competes and generates revenues, then how it values place can be an integral aspect of its mission. This paper offers litmus for identifying likely place building strategies incorporated in its business model and thus evident in its MS.

As Levin (2000) posits "an organizational mission is a broadly defined statement of purpose that specifies who the organization is and what it does" (p. 93) and what it values. As such, a MS aims at providing organizations with a strategic direction that can uncover or expose its intentions toward the places it occupies. In order to do this, we have extrapolated key terms from selected MS's that can help compare a MS to a particular type of organizational place builder. For precisely these points we found the notion of a MS as a link or connection to describing how an organization values and builds place an indication of how it will treat the places it occupies in a community.

MISSION STATEMENTS AND PLACE BUILDING: AN EMPIRICAL INVESTIGATION

This study investigates possible relationships between business mission statements (if any) and Thomas' typology of Organizational Place Building (OPB), thus producing a fair estimate of the organization's intentions in terms of how it builds place. We examined the MS's from 41 businesses selected among a group of fortune 500 firms to determine if place building attributes, as outlined in the OPB model, were evident.

Method

Qualitative document analysis (Bernard and Ryan, 2010) was employed to investigate the possible linkage between mission statements and the concepts of the place building model. For example, does a MS contain likely terms that are symbolic or indicative of its place building strategies or intentions as identified in the OPB typology? In terms of methods, the four types of organizational place building (transformational, contributive, contingent, and exploitive) served as deductive/prior codes (Bernard and Ryan, 2010) by which to exam the corporation's MS. By the process of purposefully sampling (Willig, 2001), (i.e. selecting cases that would yield data for the research purpose to be fulfilled) the study located 41 corporate mission statements for inclusion in the study.

The study located 41 corporate mission statements for examination. The sample included major US corporations representing the business sectors of medical (5), retail (2), manufacturing/distribution (5), transportation (5), communications (4), financial (5), energy (3), entertainment (3), food/beverage/grocery (6), services (2), and one unassigned. The findings of the cross-case analysis (Miles and Huberman, 1994) of the document analysis using the typologies as deductive codes are presented using a meta-matrix display (See Table 1) (Miles and Huberman, 1994).

FINDINGS

The purpose of the study was to determine if a relationship exists between MSs and OPB. A Meta Matrix of Mission Statements and Organizational Place Building by Business Sector (See Table 1) presents the results.

Table 1

A Meta Matrix of Mission Statements and Organizational Place Building Type by Business Sector

Business Sector	Unassigned	Exploitive	Contingent	Contributive	Transformational	Contributive/Transformational
Medical	23	0	2	14	0	2
Retail	2	0	1	2	0	0
Manufacturing	1	0	0	1	0	0
Transportation	3	0	0	1	0	1
Communications	3	0	1	0	0	0
Financial	3	0	0	1	0	0
Energy	3	0	0	2	0	0
Entertainment	1	0	0	1	0	0
Food	2	0	0	1	0	0
Services	2	0	0	3	0	1
	1	0	0	1	0	0

Research revealed that 23 of the 41 organization's business MS manifested *no place* building characteristics. 18 organizations had MS's that manifested *some place building values.* Of these 18 MS, two were coded contingent, 14 exhibited certain characteristics associated with a contributive type of place builder and two were a combination of contributive and transformational.

The findings in this study of organizational mission statements and place building concepts illustrates that a relationship can be found, but over half of the mission statements do not give sufficient information to warrant an assignment of a place building type. However, an organization's MS relationship to the principles of OPB may serve as a key in evaluating how it may operate in a community.

DISCUSSION AND IMPLICATIONS

Each type of OPB builds place in different ways, with a variety of results that should be coded to give organizations and their communities a chance to understand how OPB principles are subscribed to in a MS. For example, how does the organization *designate the use of space* in ways that ascribe meaning and reflect the organization's culture; *determine the significance, worth or condition of a place*, and how that organization assess or estimates the quality or condition of a place relative to its role; and most importantly, the mission statement, signals its *intentions toward the wider community*: how it will *use resources and engage in activities that impact the community*, and what social and ethical responsibilities it acknowledges and strives to meet. This article concludes by predicting that mission statements will continue to be a significant reporting tool to identify the type of place building organization.

Research Limitations/Implications

Thinking theoretically OBP theory can contribute to the study of organizations and their roles in a community in several practical ways: First, as a way to co-join place as an interdisciplinary study with some larger issue such as the growing emphasis on organizational and community social responsibilities, especially to each other. Second, this study offers a critical perceptive on the traditional view of CSR which has come to be regarded as an appearance of responsibility geared toward some particular business objective that may be connected to its MS. And third, offers an anthropological view of an organization as an *interdependently* acting agent with varying degrees of contributions to the places they occupy at some point in the time of their development.

OPB is more holistic approach that is a shift in thinking about the relationship between place and organization that proffers new questions about the organization and its place in a community. For example it's clear that replacing traditional commerce and modern industry is upon us. How will we respond? What new systems will emerge and from whom do we or will we take our quest? Certain organizations are in a better position to innovate and create places in which shareholders can become placeholders. Or will larger economic forces reconfigure and change how our organizations value place? What new metrics will we use to create new thinking about what kind of organizations communities need and what will be their role in the places we call important? Place building emerges as a practical method for identifying, describing, evaluating and making some reasonable guesses at the level of contribution beyond what is known as being socially responsible.

In essence OPB excels beyond stakeholder thinking and redefines socially responsible behavior as a strategy for protecting and advocating for place, enhancing an organization's role in a community as a "place holder" resulting in building a competitive advantage for both the organization and the community.

This study is the first to assess whether or not place building performance is evident in an organization's MS. Clearly we would need to explore other dimensions of performance, operational activities, marketing, consistencies in financial reporting for example which is outside this article, rather we attempt to discern if and how PB principles are evident in the MS and provide a method for doing so.

REFERENCES

Agnew, J. A. (1987). *Place and Politics.* Boston: Allen & Unwin.

Alvesson, Mats. (1990). On the popularity of organizational culture. *Acts Sociologica*, 33, 1:31-49.

Amit, R., and C. Zott. (2001). "Value Creation in E-Business," *Strategic Management Journal* 11(22), 493–520.

Bart, C. K. (2001). Exploring the application of mission statements on the World Wide Web. *Internet research: electronic networking applications and policy.* 11, 360-368.

Bart, C. K. (1998). Mission matters. *CPA Journal*, 68 (6), 56-57.

Bart, C. K. and Baetz, M. C. (1998). The relationship between mission statements and firm performance: an exploratory study. *The journal of management studies.* 36, 823-853.

Bart, C. K. (1997). Industrial firms and the power of the mission. *Industrial marketing management*, 26. 371-378.

Bernard, H.R. and Ryan, G. W. (2010). *Analyzing qualitative data: Systematic approaches.* Thousand Oaks: Sage.

Buttimer, A. & Seamon, D. Eds. (1980). *The human experience of space and place.* London: Croom Helm.

Cetro, S. & Peter, P. (1992). Strategic management: A focus on progress. New York: McGraw-Hill.

Chaskin, R. J., Brown, P., Venkatesh, S., and Vidal, A. (2001). *Building community Capacity.* New York: Aldine de Gruyter.

Entrikin, J. N. (2000). The betweenness of place: Towards geography of modernity. New York: Routledge.

Gans, H. J. (2002). The sociology of space: a use-centered view. *City and Community*, 1(4): 329-339.

Geertz, C. (1983). *Local knowledge.* New York: Basic Books.

Gieryn, T. F. (2000). A Space for Place in Sociology. *Annual Rev. Social.*, 26:463-496.

Gustafson, P. (2001). Meanings of place: Everyday experience and theoretical conceptualization. *Journal of Environmental Psychology.* 21, 5-16.

Glaser, B. and Strauss, A. (1967). *The discovery of grounded theory: strategies for qualitative research.* New York: Aldine de Gruyter.

Harsh, V. V. (2009). Mission statements: A study of intent and influence. *Journal of Services Research*, 9(2).

Hatch, M. J. (1993). The dynamics of organizational culture. *The academy of management review*, 18(4):657-693.

Hudson, R. (2001). *Producing places.* New York: The Guilford Press.

Sagoff, M. (1996). Values and preferences. *Ethics*, 2: 301-316.

Ireland, R. and Hitt, M. (1992). Mission statements: Importance, challenge and recommendations for development. *Business Horizons*, 35(3). 34-42.

Kotter, J. P. (1997). Leading Change. Cambridge, MA: Harvard Business School Press.

Kimball, M. & Thomas, D. (2012). Place-Building Perceptions: A New Model for Catalyzing change in University-Community Relations and Student Civic Development. *Michigan Journal?*

Larwood, L., Falbe, C. M., Kreieger, M. & Miesing, P. (1995). An empirical study of the structure and meaning of organizational vision. Academy of Management Journal. 38, 740-769.

Levin, (2000). Vision revisited. The journal of Applied Behavioral Science. 36, 91-108.

Miles, M. B. and Huberman, A. M. (1994). *Qualitative Data Analysis* (2 Ed.). Thousand Oaks: Sage Publications.

Rodman, M. (1992). Empowering place: Multilocality and multivocality. *American Anthropologist, New series.* 94. (3), 640-656.

Schoenberger, E. (1997). *The cultural crisis of the firm.* Cambridge: Blackwell.

Sheaffer, Z. Landau, D., & Drori, I. (2008). Mission Statement and Performance: An Evidence of "Coming of Age" *Organization Development Journal*, 26(2), 49-62.

Shafer, S., Smith, H. J. & Linder, J. (2005). "The Power of Business Models," *Business Horizons* 48(3), 199-207. pg. 202.

Schneider, B., Brief, A. P., & Guzzo, R. A. (1996). Creating a climate and culture for sustainable organizational change. *Organizational Dynamics.* Spring: 7-18.

Snyder, G. (1995). *A place in space: Ethics, aesthetics, and watersheds.* Washington D.C.: Publishers Group West.

Staeheli, L. A. Chapter 11 *in A companion to Political Geography edited by john Agnew, Place Mitchell, K and Toal, G. Blackwell publishing.*

Sheaffer, Z., Landau, D., Drori, I. (2008). Mission Statement and Performance: An Evidence of "Coming of Age". *Organization Development Journal* 26.2 (summer): 49-62.

Thomas, D. F. (2004). *Toward an understanding of organization place building in communities.* Unpublished doctoral dissertation, Colorado State University, Fort Collins, CO.

Thomas, D. & Cross, J. (2007). Organizations as Place Builders. *Journal of Behavioral and Applied Management*, 9(1).

Thomas, D. F., Gaede, D., Jurin, R. & Connolly, L. S. (2008). Understanding The Link Between Organizational Behavior And Community Sense Of Place. *Community Development*: 2008; 39(3).

Thomas, D. F., Gould, J., Gaede, D., & Jurin, R. (2012). Transformational Place Building: A Mixed Method Exploration of Small Businesses. *Journal of Enterprising Communities: People and Places in the Global Economy.*

Vandijck, D. & Desmidt, S. (2007). Relevance of mission statements in Flemish not-for-profit healthcare organizations. *Journal of Nursing Management,* 15 (2), 131-141.

Verma, H. V. (2009). Mission Statements: A Study of Intent and Influence. *Journal of Services Research* 9.2 (Oct 2009-Mar 2010): 153-172.

Weick, K. E. (1995). *Sensemaking in organizations.* Thousand Oaks: Sage.

Werlen, B. (1993). Society, Action, and Space: An Alternative Human Geography. London: Routledge.

Williams, L. S. (2008). The mission statement: a corporate reporting tool with a past, present, and future. *Journal of Business Communication, 45*(2), 94-119.

Willig, C. (2001). *Introducing qualitative research in psychology: Adventures in theory and method.* Berkshire, UK: Open University Press.

Wright, S. (1994). (Eds.). *Anthropology of organizations.* New York: Routledge.

Vogel, D. (2005). *The market for value: The potential and limits of corporate social responsibility.* Brookings Institution Press: Washington D.C.

APPENDIX A

Meta-matrix Display of Deductive Codes

Company	Industry	Mission Statement	Exploitive	Contingent	Contributive	Transformational
ADM	Agriculture	To unlock the potential of nature to improve the quality of life.			Improve the quality of life	Improve the quality of life
Albertsons	Grocery	Guided by relentless focus on our five imperatives, we will constantly strive to implement the critical initiatives required to achieve our vision. In doing this, we will deliver operational excellence in every corner of the Company and meet or exceed our commitments to the many constituencies we serve. All of our long-term strategies and short-term actions will be molded by a set of core values that are shared by each and every associate.			Commitments to the many constituencies we serve. Core values that are shared	
Ashland	Chemical	We are a market-focused, process-centered organization that develops and delivers innovative solutions to our customers, consistently outperforms our peers, produces predictable earnings for our shareholders, and provides a dynamic and challenging environment for our employees.				

Company	Industry	Mission Statement			
Amerisource Bergen	Pharmaceutical	To build shareholder value by delivering pharmaceutical and healthcare products, services and solutions in innovative and cost effective ways. We will realize this mission by setting the highest standards in service, reliability, safety and cost containment in our industry.			
American Standard	To "Be the best in the eyes of our customers, employees and shareholders."				
AutoNation	Car dealerships	To be America's best run, most profitable automotive retailer.			
Avaya	Communication systems	Provide the world's best communications solutions that enable businesses to excel			
AGCO	Manufacturer and distributor of agricultural equipment	Profitable growth through superior customer service, innovation, quality and commitment.			

Company	Industry	Mission Statement	Exploitive	Contingent	Contributive	Transformational
Aflac	Aflac is a supplemental insurance company in the US. Its main business is into health and life insurance policies that cover special conditions, particularly cancer.	To combine aggressive strategic marketing with quality products and services at competitive prices to provide the best insurance value for consumers.		Combine aggressive strategic marketing		
Computer Services Corp	IT	To use our extensive IT experience to deliver tangible business results enabling our clients in industry and government to profit from the advanced use of technology. We strive to build long-term client relationships based on mutual trust and respect.				
CHUBB	Insurance	We are dedicated to providing excellent underwriting and loss control advice up front, and to ensuring superior customer service through the life of the policy.				
Becton, Dickinson and Company	Medical/ Manufacturing	To help all people live healthy lives.			To help all people live healthy lives	

Company	Industry	Mission		Values
Barnes and Noble	Specialty retail	Our mission is to operate the best specialty retail business in America, regardless of the product we sell. Because the product we sell is books, our aspirations must be consistent with the promise and the ideals of the volumes which line our shelves.		Consistent with the promise and the ideals of the volumes
Cooper Tire and Rubber	Manufacturing	Earn money for its shareholders and increase the value of their investment		
Coventry Health Care	Coventry Health Care is an institution that offers health care services that includes HMOs, PPOs, Medicare, Medicaid products, Worker's Compensation and Network Rental	Our mission is to provide high quality care and services to our members and to be profitable in the process. Coventry Health Care is also committed to maintaining excellence, respect, and integrity in all aspects of our operations and our professional and business conduct. We strive to reflect the highest ethical standards in our relationship with members, providers, and shareholders.		Maintaining excellence, respect, and integrity in all aspects of our operations and our professional and business conduct.
CSX	Transportation	To be the safest, most progressive North American railroad, relentless in the pursuit of customer and employee excellence.		

Company	Industry	Mission Statement	Exploitive	Contingent	Contributive	Transformational
Chevron,	Energy	To be the global energy company most admired for its people, partnership and performance.			Admired for its people, partnership	
Conoco Philips		Use our pioneering spirit to responsibly deliver energy to the world.			Responsibly deliver energy	
Disney	Entertainment	The mission of The Walt Disney Company is to be one of the world's leading producers and providers of entertainment and information. Using our portfolio of brands to differentiate our content, services and consumer products, we seek to develop the most creative, innovative and profitable entertainment experiences and related products in the world.				
Darden Restaurants	Restaurant	"To nourish and delight everyone we serve."			To nourish	
Dean Foods,	Food and beverage	Maximize long-term stockholder value, while adhering to the laws of the jurisdictions in which it operates and at all times observing the highest ethical standards.			Adhering to the laws of the jurisdictions in which it operates and at all times observing the highest ethical	

			Essential to human progress
Dow Chemical	Chemical	To constantly improve what is essential to human progress by mastering science and technology.	
Dole Food Company,		Committed to supplying the consumer and our customers with the finest, high-quality products and to leading the industry in nutrition research and education.	
		A corporate philosophy of adhering to the highest ethical conduct in all its business dealings, treatment of its employees, and social and environmental policies.	Highest ethical conduct
Este Lauder	Skin care	"Bringing the best to everyone we touch".	
Eco Lab	Sanitizing and cleaning	We will achieve aggressive growth and fair return for our shareholders. We will accomplish this by exceeding the expectations of our customers while conserving resources and preserving the quality of the environment.	Conserving resources and preserving the quality of the environment.
Fed Express	Transportation	FedEx will produce superior financial returns for shareowners by providing high value-added supply chain, transportation, business and related information services through focused operating companies	

Company	Industry	Mission Statement	Exploitive	Contingent	Contributive	Transformational
Ford Motor Company	Automotive	We are a global family with a proud heritage passionately committed to providing personal mobility for people around the world.				
Family Dollar Stores	Retail	For Our Customers A compelling place to shop... by providing convenience and low prices For Our Associates A compelling place to work... by providing exceptional opportunities and rewards for achievement For Our Investors A compelling place to invest... by providing outstanding returns				
Golden West Financial Corporation,	Financial services	Golden West Financial Corporation's vision is to create long-term value for customers, shareholders, employees, and neighbors by providing high quality consumer financial services through our World Savings and Atlas subsidiaries.				
Hersey Company	Food	Undisputed Marketplace Leadership				

Kindred Heathrow	Health care	The Compliance and Quality Committee is appointed to assist the Board of Directors in monitoring (1) the Company's compliance with applicable laws, regulations, and policies; (2) the Company's compliance with its Corporate Integrity Agreement and its Code of Conduct; and (3) the Company's programs, policies and procedures that support and enhance the quality of care provided by the Company.			
H&R Block	Financial services	To help our clients achieve their financial objectives by serving as their tax and financial partner.			
Hughes Supply, Inc.	A wholesale distributor of construction	To supply outstanding service and solutions through dedication and excellence.			
IBM	Technology	Operating a safe and secure government.			
Kelly Services	Human resources	To serve our customers, employees, shareholders and society by providing a broad range of staffing services and products.			

Company	Industry	Mission Statement	Exploitive	Contingent	Contributive	Transformational
Lucent	Telecom	Philanthropy supports the social responsibility cornerstone of Lucent's mission: To live up to our responsibilities to serve and enhance the communities in which we work and live and the society on which we depend.			Supports the social responsibilities to serve and enhance the communities in which we work and live and the society on which we depend.	
McGraw Hill	Publishing	Dedicated to creating a workplace that respects and values people from diverse backgrounds and enables all employees to do their best work. It is an inclusive environment where the unique combination of talents, experiences, and perspectives of each employee makes our business success possible. Respecting the individual means ensuring that the workplace is free of discrimination and harassment. Our commitment to equal employment and diversity is a				

			and employ people around the world. We see it as a business imperative that is essential to thriving in a competitive global marketplace.
MBNA	Banking		We strive to be the acknowledged global leader and preferred partner in helping our clients succeed in the world's rapidly evolving financial markets.
MGM Mirage			MGM MIRAGE supports responsible gaming and has implemented the American Gaming Association's Code of Conduct for Responsible Gaming at its properties. MGM MIRAGE also has been the recipient of numerous awards and recognitions for its industry-leading Diversity Initiative and its community philanthropy programs. For more information about MGM MIRAGE, please visit the company's website at www.mgmmirage.com

Company	Industry	Mission Statement	Exploitive	Contingent	Contributive	Transformational
Mutual of Omaha	Insurance	We will continue to build a corporate culture that respects and values the unique strengths and cultural differences of our associates, customers and community.			Respects and values the unique strengths and cultural differences	
Mattel Toy	Manufacturing	Mattel makes a difference in the global community by effectively serving children in need. We also enrich the lives of Mattel employees by identifying diverse volunteer opportunities and supporting their personal contributions through the matching gifts program.			Makes a difference

Enrich the lives of Mattel employees | Makes a difference |

APPENDIX B

Descriptive

Type	Description
Exploitive	Organization values place in quantifiable terms that describe place as a product or commodity. The organization negotiates its position in the community without regard to the impact of its operations and operates outside acceptable practices – no local knowledge of the place and its historic or cultural history.
Contingent	Values place primarily in measureable terms. What is the return on its contributions to place (i.e. how does the organization gauge its investments and estimates of the economic and financial worth to the organization). What economic and political advantages can be gained that advance its mission.
Contributive	Values place in terms of its social network. The organization's contributions are intended to gain recognition and favorably position the owner or leader as an important player in the community.
Transformational	Values place equally on all five place dimensions. The organization invests its assets to build competitive advantages for both place and organization. Assumes a leadership role in advancing new community capacities and competencies that improve community well-being.

APPENDIX C

Type	Prescriptive
	Designates the use of strategic resources and assets that value and/or de-value place.
Exploitive	To capture financial gains through aggressive and organization-centric strategies that often value place as an acquisition or commodity.
Contingent	Conditional development of resources and assets to attain some good or purpose for the firms benefit.
Contributive	Commits resources and assets to help build place, seek membership community organizations as a way of enhancing its reputation as a contributor.
Transformational	Commits resources and assets to lead and create new opportunities for civic participation and economic partnerships. An advocate for change and improvements consistent with it's and the community's business mission and purposes.

APPENDIX D

Evaluative

Type	Description
Exploitive	Assesses value of place primarily as an economic factor. It monetizes place and spaces as resources for its own purposes.
Contingent	Calculates the value of place in terms of its worth based on what it can contribute to the organization. What place affords that can enhance its market position and business model.
Contributive	Determine values based on the organization's relationship to some propositional good, such as the owners "fit" in the community.
Transformational	Determines the value of place based on the shared qualities of all five dimensions (economics, ethic, social, nature and the built environment). Each of which are viewed for their intrinsic values that gain prominence from an integrated and complex setting in which it operates. Transformational organizations can help revive the long dormant assets in a community by changing their business structure(s) to facilitate new investments in community capacity and or adopting new policies that value place on all five dimensions.

6

THE ORGANIZATIONAL PLACE BUILDING INVENTORY: AN INSTRUMENT FOR ASSESSING AND FACILITATING PLACE-BASED CORPORATE SOCIAL RESPONSIBILITY

David F. Thomas

Dr. Thomas is an Assistant Professor of Management. He is responsible for program development of UNC's Entrepreneurship program. This innovative program concentrates on the applied aspects of the entrepreneurship with an emphasis on supporting student start up opportunities and collaboration with the Northern Colorado business community.

Dr. Thomas received his Ph.D. from Colorado State University. He has held various senior level positions in the travel and tourism industry. In addition, he has managed corporate start-up enterprises and small business turn around operations. UNC has recognized his contributions to students and faculty as both advisor of the year and professor of the year in the Monfort College of Business.

His research has produced a new model for describing and evaluating how an organization contributes to their community. His research models have been instrumental in developing economic programs that advance community's recruit and retain best fitting firms.

Assistant Professor Management / Management/University of Northern Colorado/ Campus Box 128 Kepner Hall / Greeley, Co 80639/ USA

David.thomas@unco.edu

Michael Kimball

Associate Professor of Anthropology whose research focus on applied anthropological approaches to studying and facilitating place building in community, organizational and heritage contexts.

Anthropology Department, University of Northern Colorado, Candelaria 2200, Campus Box 90, Greeley, Colorado, 80639, USA

michael.kimball@unco.edu

Diane Suhr Lecturer University of Northern Colorado

Diana Suhr, Ph.D., is an Adjunct Professor, Monfort College of Business, University of Northern Colorado. She holds an M.S. in Research and Statistics, an M.A. in Special Education: Gifted and Talented Education, and a Ph.D. in Educational Psychology. Her research interests include analyzing data with exploratory factor analysis and structural equation modeling.

Diana Suhr, Ph.D., Monfort College of Business, University of Northern Colorado, Greeley CO 80639, USA.

SuhrSirs@msn.com

ABSTRACT

Purpose

Through a discussion of Organizational Place Building Theory (OPBT) and the presentation of a professional services firm (PSF) case study, the purpose of this paper is to present the justification for and efficacy of the Organizational Place Building Inventory (OPBI).

Design/methodology/approach

The OPBI is an objective instrument designed to assess an organization's values and strategies along five dimensions or latent constructs of place building: ethical, social, natural, built environment and economic.

Findings

The paper discusses the significance of the OPBI's scores with respect to four place building profiles – exploitive, contingent, contributive and transformational. It concludes by offering a three-phase process in which the OPBI may be incorporated into participatory research.

Originality/value

Although the literature provides several methods for measuring corporate social activities, they do not include corporate social responsibility from a place perspective, that is, one that recognizes, values and integrates the meanings individuals and groups give to a place in terms of its geographic and social contexts. This perspective focuses on how place can and should play an important role in the strategic relationships organizations have with their communities, their clients and employees.

Organizational Place Building serves as both a mirror and a lens through which organizations can (1) locate themselves on a continuum of values and strategies with regard to place (i.e., their relations to its social, natural, material, economic and ethical dimensions); (2) develop strategies for how they might stay where they are or get where they would rather be.

Key Words

Place Building, Place, Corporate Social responsibility, organizational behavior, case study

INTRODUCTION

The term corporate social responsibility (CSR) is often used interchangeably with corporate responsibility, corporate citizenship, social enterprise, sustainability, sustainable development, triple-bottom line, corporate ethics, and in some cases corporate governance. Though these terms are different, they all point in the same direction: throughout the industrialized world and in many developing countries there has been a sharp escalation in the social roles corporations are expected to play. Companies are facing new demands to engage in public-private, multi-stakeholder and cross-sector partnerships (Drexler, 2016; Rein et al, 2005) and are undergoing pressure to be accountable not only to shareholders, but also to stakeholders such as employees, consumers, suppliers, local communities, policymakers, and society-at-large (Anderson, 2005; Cavanagh, Oza, and Bennett, 2005).

CSR is a concept with multiple definitions. Investors use an internal definition including transparency, governance and ethics as key citizenship elements (Cavanagh, Oza, and Bennett, 2005). Heslin and Ochoa (2008) posit that CSR is an engagement in economically sustainable business activities that go beyond legal requirements to protect the well-being of employees, communities, and the environment. Carroll (1991) views CSR as those discretionary actions above and beyond the economic, legal and ethical requirements of business, i.e., acting when no one is watching.

This study advances place building as a new perspective of CSR that is built on Organizational Place Building theory (Thomas, 2004; Thomas and Cross, 2007). OBP theory can contribute to the study of organizations and their roles in a community in two practical ways: first, as a way to join organizational studies with some larger issue or body of knowledge such as place from the sociological and geographical disciplines and organizational behavior; second, place building represents a shift in thinking about the relationship between places and the organization. How an organization balances its fiscal success with community well-being is the hallmark of Organizational

Place Building (Thomas and Cross, 2007). This balancing act is a shift in the organization's relationship with its community from occupant and part time contributor to partner in the co-construction of place (Thomas and Cross, 2007).

One of the challenges faced by those who wish to investigate and foster CSR is how to assess an organization's practices relative to some set of CSR principles, guidelines or rubrics. As a result, over the years there has been a proliferation of quantitative assessment instruments, from measures concerned with CSR's relations to profitability (Aupperle, Carroll and Hatfield, 1985), to multidimensional scales measuring performance and competitive success (Gallardo-Vázquez and Sanchez-Hernandez, 2014) or even psychosocial characteristics (D'Aprile and Talò, 2014). Until now, however, no instrument has been developed and tested that measures an organization's role as place builder. To what extent does an organization invest its resources in building place in its community? Is there internal consistency in an organization's values and strategies as held and delivered at each level – employees, management, and executive leadership? Does an organization focus its place building mission on one or more dimensions, e.g., social, natural, ethical, human-made, and economic?

The purpose of this paper is to unveil the Organizational Place Building Inventory (OPBI) (See appendix A), an instrument designed for use by both investigators and practitioners to not only identify where an organization currently resides on a continuum of sets, or profiles, of place building values and strategies, but also to collaborate with organizations on changing this location if they so choose. In the following pages, the OPBI is explicated through a case conducted within a single professional services firm (PSF). The paper begins with a brief review of earlier theoretical and empirical research on place and place building and then presents and discusses the PSF case study, in which a cohort of partners and managers completed the OPBI and an exploratory factor analysis was used to identify patterning and explain variation in the data. The paper concludes with a consideration of the utility of both Organizational Place Building Theory and the

Organizational Place Building Inventory for assessing place-based Corporate Social Responsibility.

PLACE BUILDING THEORY

Place is defined as both geographic and social and is organized around the meanings individuals and groups give to a place in its setting (Rodman, 1992). Collinge and Gibney (2010, 388) draw from the work of Patsy Healey (Healey, 1998) and Doreen Massey (e.g., Massey, 2005) to conceive place "in terms of the intersection of flows (people and goods and services)." Places take on the meaning of events that occur there, and their descriptions are fused with human goals, values, and intentions. These shared meanings are held in common by the collective, and are historically generated and tend to be durable (Alvesson and Berg, 1991). Geographers refer to place as context explaining how social relations attach to space and place and only secondarily to people (Staeheli, 2007). Place is therefore described in this sense as a setting for social action such as in an organization. Entrikin (2000) found that place shares meanings or interpretive frames of events for different actions, and second it provides resources for action (p. 6). Thus, place as a platform can mediate between individuals, social groups and broader political structure (Thomas and Cross, 2007).

In the past thirty years the concept of place has received examination from scholars in a variety of disciplines. Place in the context of community development, local and regional economic development, leadership, corporate culture, and organizational behavior have been studied by sociologists (Gans, 2002; Gieryn, 2000), geographers (Agner, 1987; Buttimer and Seamon, 1980; Entrikin, 2000; Werlen, 1993), anthropologists (Geertz, 1983; Wright, 1994), urban planners (Collinge and Gibney, 2010; Sotarauta, 2014), and business and policy scholars (Ayres, 2014; Beer and Clower, 2014; Delheim, 1986; Hatch, 1993; Morgan, 1986; Weick, 1995). Place building, referred to elsewhere as place-shaping or place-making (Collinge and Gibney, 2010), as a concept is alluded to by anthropologists, sociologists, geographers, and other social scientists interested in matters such as enterprise movement, community and systems sustainability (Schneider, Brief, and Guzzo, 1996), sustainable development, and enterprise attributes of communities (Hudson, 2001; Jacobs, 1984; Kimball, McBeth, Brunswig and Thomas, 2013; Sagoff, 1996; Schoenberger, 1997; Wright, 1994).

OPB theory contributes to the studies mentioned above by including a *prescriptive* approach that frames and investigates place building relations between organizations and their associated communities and environment. In other words, OPB theory asks not only what these place building relations are and how and why they exist, but also whether an organization and its constituents wish to change these relations and how they might do so. Below, three key components undergirding this approach are explained: (1) place building dimensions; (2) agent perspectives; and (3) place building profiles.

Five place building dimensions. Place-building theory explains how an organization values place on five dimensions: nature; social relationships; material environment; ethics; and economic relationships. Nature includes the natural as opposed to man-made, such as landscape, earth, geography and natural resources, and asks how an organization relates and contributes to nature and the environment. The social relationships dimension includes the full spectrum of interactions between an organization's employees and stakeholders and among and between other organizations. It is concerned with how certain space is treated in such a way that reflects the culture, strategies and values of the organization. Built environment includes man-made buildings, roads, and other structures such as the exterior and interior space of office buildings an organization occupies and how these spaces are treated. This also reflects the value placed on a structure's architecture, landscaping and historical construction (if any). The ethics dimension describes the organization's business practices and its implicit and explicit contract with the community that seeks to establish itself as legitimate. This dimension asks how an organization's practices are modeled in its industry, its culture and all stakeholders. The economic relationships dimension defines the organization's level of investment in the fiscal well-being of the community. For example, how does the organization attract skilled labor to the community? How does it seek to improve the economic viability of the community? How does the organization create new opportunities for economic growth? How the organization values place in each of these five dimensions suggests its place building profile and its strategies for building place.

Agent perspective. An organization's agent perspective distinguishes two distinct viewpoints held by organizations, which encompass not only how organizations conceptualize themselves in relationship to place, but also the meaning they give to place, which then influences their goals, contributions to place, and all variety of their behavior. It is possible to distinguish two types of agent perspectives: one perspective conceptualizes organizations and their success as *interdependent* with the well-being of place; the other conceptualizes organizations and their success as *independent* of place (Thomas, 2004; Thomas and Cross, 2007; Thomas and Banning, 2014).

Organizations with the interdependent perspective view themselves as members of a community and recognize that organizations and places are mutually dependent on each other. Interdependent organizations consider themselves responsible for the well-being of place view their success as intimately tied with the greater well-being of the place, and actively seek a variety of opportunities to invest and contribute to the multiple aspects of place. In contrast, organizations with an independent perspective view themselves merely as occupants of place and economic agents, rather than integral members of place. Organizations that see themselves as independent agents focus their activities on satisfying internal goals while viewing the realms of place as resources to satisfy their needs. Their primary responsibility is to their shareholders, not the places in which they do business. They consider generating jobs and tax revenues as their primary, if not their only, contribution to place. Independent organizations are not committed to the well-being of place and will only maintain the relationship as long as it benefits their shareholders (Thomas, 2004; Thomas and Cross, 2007; Thomas and Banning, 2014).

Place building profiles. Four profiles (See appendix B) have been identified through the development of Organizational Place Building Theory (Thomas, 2004). It is important to emphasize here that these are not monotypes (aggregates of fixed, unvarying traits), but rather polythetic sets (Needham 1975). In other words, in the taxonomy of place building, there are sets, or profiles, comprising values, strategies, perspectives, and so on, each of which is neither necessary nor sufficient for the definition of the set, but which often co-occurs with other attributes inside it. This approach allows for the fact that, in nature, i.e., in the real world of social and economic interactions, there are no fixed categories into which organizations can be usefully shoehorned. As Needham (1975, 357) writes, citing the work of Sokal and Sneath (1963, 15):

> ... the advantages of polythetic groups are that "they are natural, have a high content of information, and are useful for many purposes"; the disadvantages are that "they may partly overlap one another (so that hierarchies and keys are less easy to make than with monothetic groups) and that they are not perfectly suited for any single purpose.

From the standpoint of OPBT, the disadvantages of polythetic sets are also strengths – they affirm OBPT's focus on the place building process, support its deliberative and participatory orientation, and facilitate its analyses of complex data.

Each of the four profiles are reflected in the mission, statement, which demonstrates different levels of commitment to place well-being and fiscal success. Organizations with the same agent perspective, but different profiles, develop similar although not identical missions and strategies, which include similar commitments to place well-being and/or fiscal success. Organizations with an interdependent perspective strive for a relatively equal balance between place well-being and their own fiscal success, whereas those organizations with an independent agent identity put much more emphasis and weight on fiscal success with little concern for place well-being. The place building model illustrates the minor differences between types of place building organizations that share the same agent perspective, but distinct differences between organizations with different place building profiles (Thomas, 2004; Thomas and Cross, 2007).

The four profiles differ in how they express agent perspectives, the value organizations assign to the dimensions of place, their corporate culture, and their strategies and behavior. For examples, transformational organizations conceptualize or identify themselves as change agents acting to improve the lives of individuals and groups in a place. Contributive organizations conceptualize themselves as investors and contributors to the well-being of places in which they operate. Contingent organizations view themselves simply as participants in places and exploitive organizations view themselves as independent agents with little to no obligations to the places in which they operate.

Exploitive profile. Organizations exhibiting this profile view themselves as occupants to place and are more isolated from the values of the community. They are active users of the economic, cultural, social, and political resources, valuing place as a commodity that they use to their greatest economic benefit (Entrikin, 2000; Rodman, 1992; Sagoff, 1996). They largely plan and organize to control space in which short term financial progress and cost effectiveness trump local needs (Thomas, 2004) and their preference is to be granted the rights and legal protections typically afforded only to individual citizens (Vogel, 2005).

This type of organization's mission to maximize profit determines their organizational philosophy, and it is usually practiced by deliberately targeting certain places for the potential to extract resources without accountability for the risks posed to the local population. While these organizations may employ local people and deal with local suppliers, they practice a separatist strategy in that they are not invested in ways that contribute to a sense of place. These organizations are likely to leave a place once they have determined they don't fit or the return is not as lucrative as originally anticipated (Thomas & Cross, 2007).

Contingent profile. Organizations exhibiting tis profile view themselves as disassociated and autonomous agents. They narrowly define correct corporate behavior as corporate social responsibility with obeying existing laws, regulations, and ethical codes, yet they make a concerted effort to act accordingly. Rather than viewing themselves as interdependent with place (transformational), or key members of place (contributive), they view themselves as control agents. This type of organization practices a separatist strategy that centers on a plan that distinguishes the organization in terms of its economic power. These organizations value place for what it provides for the company, such as workers for its labor force. They practice philanthropy only as a method for advancing their own causes, not out of any intrinsic commitment to place and their principle contribution is their economic contribution and adherence to laws and regulations (Thomas and Cross, 2007).

Contributive profile. Organizations exhibiting this profile view themselves as being a contributing member of a network of business people and community leaders who share a common ideology. Their identity as a local contributor is affirmed by engaging with local organizations, fundraising, and by philanthropy that builds place (Chaskin, Brown, Venkatesh and Vidal, 200; Schneider, Brief, and Guzzo, 1996). In contrast to transformational organizations that view themselves as responsible for the well-being of place, a contributive organization view itself as a contributor to the well-being of place. The organizational culture is focused on investing in its community and conforming to local norms and values (Thomas, 2004).

These organizations value place first for its social relationships and second for its economic opportunities and potential for business growth. The natural world may simply be the geographic location of their business. These organizations need a place that needs them, where they can simultaneously prosper and give back. They practice an integrative strategy that cultivates their role as a key contributor in their community, through the network of organizations that facilitate social and philanthropic activity (Thomas, 2004; Thomas and Cross, 2007).

Transformational profile. Organizations exhibiting this profile view themselves as critical agents with a mission and focus on improving life and creating positive change for both the organization and the place (Thomas, 2004; Thomas and Cross, 2007). A transformational organizational culture is highly focused on team learning, collaboration, openness to change, and building partnerships. These organizations view themselves as interdependent members of a place and their success contributes to advantages beyond those of the organizations (Thomas, 2004).

Further, transformational place builders demonstrate an integrative strategy that focuses on building a shared vision with the community and holding itself accountable to the community for the quality of its contribution to place. These behaviors are not solely for public relations advantage but an effort to surpass community business trends and regulations, perhaps even at a cost to the organization (Thomas and Cross, 2007). These strategies include initiating new policies and business practices for protecting the natural environment, neighborhoods, cultural heritage, local economy, and other local resources (Thomas and Cross, 2007).

Transformational organizations orchestrate their contributions in ways that transform themselves and place. As agents of change, they are distinguished from other organizations in that they view place in a holistic manner in which all five dimensions are interactive and interdependent. Consequently, the business practices of transformational organizations contribute to place well-being through learning and teaching in partnership with clients (Thomas, 2004; Thomas and Cross, 2007). And so it is with organizations that wield the power to create strategies and actions that will (intentionally or otherwise) create business strategies and activities that have the potential to destroy in some cases, recreate in others and in all cases change the reality of a place.

OPBT make no value-laden judgments about where an organization should belong on the place building continuum. Instead it invites organizations to engage in a journey of self-discovery through which they have an opportunity to take an unvarnished look at relations among their history, mission, vision, core values, strategies and goals and how these communicate, contribute to or detract from their place building roles. The OPBI is an instrument with which this place building journey can be investigated and charted.

METHOD

The purpose of this paper is to present the justification for and efficacy of the Organizational Place Building Inventory (OPBI) (See Appendix A). This objective instrument is designed to assess an organization's values and strategies along five dimensions of place building: ethical, social natural, built environment and economic. Based on place building theory, a scale was developed through a systematic scale development process. In the study, exploratory factor analysis was conducted to determine the underlying factorial structure of the organizational place building scale. Data were collected from a single professional services firm. The results of the analysis provided evidence of a set of place building profiles with specific characteristics of place building that can be used to describe and predict certain place building tendencies. The instrument can be used as a method to assess an organization's investments in community and socially responsible activities from a place perspective. The case study approach focused on collecting, analyzing, and interpreting quantitative data in a single case study of a Professional Services Firm (PSF).

Criterion sampling. The Front Range region of Colorado was selected as the business community from which an organization was selected. Access to research resources and its proximity to the university were the principal reasons for this selection. The other criteria included the selection of a PSF with at least 15 years in the community, local knowledge of the community, and a record of investment in the community on multiple levels – philanthropy, employee and client relationships. These levels of investment are an indication of this organization's commitment to the social and economic wellbeing of the community and thus a likely resource for our study.

Participant Selection Criteria. A form of theoretical sampling involved the process of selecting people on the basis of their position and responsibilities (Patton, 2002). In this case, the Executive Vice president (EVP) of PSF facilitated access to the firm's business model and participants and championed the research as compatible with their culture. Further, the EVP was eager to learn more about place building and where the firm might fit in the typology. The EVP was the best contact in the organization to describe the organization's strategies and community relationships.

In addition, the EVP had the credibility to promote the research and facilitate participation in data gathering activities. All 40 of the firm's partners (each of whom owned equity in the firm) and 66 managers were invited to participate in the survey questionnaire. Twenty-six of 40 forty partners completed the survey. Twenty out of the 66 managers were available to participate. A total of 46 completed the survey questionnaire. In all, 26 of 40 (62%) partners, and 20 of 66 (64%) managers participated in the research.

Quantitative data collection and analysis. The OPBI was constructed and based on the findings from an expert panel convened in 2013. The expert panel provided insights in two key areas. First, terminology appropriate to the content of place and organizational behavior was identified. This was key in communicating the language of place building and its relevance to organizational behavior. Second, the survey was tested on both a group of academics and small business owners. The survey used in this paper's case study emerged from these findings and the panel. The researchers, in collaboration with an expert panel and other subject matter experts, including pilot interviews with business owners, worked together to probe for specific aspects in creating the survey questions. Because no existing instrument that measures the importance of place building activities was available, these qualitative methods were relied upon in building questions that were pertinent to the assessment of place building and the metrics used in approximating the type of place builder.

The OPBI is a measurement instrument designed to assess an organization's values and strategies along five dimensions or latent constructs of place building: ethical, social natural, built environment and economic. Exploratory factor analysis (EFA) provides a means to explain variation and condense information among OPBI items by using fewer items (dimensions or latent constructs). Factor analysis explores the possible underlying factor structure of a set of interrelated variables (survey items) without imposing any preconceived structure on the outcome (Child, 1990). By performing an exploratory factor analysis (EFA), the number of dimensions (latent constructs) and the underlying factor structure of the Place Building Survey (PBS) were identified. Knowledge of theory identifies the dimensions while empirical research confirms that the survey items measure the dimensions (latent constructs).

The five dimensions of place building are ethics, social relationships, economics, built environment and nature. The underlying structure of each dimension can be measured with a set of interrelated variables (survey items) (See Table 1). Questions 1–6 on the OPBI measure Social Relations; questions 7–12 measure Economic Relations; questions 13–18 measure Nature; questions 19–24 measure Ethics; and questions 25–29 measure Built or Material Environment. Knowledge of theory identifies the dimensions while empirical research confirms that the survey items measure the dimensions.

Participants scored the importance of certain place building activities across the five place building dimensions described earlier. The sum of the scores approximated the importance of certain place building activities exhibited by the organization. Recognizing that some dimensions may score higher in terms of importance allows researchers to isolate the organization's preferences; it also provides some indication of how the firm evaluates, describes and prescribes certain policies towards place. For example, an organization scoring between 34 and 42 indicates an exploitive type; scores between 25 and 33 indicate a contingent type; scores between 16 and 24 indicate a contributive type; scores between 1 and 15 indicate a transformational type. Using the place building model (See Appendix B), an investigator can thus discern the characteristics of the profile. Earlier research (Thomas, Gaede Jurin, and Connolly, 2008) discovered that business organizations evolve over time, financial and economic conditions. This research gave rise to the interest to delve deeper to explaining place building in a single organization (Thomas and Banning, 2014).

Table 1. Scoring Type by Dimension

Dimension	Exploitive	Contingent	Contributive	transformational
Social	34-42	25-33	16-24	1-15
Economic	34-42	25-33	16-24	1-15
Nature	34-42	25-33	16-24	1-15
Ethics	34-42	25-33	16-24	1-15
Built environment	34-42	25-33	16-24	1-15

RESULTS AND DISCUSSION

The analysis included internal reliability and exploratory factor analysis of the total group, of partners and of managers. The five dimensions of place were measured with the survey as well as determining a company profile (exploitive, contingent, contributive, or transformational place building profile). It must be noted that the small size does not allow statements to be made pertaining to a population.

Reliability Analysis (total sample, n=46)

Table 2. Internal Reliability of the OPBI

Dimension	Dimension Description	Items	Reliability Cronbach Alpha	Comments
1	Social	1-6	0.61	Low correlation of items 1,2,5 with total
2	Economic	7-12	0.59	Low correlation of items 9 with total. Negative correlation item 12 with total
3	Nature	13-18	0.88	
4	Ethics	19-24	0.81	
5	Built Environment	25-29	0.75	
Total	PLACE	1-29	0.91	

Table 3. Comparison of Reliability Analysis between Partner and Manager Responses

Dimension	Items	Reliability Combined (Cronbach Alpha)	Managers Reliability (Cronbach Alpha)	Partners Reliability (Cronbach Alpha)
Social	1-6	0.61	0.52	0.62
Economic	7-12	0.59	0.40	0.82
Nature	13-18	0.88	0.90	0.88
Ethics	19-24	0.81	0.82	0.77
Built Environment	25-29	0.75	0.77	0.80
PLACE	1-29	0.91	0.92	0.93

Reliability analysis of the total and each of the five dimensions according to OPBI found Cronbach Alpha values ranging from 0.59 to 0.91 (Table 2). This suggests that, while most of the scores associated with OPBI dimensions are reliable, two of them, social and economic, fall below the conventionally accepted Chronbach's Alpha limit of 0.70. The analysis further indicates that OPBI social dimension items 1, 2 and 5 and economic dimension items 9 and 12 reduced the internal reliability of the OPBI in this context. To further investigate this finding, the responses from partners and managers were analyzed separately. Table 3 shows that, for both dimensions, managers' scores were less reliable than those of partners. This is especially pronounced for the economic dimension, where managers' Cronbach's Alpha is 0.40 compared to partners', which is 0.82. The Cronbach's Alpha for partners, however, still falls below the acceptable limit (0.62 vs. 0.70) for the social dimension.

These results suggest two things: (1) the reliability of the scores for the social dimension is somewhat low for both partners and managers and (2) the reliability of the scores for the economic dimension is very good for partners, but quite poor for managers. Why is this? For the social dimension, there might have been uncertainty or ambiguous definitions associated with concepts such as "positive change" (item 1), "education programs" (item 2) or "philanthropic activities" (item 5). For the economic dimension, there might have been ambiguity around the notion of "business practices" (item 9) for managers with respect to how PSF might improve these for their clients. Interestingly, item 12 ("My organization's sole contribution is to the community's economy, i.e. creating jobs, taxes, etc.") was negatively correlated with this dimension's total. This suggests that this item is not only an especially poor one for managers, but also that their assessment of PSF's economic place building tends to contradict their response to this item.

The existence of some combination of random and systematic error in the responses to particular questions associated with the social and economic place building dimensions provides an opportunity for interaction with respondents to identify and clarify their interpretations of concepts presented in the OPBI and further differentiate and explore perceptions held by different levels of the organization, in this case managers and partners.

Table 4. Exploratory Factor Analysis Results

Dimension	Variance Explained Combined (n=46)	Variance Explained Managers (n=20)	Variance Explained Partners (n=26)
Social	0.4787	0.4285	0.4378
Economic	0.1003	0.0872	0.1385
Nature	0.0777	0.0761	0.1132
Ethics	0.0729	0.0706	0.0948
Built Environment	0.0577	0.0618	0.0740
PLACE	0.7872	0.7242	0.8583

Exploratory factor analysis explained 78.7% of the variance when extracting a five factor solution (n=46). According to Table 4, the exploratory factor analysis reveals that the first factor's eigen value accounts for approximately 48% of the variance and, consistent with expectations for unidimensionality, the subsequent factors' eigen values explain significantly less variance. This suggests that each of the OPBI's dimensions are well measured by their respective scales.

Table 5. OPBI Average Scores

Dimension	Partners	Managers	Place Building Profile
Social	10.33	13.57	Transformational
Economic	13.75	14.61	Transformational
Nature	21.25	21.45	Contributive
Ethics	11.33	11.91	Transformational
Built Environment	14.50	14.24	Transformational

PSF Place Building Profiles.

The average OPBI scores (Table 5) for each dimension demonstrate consistency between the perceptions of partners and managers. Except for the nature dimension, both groups viewed the organization as transformational. These results suggest that both partners and managers maintain an interdependent agent perspective and understand their firm's mission to include transformational roles in the social and economic aspects of their local community, both internal external to the organization; ethical practices that are focused on how the organization interacts with its community and internal constituents; and perceptions and use of the built environment that encourage safe and collaborative work spaces. As the mission of PSF is oriented around the provision of financial services it is perhaps no surprise that respondents scored in the contributive range of the place building continuum and view their organization as a contributor to, rather than responsible for, the well-being of the natural environment.

Conversations with respondents during administration of the OPBI support these results. The partners advocate for and encourage individual growth and pursuit of activities that can expand their skills and build the firm's reputation. Indeed, characteristic of the transformational profile is the firm's support of this research project. The firm's culture of support and advocacy for creating opportunities that improve the firm and its community's economic and social well-being, and the emphasis on creating new opportunities, for firm and employees, was evident in the EVP's reasons for participating in the research. He pointed to the following objectives: to (1) identify where the PSF is located on the place building continuum; (2) determine how both groups of managers and partners view the organization's responsibility to community and place; and (3) explore how this new information will inform their place building strategies.

CONCLUSION

In the case study presented above, PSF invited the researchers to explore how the firm values and builds place and what import this may

The Organizational Place Building Inventory   175

have for the business. Can the OPBI support a strategy for building on its existing CSR strategies? Can place building assess its current activities and outcomes relative to a desired profile? The case study confirmed that place and place building can resonate with executives in an organization provided similar steps taken in this research are implemented. Moreover, PSF was curious about place. Many had heard of the term, primarily as sense of place, and were very interested. In fact, the EVP remarked that "we had never really thought about place and CSR in this respect."

Below is a discussion of the significance and prospects for OPBI implementation in organizational research writ large and the interface between leadership of place and Knowledge Based Economies (KBEs) (Gibney et al. 2009).

The OPBI and organizational research. The OPBI contributes to a participatory and deliberative process through which organizations can describe and explain how they build place via their business model and possibly predict the likely contributions they will make based on their place building profiles. For example, organizations can use OPBT to assess their current practices and ask summary questions that lead to a set of policies and adjustments to its business model that move the organization to its preferred place on the continuum. Answers may reveal: (1) how the organization interfaces with its community: (2) how that interface influences the way an organization looks at its role in the community; and (3) the existence of place building artifacts in an organization that symbolize its place values.

The following discussion describes a three-step process through which an organization can assess its place building profile and shape its strategies to build value with its community and stakeholders: (1) *securing company buy-in and commitment* to exploring how the organization values and builds place; (2) *creating a pathway for conducting research,* which includes establishing a company-wide effort and identifying an executive to champion the research process; and (3) revealing the findings and gathering a group to *layout the strategies and tactics.*

To *secure company buy-in and commitment,* an organization must self-assess its current relationships with its community and place by looking at how it invests and engages in the community and places it occupies. The organization must then elect a champion with political and organizational, credibility to communicate place building, its relevance and connection to the organization's mission and vision.

To *create a pathway for research,* employees must be asked to work with management to frame the place building research, including the questions and OPBI distribution. For example, the following questions can help participants understand and explain OPBT:

> Initial open ended questions: Does this makes sense and can you think of any companies that fit in each type? What is characteristic of these types? For example, do you recognize these types?
>
> Intermediate questions: Are there certain variables that place an organization in each type and can you suggest the factors that move an organization across the continuum? Do you think that an organization goes about this strategically in terms of how it values place?
>
> Ending questions: Where would you place your organization on the typology? What are the factors that move an organization across the continuum? Do you think there are any benefits to a company in each type? Do you do business with each type? If so, how?

To ensure that participants understand the purpose and design of the project and its import to the business model or the company's mission, the OPBI should be distributed in person and not electronically via small groups. The survey results should be shared by bringing people together to validate and explore further actions that support the findings.

To *lay out strategies and tactics,* the findings are used to identify the organization's place profile and discuss the likely consequences and

The Organizational Place Building Inventory   177

impacts or each type and costs to the organization. Next, participants should collaborate on identifying strategies and metrics for pursuing and quantifying the organization's ideal place building profile.

OPBT, OPBI, leadership of place and KBEs. OPBT and the OPBI represent one answer to Gibney, Copeland and Murie's (2009, 5) call for "the development of a conceptual framework that will allow a better alignment between leadership studies, place-shaping and the KBE discourse" because its theory and method are fundamentally interdisciplinary, collaborative and participatory. Stough (2003) and, earlier, DeSantis and Stough (1999), concluded from a review of the leadership and development literature that there is a tendency for identifiable local (leadership-oriented) groups to emerge and cooperate to influence the regional economic future of the community. On the basis of their review, leadership was defined as "the tendency of a community to collaborate across sectors in a sustained, purposeful manner to enhance the economic performance of its region" (Stough 2003, 183).

The growing interest in leadership of place (Stough 2003, Sotarauta 2005, 2009, Gibney et al. 2009, Stimson et al. 2009) will continue to drive the need for an explicit connection between leadership and the treatment of and interaction with places. These leaders will require new tools that can help explain these relationships and more importantly how they can be assessed, which can be central to leadership in terms of guiding how communities recruit the best fitting organizations or address local or regional place building issues.

OPBT and the OPBI can be used in at least three ways to accomplish these ends: evaluative, integrative and restorative (see Kimball and colleagues [2013] for a details on how OPBT has been used in all three of these modalities with respect to cultural heritage management). An *evaluative* approach assesses the current state of place building and yields results that are useful for taking stock, planning and envisioning. An *integrative* approach uses OPBT to assess "placekeeper" (Kimball and Thomas 2012) values from across constituencies and yields results that are useful for building consensus, conducting gap analyses, and conflict management and resolution. Finally, a *restorative* approach employs OPBT as an intervention through which marginalized, subaltern or underrepresented constituencies can be recognized and invited into the place building process.

In conclusion, the results of this paper's case study provide a transparent, systematic and efficient way of analyzing and presenting data assessing an organization's place building values and strategies. As is indicated in the definition of place building profiles at the outset of this paper, constellations of these values and strategies do not exist as rigid types, but instead polythetic sets. They open a window into an ongoing process, which includes a blending of both complementary and competing values and strategies that express the dynamic nature of organizations, placekeeper constituencies, and KBEs.

Thus, OPBT, unlike a typical inventory of corporate social responsibility, is a comprehensive, participatory (Kimball and Thomas, 2012) and holistic intervention process. The OPBI serves as both a mirror and a lens through which organizations and leaders of place can (1) locate themselves and their constituencies on a continuum of values and strategies with regard to place (i.e., their relations to its social, natural, material, economic and ethical dimensions); (2) deliberate on whether they like being where they are or, if not, where they would prefer to reside; and (3) develop strategies for how they might stay where they are or get where they would rather be. OPBT's intervention process can lead to a different and richer discussion on the real verifiable reasons for being socially and environmentally responsible.

APPENDIX A
Organizational Place Building Inventory

Please answer each question by placing an X in the column that best matches your answer.	1. Strongly Agree	2. Agree	3. Somewhat Agree	4. Neither Agree nor Disagree	5. Somewhat Disagree	6. Disagree	7. Strongly Disagree
1. My organization invests its resources to create positive change for the community.							
2. My organization collaborates with other organizations to improve the community's education programs.							
3. My organization is accountable for the impact its business practices have on the community							
4. My organization invests its assets and resources to help sustain the community's culture.							
5. My organization's employees are expected to contribute their time or money to local philanthropic activities.							
6. My organization invests its resources to increase opportunities for civic participation and investments.							
7. My organization places a high priority on its economic influence in the community.							
8. My organization commits resources to the economic development of the community.							
9. My organization helps its clients improve their							

tribute to the economic success of the community.										
11. My organization is recognized for its contributions to the local economy.										
12. My organization's sole contribution is to the community's economy, i.e. creating jobs, taxes, etc.										
13. My organization's mission includes improving the well-being of the natural environment.										
14. My organization utilizes best practices that protect local resources, such as the natural environment, water, geography, etc.										
15. My organization is a leader in actions that protect the natural environment.										
16. My organization is respected for its improvements to the natural environment.										
17. My organization contributes financially to activities that build an environmentally sustainable community.										
18. My organization considers the extent of its impact on the environment in all its activities.										
19. My organization's mission includes a financial commitment to the social well-being of the community.										
20. My organization holds itself accountable for the impact its operation has on the community.										
21. My organization works to enhance its legitimacy as a leader in the community.										

Please answer each question by placing an X in the column that best matches your answer.	1. Strongly Agree	2. Agree	3. Somewhat Agree	4. Neither Agree nor Disagree	5. Somewhat Disagree	6. Disagree	7. Strongly Disagree
22. Building my organizations' influence in the community is a key business strategy.							
23. My organization invests its resources for the common good even when there is a cost to the firm							
24. My organization initiates business practices that help build a more ethical business place.							
25. My organization invests in projects that support community renewal (such as historic neighborhoods and tourism, entertainment facilities).							
26. My organization's office building and landscape help create a sense of place.							
27. My organization contributes to community redevelopment projects that advance economic development.							
28. My organization's office space is valued as a place where employees can create meaningful working relationships.							
29. My organization's mission considers the economic well-being of the entire community.							

APPENDIX B
Organizational Place Building Model

Independent Strategies

Organizations view themselves merely as occupants of place
View a community's resources only as a means to satisfy their needs
Jobs and tax revenues are the organizations' primary contributions

Interdependent Strategies

Organizations and communities are mutually dependent on each other
Organizations consider themselves responsible for the well-being of the community
Seek opportunities to invest and contribute

Exploitive

- Contributions are limited to legal requirements or to protect brand/image
- Removed from the community
- Values the community solely for its favorable economic and political policies toward business

Contingent

- Contributions are conditional and measured
- Engaged in community activities that create a financial gain
- Values the community primarily for its geographic, political and economic assets

Contributive

- Contributions are broad based and serve the firm and the community
- Supports activities that help them fit into the community
- Values the community on a number of levels but primarily for its social and business network

Transformational

- Committed to creating opportunities that build community and protect the environment
- Facilitates change that improves community economic and social well being
- Advocates for all community values: esp. its cultural and ethical heritage

References

Agnew, J. A. (1987). *Place and Politics.* Boston, MA: Allen & Unwin.

Alvesson, M., & Berg, P. O. (1992).*Corporate Culture and Organizational Symbolism.* Berlin: Walter de Gruyter.

Anderson, R. (2005). Global corporate citizenship – a trend to watch. Retrieved from: http://www.theconglomerate.org/2010/01

Aupperle, K. E., Carroll, A. B., & Hatfield, J. D. (1985). An empirical examination of the relationship between corporate social responsibility and profitability. *Academic of Management Journal,* 28(2), 446-463.

Ayers, S. (2014). Place-based leadership: Reflections on scale, agency and theory. *Regional Studies, Regional Science.* 1(1), 21-24.

Beer, A., & Clower, T. (2014). Mobilizing leadership in cities and regions. *Regional Studies, Regional Science,* 1(1), 5-20.

Buttimer, A., & Seamon, D. (Eds.). (1980). *Human Experience of Space and Place.* New York, NY: Martins.

Cavanagh, T. E., Oza, A., & Bennett, C. J. (2005). The measure of success: Evaluating corporate citizenship performance. New York, NY: Conference Board.

Chaskin, R. J., Brown, P., Venkatesh, S., & Vidal, A. (2001). *Building Community Capacity.* New York, NY: Aldine de Gruyter.

Collinge, C., & Gibney, J. (2010). Connecting place, policy and leadership. *Policy Studies,* 31(4), 379-391.

D'aprile, G., & Talò, C. (2014). Measuring corporate social responsibility as a psychosocial construct: A new multidimensional scale. *Employee Responsibilities & Rights Journal,* 26(3), 153-175.

Delheim, C. (1986). Business in time: The historian and corporate culture. *The Public Historian,* 8(1), 9-22.

DeSantis, M., & Stough, R. R. (1999). Fast adjusting urban regions, leadership and regional economic development. *Region et Development,* 10, 37-56.

Draxler, A (2016). Public-private partnerships and international education policies, in McGrath, S and Gu, Q., eds. *Routledge Handbook of International Education and Development* pp. 443-62, London & New York: Routledge/Taylor & Francis Group.

Entrikin, J. N. (2000). *The Betweeness of Place: Towards Geography of Modernity.* New York, NY: Routledge.

Gallardo-Vázquez, D., & Sanchez-Hernandez, M. I. (2014). Measuring Corporate Social Responsibility for competitive success at a regional level. *Journal of Cleaner Production,* 7214-7222.doi:10.1016/j.jclepro.2014.02.051

Gans, H. J. (2002). The sociology of space: A use-centered view. *City and Community,* 1(4), 329-339.

Geertz, C. (1983). *Local Knowledge.* New York, NY: Basic Books.

Gibney, J., Copeland, S., & Murie, A. (2009). Toward a 'new' strategic leadership of place for the Knowledge-Based Economy. *Leadership,* 5(1), 5-23.

Gieryn, T. F. (2000). A space for place in sociology. *Annual Review of Sociology,* 26, 463-496.

Hatch, M. (1993). The dynamics of organizational culture. *The Academy of Management Review,* 18(4), 657-693.

Healey, P. (1998). Collaborative planning in a stakeholder society. *Town Planning Review,* 69(1), 1-21.

Heslin, P. A., & Ochoa, J. D. (2008). Understanding and developing strategic corporate social responsibility. *Organizational Dynamics,* 37(2), 125-144.

Hudson, R. (2001). *Producing Places.* New York, NY: The Guilford Press.

Jacobs, J. (1984). *Cities and the Wealth of Nations.* New York, NY: Random House.

Kimball, M., & Thomas, D. F. (2012). Place-Building Perceptions: A new model for catalyzing change in university-community relations and student civic engagement. *Michigan Journal of Community Service Learning,* 8(2), 1-6.

Kimball, M., Brunswig, R., McBeth, S., & Thomas, D. F. (2013). Fostering local futures; place building theory and the living heritage paradigm. *The Applied Anthropologist,* 33(2), 2-6.

Massey, D. (2005). *For Space.* London: Sage.

Morgan, G. (1986). *Images of Organization.* Thousand Oaks, CA: Sage.

Needham, R. (1975). Polythetic classification: Convergence and consequences. *Man, New Series,* 10(3), 349-369.

Rein, M., Stott, L., Yambayamba, K., Hardman, S. and Reid, S. (2005) *Working Together: A Critical Analysis of Cross-Sector Partnerships in Southern Africa:* Cambridge, UK: The University of Cambridge Programme for Industry.

Rodman, M. (1992). Empowering place: Multilocality and multivocality. *American Anthropologist, New Series,* 94(3), 640-656.

Sagoff, M. (1996). Values and preferences. *Ethics,* 2, 301-316.

Schneider, B., Brief, A. P., & Guzzo, R. A. (1996). Creating a climate and culture for sustainable organizational change. *Organizational Dynamics,* 24, 7-18.

Schoenberger, E. (1997). *The Cultural Crisis of the Firm.* Cambridge: Blackwell.

Sotarauta, M. (2005). Shared leadership and dynamic capabilities in regional development. In: I. Sagan & H. Halkier, (Eds.), *Regionalism Contested: Institutions, Society and Territorial Governance* (pp. 53-72). Aldershot: Ashgate.

Sotarauta, M. (2009). Power and influence tactics in the promotion of regional development: An empirical analysis of the work of Finnish regional development officers. *Geoforum*, 40(5), 895-905.

Sotarauta, M. (2014). Reflections on 'mobilizing leadership in cities and regions.' *Regional Studies Regional Science*, 1(1), 28-31.

Staeheli, L. A. (2007). A companion to Political Geography (Ed.). New York, NY: Blackwell Publishing.

Stimson, R., Stough, R., & Salazar, M. (2009). *Leadership and Institutions in Regional Endogenous Development*. Cheltenham: Edward Elgar.

Stough, R. (2003). Strategic management of places and policy. *The Annals of Regional Science*, 37, 179-201.

Thomas, D. F. (2004). Toward an understanding of organization place building in communities. (Unpublished doctoral dissertation). Fort Collins, CO: Colorado State University.

Thomas, D. F., &Cross, J. (2007). Organizations as place builders. *Journal of Behavioral and Applied Management*, 9(1), 34-64.

Thomas, D. F., Gaede, D., Jurin, R., & Connolly, L. (2008). Understanding the link between organizational behavior and community sense of place. *Community Development*, 39(39), 32-45.

Thomas, D. F., & Banning, J. H. (2014). Place building and mission statements: A match or misfit? *Journal of Contemporary Issues in Business Research*, 3(2), 52-74.

Vogel, D. (2005). The low value of virtue. *Harvard Business Review*, 8(6), 26.

Weick, K. E. (1995). *Sensemaking in Organizations.* Thousand Oaks, CA: Sage.

Werlen, B. (1993). *Society, Action, and Space: An Alternative Human Geography.* London: Routledge.

Wright, S. (1994). *Anthropology of Organization.* New York, NY: Routledge.

7

THE APPLIED ANTHROPOLOGIST:
FOSTERING LOCAL FUTURES: PLACE BUILDING THEORY AND THE LIVING HERITAGE PARADIGM

MICHAEL KIMBALL, ROBERT BRUNSWIG, SALLY MCBETH, AND DAVID THOMAS

ABSTRACT

In contrast to essentialist and static notions of heritage, encapsulated here as the Good Old Days (GOD) and Saving the Past for the Future (SPF), the living heritage paradigm offers an alternative model that sees heritage as a social construct evolving in response to its changing relations with extant communities of people. Place building theory (PBT), an applied and explanatory theory arising from research on place-based corporate social responsibility, offers tools and perspectives to operationalize living heritage research and reveal and unpack *placekeeper* (investment in place identity) and *place user* (investment in place utility) identities and roles. Using three examples from our Colorado heritage research programs, we present three different approaches to PBT living heritage research – evaluative, integrative and restorative. We conclude with a summary discussion of PBT's broader relevance to living heritage research and offer suggestions for future applications.

KEY WORDS: living heritage, place building, placekeeper, heritage conservation, heritage management

(T)here is a failure on the part of the heritage system to concede that an old place can be recycled back into Aboriginal culture with a new meaning. There is a failure, in other words, to acknowledge that a place's significance can be up-dated, a failure…to acknowledge that an old place could be given a "local future"[1] (Byrne 2008: 164).

Our topic concerns the concept of "living heritage" (ICCROM 2013; Poulios 2010), its relevance to how cultural heritage places are and should be conserved and managed, and how place building theory (Thomas 2004; Thomas and Cross 2007; Kimball and Thomas 2012) is being applied to living heritage research in Colorado.[2] In this paper, we present and discuss the living heritage paradigm and place building theory (PBT), which, through grounded theory research, is being developed as both an applied and explanatory theory in organizational and business studies to critically examine and transform corporate social responsibility.

We then show how PBT's agent perspectives, place building dimensions and place building continuum shed light on relations between communities and heritage places and align with place attachment research to suggest heritage place building identities. Further, we apply a PBT lens to three heritage research examples – a community-engaged research project embedded in an undergraduate applied anthropology course; a collaborative archeological research project in North Park; and an ethnobotanical project in Rocky Mountain National Park – and show how they represent three different approaches – evaluative, integrative and restorative – to living heritage research. We conclude with a summary discussion of PBT's relevance to living heritage research and offer suggestions for future applications.

THE LIVING HERITAGE PARADIGM

There are arguably two hegemonic and overlapping Western paradigms that continue to frame heritage interpretation and management in the United States and beyond. First, there is the "discipline of heritage conservation" (Poulios 2010:171), inspired by the nineteenth century Western European nostalgic notion of authenticity arising from a "feeling of dissatisfaction with the present caused by its rapid change and mobility" and leading to "discontinuity between the monuments, considered to belong to the past, and the people and social and cultural processes of the present." In other words, from this point of view, heritage conservation's purpose is to help us stay in touch with the *Good Old Days* (GOD).

Second, Laurajane Smith (2006) draws on theories of discourse (Foucault 1980), hegemony (Gramsci 1971) and habitus (Bourdieu 1969) in her conceptualization of "authorized heritage discourse," which embodies power relations as expressed and reproduced through "aesthetically pleasing material objects, sites, places and/or landscapes that current generations 'must' care for, protect and revere so that they may be passed to nebulous future generations for their 'education,' and to forge a sense of common identity based on the past" (Smith 2006: 29). Authorized heritage discourse might be summed up with archaeology's well-known platitude, *Save the Past for the Future* (SPF).

In contrast, in its presentation of the concept of *living heritage,* the International Centre for the Study of the Preservation and Restoration of Cultural Property (CCROM 2013) points to the necessity for "revisiting the definition of heritage and its integration into a wide variety of socio-political and economic aspects of society" and calls for heritage conservation and management to address the following concerns: respect for diversity; a focus on both past and present; enhancement of the value of all cultural products; the influence of heritage on the contemporary life of people and how it can improve their quality of life; heritage as perceived by people, moving away from the sharp lines drawn between its various types (e.g. movable/immovable; tangible/intangible); respect for people's voices in conservation and management of heritage; the improvement of relationships between heritage and people; recognition of the living dimensions of heritage, particularly of religious heritage; consideration for the impact of globalization on living environments such as historic urban centers and cultural landscapes; the recognition of the custodianship of people for the long-term care of heritage; the link of heritage to the sustainable development of society; and relationships with a wide variety of non-professionals.

Living heritage offers a paradigm that is quite different from GOD or SPF. Unlike the relatively rigid frames the latter two paradigms impose, living heritage accommodates, indeed welcomes, "change in the context of continuity," i.e., "changes in the function, the space, and the community's presence, in response to the changing circumstances in society at local, national, and international levels" (Poulios 2010:175). This paradigm constructs neither discontinuities nor arbitrary barriers between the past and present, but instead envisions heritage places, their natural and social environments and their integral intangible assets (local and indigenous knowledge, stories, practices, etc.) as, in a sense, *living*, i.e., adaptive expressions of and full participants in dynamic relations among the past, present and future of people and their societies.

To be sure, this is not a new idea in heritage management; rather, it offers a larger context in which existing approaches may be understood and operationalized. For example, the Traditional Cultural Property (TCP) concept, associated with cultural resource management and the National Park Service's National Register of Historic Places, fits well under the living heritage umbrella. The TCP, defined fifteen years ago by Parker and King (1998; King 2003), emphasizes the role of environmentally and socially significant places – heritage sites and even landscapes – in the lives of communities that are historically interconnected with them and from which members of these communities continue to derive benefit. In King's (2005:5) phrase, "TCPs are for the living," we can see appreciation of fluid relations between past and present, change and continuity, tradition and adaptation.

We argue here that embracing, or at least engaging with, a living heritage paradigm is important for both theoretical and practical reasons. Theoretically speaking, it is difficult for one to cling to one's GOD and SPF, i.e., static definitions of heritage and heritage conservation and management, when one is faced with their obvious contingency. After all, heritage is, as Waterton and Watson (2013:6) put it, "a social and cultural process – something more than a collection of things or, indeed, resources." As such, it is socially constructed based on shifting trajectories and intersections of ideas, beliefs, values and histories. Living heritage offers an alternative frame through which one can understand, interpret and appreciate heritage in many of its evolving expressions.

Just as the idea of heritage cannot be fixed with one definition or set of expectations, so too tangible and intangible heritage themselves are always in flux, in their form (what they look like), their substance (what they are made of) and how they are treated and experienced by people. Indeed, a heritage place's "core community" (Poulios 2010:176), i.e., one whose senses of identity and place are in some way integral to the place itself, might have perspectives and practices that differ significantly from those espoused by heritage professionals. Clavir (2002:78, Table 3) quotes Miranda Wright (1994:1) regarding an Athapascan perspective: "The emphasis on preserving the Native elders' material culture was often contrary to their holistic belief that these goods should return to nature to nurture future generations."

Likewise, Chapagain (2013) discusses the example of a 15th century Buddhist temple in the settlement of Lomanthang, Nepal, in which the core community hold a Buddhist appreciation for the impermanence of physical materiality and a concern for its role as simply a "vehicle for the transmission of abstract non-material concepts" (61). Thus, "drastic physical changes, including the reconstruction ... of historic buildings and artifacts are not unusual ... and considered meritorious" (50). This philosophy and practice flies in the face of prevailing conservation ethics as the following description illustrates (51): The locals and the professional conservators had conflicting ideas on the extent to which the crumbling wall paintings should be restored. The conservators were following their professional ethics by mostly consolidating the base layer of the wall paintings and cleaning the paint layers, while leaving the missing parts as blank. The local people argued that the incomplete restoration would not make sense because they could not worship the "amputated" images of the Buddha and Bodhisattvas.

Add to this the sometimes critical role that invested "peripheral communities" (Poulios 2010:176), i.e., people who do not connect their history or whose history cannot be demonstrably connected to a heritage place, can play in conservation and management and the relevance of a living heritage framework becomes even more evident. As Lowenthal (2000:22) writes,

> Ourselves heirs of commingled legacies, we gain more from attachment to many pasts than from exclusive devotion to our "own" – assuming we could indeed decide which past was truly just ours.... Fractious claimants do not merely debase the value but threaten the survival of heritage that is never theirs alone.

Regardless of whether heritage stewards, or, as we refer to them, "placekeepers" (Kimball and Thomas 2012:19), belong to a core or periphery, their work can be hindered by discontinuities and arbitrary barriers constructed by GOD and SPF and between the past and the present, "us" and "them." Lowenthal (2000:22) puts it this way:

> A heritage disjointed from ongoing life cannot enlist popular support. To adore the past is not enough; good caretaking involves continual creation. Heritage is ever revitalized; our legacy is not simply original but includes our forebears' alterations and additions. We treasure that heritage in our own protective *and* transformative fashion, handing it down reshaped in the faith that our heirs will also become creative as well as retentive stewards.

Returning to ICCROM's (2013) criteria for a living heritage approach, it is clear from the above that an abiding concern for reciprocal relations among local communities and heritage places is imperative for sustainable and adaptive heritage conservation and management. Questions about how heritage is perceived by people; how it might improve the quality of their lives; whose voices are being heard and whose are inaudible; what links exist or could be established between heritage and the sustainable development of society, etc., become not only possible, but essential to ask and explore.

PLACE BUILDING THEORY

As the geographer, Yi-Fu Tuan (1977:6), wrote in his classic text, *Space and Place: The Perspective of Experience*, "What begins as undifferentiated space becomes place as we get to know it better and endow it with value." Place, like heritage, is a social construct. It is *built* at the intersections among, as anthropologist Margaret Rodman (1992:643, following Agnew and Duncan 1989:2), delineates them, "*location* (i.e., the spatial distribution of socioeconomic activity such as trade networks), *sense of place* (or attachment to place), and *locale* (the setting in which a particular social activity occurs, such as a church)." Thus, exploring living heritage is fundamentally about whether, how and why individuals and groups build place through their interactions with their own and others' heritage. From an applied perspective, the purpose of this exploration is to use insights gained from the study of place-building to improve living heritage conservation and management.

The living heritage paradigm offers a community-engaged, socially responsible theoretically sound and pragmatic frame through which to interpret, conserve and sustainably manage heritage. It does not, however, inherently possess its own means for achieving these ends. Although there are large bodies of literature on the assessment of community interests and values for the purpose of improving cultural resource and heritage management and research on sense of place and related phenomena, there is significantly less concerned with how people build place through their experience of heritage. Further, the living heritage paradigm's transformative mission (progressive and reciprocal relations between heritage and people's lives) asks for a complementary focus on the transformative roles and potentials of heritage place-building.

This need within the living heritage paradigm calls for a framework that integrates applied and explanatory theory. We argue here, through exposition and example, that place building theory (Thomas 2004; Thomas and Cross 2007) offers such a framework. PBT is rooted in theories of place from fields such as anthropology, sociology and geography that focus on place as a social construct, defined by relations of meaning, feelings and human interaction (e.g., Sauer 1925; Lynch 1960; Zelinsky 1973; Relph 1976; Tuan 1977; Eyles 1985; Agnew 1987; Sack 1988; Rodman 1992; Schein 1992; Light and Smith 1998; Lofland 1998; Hudson 2001; Ingold 2002; Stokowski 2002).

Arising from grounded theory (Glaser and Strauss 1967) and organizational research (Morgan 1986, 1997; Schoenberger 1997; Smircich 1983; Weick 1995; Wright, S. 1994) focused on the assessment of place-based corporate social responsibility, PBT seeks to identify and explain the values and level of investment organizations have for and in their locales. Further, PBT was developed as a *participatory* modality. As Kimball and Thomas (2012:19) write, PBT's "origins are situated in the desire not only to identify and define motivating factors and strategies, but also to engage *placekeepers* (place-based stakeholders) as participants in an evaluative and proactive process." For the purposes of this paper, we next present three key PBT components – agent perspectives, place building dimensions, and the place building continuum – and show how each articulates with the living heritage approach. For a more indepth explanation of PBT, we refer readers to Thomas and Cross (2007) and Kimball and Thomas (2012).

Agent perspectives

An agent perspective consists of an organization's concept of its relationship to and the meaning it makes from and confers on its locale. This perspective conduces to the organization's goals, behavior, and contributions to its locale. PBT identifies two agent perspectives, *interdependent* and *independent*. As Kimball and Thomas (2012:20) write:

> Organizations with the *interdependent* perspective view themselves as members of a community and recognize that

organizations and places are mutually dependent upon each other.... In contrast, organizations with an *independent* perspective view themselves merely as occupants of place and economic agents of place rather than integral members of place.

From a living heritage standpoint, it is critical to determine the agent perspectives of a place's core and peripheral communities because these have a direct impact on how these communities use heritage to "express, facilitate and construct a sense of identity, self and belonging" (Smith 2006:75). Those individuals and communities with an interdependent perspective see their identity and sense of belonging as inextricably linked to a place, how they experience interpret and interact with it. The disposition of the place speaks to their own disposition. They are place-keepers. Those individuals and communities with an independent perspective might choose to visit a heritage place, but their relationship to it is transactional. In other words, they do not see it as part of who they are – they go there for less of the emotional, recreational, or educational returns. Regard for psychological benefits they receive from services rendered (i.e., they may "love" going there), they do not identify with the place. They are place users, not place-keepers.

In reality, of course, people and certainly communities of them, do not fall neatly into categories. For example, it is quite easy to imagine a person who resides somewhere in between interdependent and independent agent perspectives: this person might not think of a heritage place as an inextricable part of who he or she is, but, on the other hand, he or she might visit the place to experience spiritual rejuvenation or perhaps get in touch with ethnic roots and would feel heartbroken if something bad happened to it (e.g., it was slated for closure or succumbed to an environmental disaster). Alternatively, a person could have an interdependent perspective with regard to the natural environment of a heritage place, but maintain an independent perspective concerning its social aspects (e.g., how other visitors or "traditional" people use it). To explore this range of perspectives, PBT offers place building dimensions and the place building continuum.

Place building dimensions

Thomas and Cross (2007:38) point out that place is a "multi-dimensional concept including the natural world, the built environment, social relationships, economic relationships, patterns of interaction, as well as socially constructed meanings about each dimension." Drawing on models of place in geography (Sack 1997) and sociology the five place building dimensions, i.e., by asking questions intended to probe each dimension's relations to agent perspective, it becomes possible to develop a fuller understanding of these perspectives in the context of living heritage. We present these dimensions, their respective definitions and examples living heritage-related queries in Table 2.

Place building continuum

Place building research has identified a set of agent perspectives by interrogating identities (Thomas 2004; Thomas and Cross 2007) that emerge from values and strategies associated with agent perspectives. These identities are not and cannot be discrete or fixed because of the variability inherent in individual and group perspectives. Rather, they mark four regions along a place building continuum between, on one end, independent and, on the other, interdependent perspectives. These four identities are, respectively, exploitive, contingent, contributive and transformation. We present these agent identities and their definitions in Table 3.

As we mention above, an important aspect of PBT, one that makes it an applied as well as explanatory theory, is its focus on movement along the continuum. PBT practitioners are interested in not only how and why organizations are located in a certain region of the continuum, but also in engaging their collaborators in a deliberative and participatory process to determine whether, in

What direction and how they might like to traverse it.

The three realms of place speak to material variety of personal and relative-corporate relationships. Cross and investments in core peripherals has derived five with respect to building dimensions from these realms (Table 1), i.e., consider five dimensions along attachment research define place *identity* and *place* role. In contrast, place dependence captures the degree to which a place is an integral part of *what you want to do or get*. From a heritage place management and conservation perspective, the former is concerned with a commitment to preserving and restoring a place's *integrity*; the latter is concerned with a commitment to improving its *utility*.

Transformation of place building identities reflect a deep commitment to integrity over utility and strong attachment to place through reciprocal relationships with it; thus, they might be expected to possess high place identity and some measure of place dependence. In contrast, exploitive identities reflect deep commitment to utility over integrity; thus, they might be expected to have a low degree of both place identity and dependence, for, as Kimball and Thomas (2012:22) put it, "The place building agent identifies environment, nature, social and ethical relationships as key to building places" (Thomas and Cross 2007:39, Figure 1). Contributive place building identities reflect a commitment to the social dimension of place; thus they might possess some degree of both place identity and dependence because of their focus on "giving back" (Kimball and Thomas 2012:21). In contrast, the independent agent perspective of contingent identities as well as their emphasis on utility suggests some degree of place dependence, but a low degree of place identity.

Based on these expectations, we locate two separate but overlapping regions on the place building continuum: *place-keepers*, or those individuals and communities of people with transformational and contributive agent identities and whose place attachment includes place identity, and *place-users*, or those with contingent and exploitive identities and whose place attachment, when present at all, emphasizes place dependence.

These regions represent heritage place building identities comprising distinct sets of roles for members of both core and peripheral living heritage communities. Placekeeper roles, being contributive and transformational, would focus on the place as consist of, for example, leadership, stewardship, and transformative relations with the place (ritual, traditional use, oral history, etc.). In contrast, place user roles, being contingent and exploitive, would primarily focus on the place as a resource or backdrop and consist of transactional relations with the place (recreation, education, entertainment, sales, public relations, marketing, etc.). Just as place agent identities are not and cannot be fixed types, so too these heritage place building identities contain variability that can be unpacked and examined by interrogating the place building dimensions (cf. Table 2; also see evaluative example below).

Below, we present three examples from our research, each offering a different approach to how PBT might address living heritage issues. The first is an *evaluative* example focusing on the Meeker Museum in Greeley, Colorado. This exampls highlights the five place building dimensions as well as the place building continuum and shows, through the results of a community engaged undergraduate applied anthropology course, how PBT is beginning to be incorporated directly into heritage research. The second is an *integrative* example focusing on the North Park Cultural Landscapes Project (Brunswig 2012) and interprets collaborative research on sacred places as seen through a PBT lens. The third is a *restorative* example focusing on the Ute Ethnobotany Project (Chapoose et al. 2012) and shows how PBT might be used to identify and explain movement across heritage place building identities.

Table 1. Place building dimensions and definitions

Dimensions	Definitions
Social Relations	Includes the full spectrum of interactions between an organization's employees and stakeholders and among and between other organizations, e.g., how an organization encourages the development of social capital and how its treatment of certain spaces reflects its culture and values.

Economic Relations	Includes the organization's level of investment in the fiscal well-being of the community, e.g., how it attracts skilled labor to the community; how it seeks to improve the economic viability of the community; how it creates new opportunities for economic growth.
Material Environment	Includes human-made buildings, roads, and other structures such as the buildings an organization occupies and how that space is treated, including interior office spaces. This also reflects the value placed on a building's architecture, landscaping, and historical significance (if any).
Ethics	Includes the organization's practices and its implicit and explicit contract with the community, e.g., how an organization's practices are modeled in its industry, its culture, and with all its placekeepers.
Nature	Includes the natural, as opposed to human-made, elements, forces, and spaces, such as the landscape, earth, geography, and natural resources, e.g., how it relates and contributes to nature and the environment.

Table 2. Place building dimensions and example living heritage queries.

Dimensions	Definitions
Social Relations	What are and should be the roles of the heritage place in the life of this community? What are core communities and how are they defined? What are peripheral communities and how are they defined? What are points of contention and collaboration?
Economic Relations	To what extent and what kind of resources (time, money, energy, etc.) are and should be invested in maintaining the heritage place? To what extent and what kind of resources does and should the heritage place invest in the sustainability of this community?
Material Environment	How important are human-made components (architecture, features, artifacts, walkways, etc.) to the significance of the heritage place? What are and should be their roles? To what extent must they be preserved or might they be modified and how? What are their relationships, and what do they mean to this community?
Ethics	What does preservation mean to this community? What should be preserved and what should not? How do treatment of and interaction with the heritage place reveal this community's ethical orientations?

Table 3. The Place Building Continuum

Agent Identities	Definitions
Transformational ⟷	Conceptualize themselves as change agents acting to improve the lives of individuals and groups in a place, sometimes even at a cost to the organization. They view themselves as interdependent members of place.
Contributive ⟷	Conceptualize themselves as investors in the well-being of places in which they operate. They view themselves as stewards of place and contributors to, but not directly responsible for, the well-being of place. They value place first for its social relationships and second for its economic opportunities.
Contingent ⟷	Conceptualize themselves simply as participants in places, as dissociated and autonomous agents. They narrowly define "organizational social responsibility" as obeying existing laws, regulations and ethical codes. They view themselves a control agents but neither interdependent nor key members of place. They value place for what it provides their organization, such as workers for its labor force.
Exploitive ⟷	Conceptualize themselves as independent agents with little to no obligation to the place in which they are located. They are active users of the local economic, cultural, social, and political resources, valuing place as a commodity that they utilize to their greatest economic benefit.

LIVE HERITAGE PLACE BUILDING: THREE EXAMPLES

Evaluative: Meeker Home Museum Property Redevelopment

The late 19th century home of Nathan Meeker, a founder of Greeley and controversial figure in the history of the Westward expansion of European Americans (Silbernagel 2011), is the site of a redevelopment project aimed at enhancing the Museum's grounds to attract more visitors and commemorate the seven principles of Meeker's Union Colony: faith, family, education, irrigation, temperance, agriculture and home. The first author's research project was based on a partnership with Greeley's Assistant City Manager and its purpose was threefold: (1) to train undergraduate students in applied anthropological methods; (2) to identify key values community members hold concerning the Meeker property and its redevelopment plan; and (3) to begin to lay a methodological foundation for heritage place building research.

Student research teams consisting of a lead interviewer and research assistant interviewed 15 stakeholders. The interviewee sample was drawn from participants in a community meeting convened by the Assistant City Manager at the beginning of the fall 2012 semester. Semi-structured interviews were based on an interview guide that explored values and attitudes for each of the five place building dimensions (social relations, economic relations, material environment, ethics and nature) with respect to the Meeker Home and property. Interviews were digitally recorded and transcribed by the research teams. Qualitative analysis consisted of open-coding (reading and re-reading a transcript to identify and code key values) by each interviewer and verification of resulting codes by team members (Stolp et al. 2002; LeCompte 1999). Coding sheets were then constructed in which codes were presented and defined and their associated concepts flagged, delimited, and illustrated with example quotes from the transcript. Each lead interviewer then analyzed their data with respect to the place building dimensions. The first author and his research assistant compiled and analyzed the students' work and produced a summary report for the Assistant City Manager (Clay and Kimball 2013).

Bearing in mind this study's limitations – its small sample size (n=15) based on convenience sampling and the fact that it was a semester-long project conducted by undergraduate researchers-in-training – the project's results were suggestive. The following information summarizes our findings across the place building dimensions.

Social Relations. Results suggest that, from a social relations standpoint (but not necessarily along other dimensions; see below) many of the interviewees belong to a kind of core community (*sensu* Poulios 2010) for the Meeker Home. Perspectives appear to cluster in the *contributive/transformational* region, which suggests participants see the Meeker Home as a place whose significance transcends transactional relations with the community. For example, one interviewee saw her residence (which is in close proximity to the Meeker Home) and her neighborhood as integral, "figuring that that's part of our neighborhood, our place, that's part of the Meeker Museum."

Economic Relations. Interviewees cluster in a *contingent/contributive* region of the continuum with regard to attitudes toward economic investment, which may indicate moderate to high place dependence, i.e., investment in historic properties as recreational destinations rather than a kind of "pilgrimage" site which would reflect more transformational values. For example, one interviewee said, "If it results in more business for all of the businesses in Greeley, then I doubt too many people would object."

Material Environment. Interviewee perspectives on this dimension could be located primarily in a *contingent/contributive* region with respect to the importance and preservation of the material environment associated with the Meeker Home (e.g., the buildings, interior spaces, landscaping, etc.). For example, one interviewee expressed a contingent perspective when he said, "… the only thing that is really preserved down there is the house itself but even that's been disturbed so much … (you are) trying to preserve an adobe situation. But now you want to bring it up to the next level, so the grounds are more appealing. To me that's not preservation." In contrast, another interviewee's perspective was more contributive; "I just liked the old neighborhood.... I could see keeping the home intact of course . . . but also doing something with the grounds and things to encourage people to go downtown more."

Ethics. Participants appear to be in general agreement about their ethical investment in historic properties: there is a trend toward *contributive to transformational* values concerning the preservation and treatment of them. For example, one interviewee said, "Heck, they can't rip that down. I mean, how could you do that? The person . . . founded the community."

Nature. With respect to place building identity, the spread of perspectives is diffuse, suggesting that there is a variety of values about the role and significance of the natural environment in the context of the heritage site. For example, the following statement from one interviewee can be readily located in a *contingent/exploitive* region: "The landscaping won't mean it's open any more hours in the day and making it pretty won't get anyone else inside the door." In contrast, another interviewee expressed a *contributive/transformative* viewpoint when he said, "Once in a while we see a bird of prey like a hawk over there … it's nice to have that nature feeling about it and in fact it could be enhanced a lot."

Interestingly, additional results emerging from our research suggest the possible existence of another heritage place building continuum: *perceptions of and attitudes toward change* (cf. Davenport and Anderson 2005). These appear to fall somewhere between two poles that we are provisionally naming attributes and ben-*traditionalist* (culturally conservative; nostalgic; focused on fixed meaning, use, development and display of a place) and *relativist* (culturally relative; interpretively flexible; accommodate multiple definitions of meaning, use, development and display of a place). Future research might include individual and/or focus group interactions in which results are shared and discussed with interviewees as well as City of Greeley administrators and planners.

Integrative: North Park Cultural Landscapes Project

To successfully and sensitively conserve and manage heritage places, it is essential to find ways to integrate the values, attitudes, interests and practices of a variety of communities, both core and peripheral. The history of research by the second author and his teams in the Southern Rockies has led us to identify at least seven place building communities we view as making up a complex, sometimes competing, sometimes collaborative, socio-cultural-economic ideological interaction system (Table 4). Members of these communities range widely between place user and place-keeper identities. Each of these communities forms an interactive system that affects both opinions and the treatment (ranging from preservation to exploitation) of prehistoric and historic heritage places. In our fifteen years of cultural heritage projects in the Colorado mountains, we have partnered with most of the seven place building communities (cf. Brunswig and Sellet 2010). The following section briefly presents some of the place building benefits of our North Park Cultural Landscapes Project, based on BLM administered public lands and part of the Cooperative Ecosystems Study Unit system (CESU 2001, 2013), which encompasses 17 regions within the boundaries of the continental United States, Mexico, and Canada. As one example of CESU-based programming, UNC's North Park Cultural Landscapes Project combines two important CESU centered member academic institution and federal lands agencies' mission objectives: civically engaged research and technical assistance. Civic Engagement, as related to public lands, has been defined by the National Park Service as a "continuous, dynamic conversation with the public on many levels that reinforces the commitment of federal agencies and the public to the preservation of heritage resources, both cultural and natural, and strengthens public understanding of the full meaning and contemporary relevance of these resources" (NPS 2007). Federal land management agencies, universities, and private cultural resource management (CRM) companies, and, frequently, Native American tribes, engage with local communities surrounded by or bordering public lands at the place-building continuum's contributive level (Table 3), promoting stewardship of place and sustainability of public lands' natural environments and heritage resources.

The university, operating within the CESU system, interacts regularly with administrators, heritage and natural resource specialists, and its own and other institution's faculty. Our annual summer field programs routinely involve university students enrolled in summer field schools for academic credit, international student volunteers, local community volunteers, avocational archaeological society members, non-archaeologist faculty, Native American consultants, and federal land managers, encompassing most of the place building communities outlined in Table 4. Integration of our sacred landscapes research program with field archaeology investigations has allowed all the above groups to interact directly with Native American consultants in field settings. Local community members are further engaged through public presentations to civic and business organizations. Our active role in scholarship and engagement with a wide range of communities helps diminish viewpoints and attitudes which may be (often unconsciously) exploitive and contingent in nature and channel them toward more contributive and transformational views and personal behavior.

We have, for the past decade and a half, surveyed tens of thousands of acres and excavated scores of sites from valley bottoms to alpine pastures, providing evidence of rich cultural histories essential for public lands stewardship and management (Brunswig 2008, 2012). Several high-ridgeline game drives have been documented along with partial excavation of buried late prehistoric camp levels associated with the region's latest indigenous native inhabitants, ancestors of the modern Ute tribe removed to reservations in northeastern Utah and southwestern Colorado in the late 1800s.

Since 2000, when our archaeological field programs discovered sacred sites in RMNP, we have conducted sacred landscapes research, combining archaeological, ethnohistoric, and Native American consultation approaches, in tandem with archeology and paleoenvironment studies (Brunswig, Diggs, and Montgomery

2009; Brunswig, McBeth, and Elinoff 2009; Diggs and Brunswig 2013). One such sacred feature in the mountain valley of North Park, identified by a university field team in 2006, was situated at a location designated for construction of a cell phone tower. In 2012, after extensive consultations and negotiations between representatives from the Ute and Arapahoe tribes, the BLM, and the cell phone tower company, an agreement was reached allowing tower construction but which also preserved the feature and provided Native American site access for religious ceremonies. Identification of a place special to descendants of Native Americans who once called North Park their traditional lands and the bringing together of diverse place building communities (industry, Native Americans, academic archaeologists, and federal land managers) transformed a potential conflict into a healthy, consensual accommodation of cultural beliefs and contemporary needs. During the consultative process, action was collectively decided upon which required stakeholders with quite different contingent (or even exploitive) perspectives and agendas to shift toward a greater sense of place-based stewardship (contributive) and transformational action. In the end, all sides acknowledged each other's cultural, economic, and technical positions and, in a practical way, came to view themselves as "interdependent members of place", preserving the past, present, and future for new generations.

Finally, the project's decade of research has produced sufficient knowledge on Native American prehistory and history in its central valley research areas to initiate plans to nominate several thousand acres to the National Register of Historic Places as an Archaeological District and Traditional Cultural Property. That effort will further ensure progress from often exploitive/contingent toward more transformational living heritage place building identities in the Colorado Rockies.

Table 4. Listing and definitions of place building communities in Colorado's Southern Rocky Mountains.

Place Building Communities	Place Building Community Values and Practices
Traditional inhabitant cultures	Native Americans-Spiritual and heritage attachments, historical resentments. Individual communities and tribal organization are often fraught with their own internal divisions driven by socio-economic and political agendas. Tribal and intertribal relations associated with interest in any particular place (e.g. historical traditional lands) vary widely ranging from intense engagement to total non-engagement.
Modern settler/ colonizer communities	Multi-Generational attachments to a particular place by normally Euro-American heritage communities with broadly common backgrounds and interest in local and regional heritage, economic lifeways, local recreation, a shared sense of established community, and sometimes conflicted views of "outsiders". Such communities are closely tied, either directly or indirectly, to substantial tracts of publically managed lands dedicated to open or limited public access for recreation, resource extraction (timber, minerals…) and leases for livestock grazing.
Federal and state public lands managers/ stewards	Public lands employees operating from federal, and some state, legal mandates to preserve, manage, and in some cases, manage extraction of, public lands resources, natural & cultural) for all American people. Goals, missions, managerial organization and individual policy mandates vary widely from agency to agency as does their interpretation and emphasis of heritage resources.
Non-local recreationalists	Hunters, fishers, campers, hikers, skiers, all-terrain vehicle drivers, etc. who periodically, occasionally, or even as single "passing-through" events use public land places for recreation and self-expression. Such use ranges from good stewardship to extreme exploitation and destructiveness of heritage and natural resources.

Natural resource extractors	Oil, gas, minerals mining, logging, water diversion…companies with a varying degree of positive to highly negative concern with policy and operating principles sympathetic to heritage and/or cultural resources. A common perspective is annoyance to direct hostility about the inconvenience and cost of adhering to heritage and natural resource protection laws (e.g. NAGPRA, ARPA…). There are, however, notable exceptions.
Environmental and heritage conservationists	"Professional", ranging from informal to formally constituted, chartered and legally franchised, environmental & heritage (historical/archaeological) societies and avocational organizations which seek strong stewardship and protection of heritage resources, often coincident with natural resource protection.
Public and private education sector	Universities, colleges, public schools, research, teaching, public outreach, technical assistance. Education sector agencies, institutions, museums, and NGOs typically advocate, support, and even conduct heritage resource preservation and research, often through alliances with and financial support from other groups listed above who are ideologically or economically motivated or even legally-mandated to support heritage resource stewardship and protection.

Restorative: Ute Ethnobotany Project

In 2005, a Centennial Service Challenge Grant was awarded to the Grand Mesa, Uncompahgre, and Gunnison National Forest for the Ute Ethnobotany Project. The project had four goals: (1) to bring youth and elders together in a field setting at recorded archaeological sites to identify and discuss plant use and associated practices; (2) to create an herbarium catalogue with the assistance of Mesa State College's Biology Department to be housed at the Northern Ute tribal offices; (3) to begin to identify plant communities that are associated with specific kinds of archaeological sites; and (4) to compile a final report of the accomplishments of the project, including an ethnographic overview of Ute plant use. The results of the project are presented in a summary report (McBeth 2008) and discussed in a recent issue of *The Applied Anthropologist* (Chapoose et al. 2012).

The outcomes of Ute Ethnobotany Project include Northern Ute (traditional inhabitant cultures) reflections on a return to Rocky Mountain National Park (RMNP), ancestral Ute homelands. The Ute were forcibly removed from their ancestral homelands in 1881 as a direct result of the Meeker Massacre of 1879. From a PBT perspective, it is possible to identify movement over the course of the project from a contingent region of the continuum to transformational.

In the twenty-first century, the Ute world is sacramental and it is a world thoroughly impregnated with the energy, purpose, and sense of creative natural forces. A sense of identity with a particular locale, however, can be severed by displacement. When Venita Taveapont, Director of the Northern Ute Language Program approached Northern Ute Tribal Council to use their vans (the National Park Service grant paid for the rental) to travel to RMNP, the response was: "Why would you want to go to Colorado? They pushed us out—why would you want to reconnect with a state whose slogan was 'The Utes Must Go!'"

Thus, we suggest that Northern Ute tribal members who have visited locations of ancestral homelands (including Rocky Mountain National Park) began as autonomous agents with a contingent place building identity. In terms of the economic and social relations place building dimensions, the Ute Tribal Council perceived of itself as well as Ute tribal members (who reside in Utah) as separate from any lands that they were dispossessed of in the state of Colorado.

Tribal members then appeared to move, provisionally, to the contributive region of the continuum. Their interest in engaging with the National Park Service to assist with the Park's mission to consult with tribal members on the significance of archaeological sites in a tribes' ancestral homelands brought them to RMNP.

> Venita's response (echoed by others) to their initial, negative reaction was, If we don't (go) those places where we lived, interacted with the environment, and prayed will be lost to us. They will be lost to the next generation. We still need to have

a reconnection. We still need to know and have knowledge of that area. Because it is our ancestral home, and the children—the youth and the ones that are yet to come, they need to know that because this is our traditional homeland (Taveapont, pers. Comm.).

The final move to the transformational region of the continuum came slowly. After spending a week in RMNP and getting to know the landscape and the players (National Park Service and the University of Northern Colorado) who had brought them there, the participants' prayers and offerings to the spirits of the mountains and their evocative statements have led us to believe that they did, indeed, restore their placekeeper identities. For example, participant Loya Arrum (pers. Comm.) said,

> I'm seeing the same mountains that (our ancestors) saw. I'm walking the same trail—the path that they walked, possibly helping one another giving a hand—the rocks are sharp so the trail is not easy to walk. Children are being carried, walking hand and hand to help one another—those are the kinds of things they saw. That's what I feel when I'm in the mountains, that their spirits are there and they are reminding us that we need to come back."

Geneva Accawanna (pers. Comm.) said,

> I feel so humbled that I'm here and I can feel them; I can feel the spirits; it makes me cry to feel that I'm home. It's like a person leaving home or taken from their home and then finally they come back. I know I can't stay here. I have to go back to the reservation. But I need to share that I just have a humble feeling being here, and being on the Ute Trail, and being on the mountains. Seeing the medicine wheel and praying there, I knew that my ancestors heard me.

Helen Wash (pers. Comm.) said,

"We have to take care of it and we want to save as much as we can for the next generation and on and on. So it has to start somewhere and we're doing it with your help you know. So when we go back we'll be able to tell—share our experiences."

Mariah Cuch (pers. Comm.) said,

But we're here today aren't we and it's because of that pain and that hurt that we're here. And I hope that we're able to give that on, and I know we will because we have it. It's not gone, nothing is lost in this world. We just need to open our hearts to it. It belongs to us just the same as we belong to each other. That's the blessing we have from it and you can get through anything 'cause you're never alone.

Conclusions

In presenting the living heritage paradigm and showing how PBT might operationalize it, we hope to contribute to discussion among heritage professionals, scholars and other communities of practice and place-keeping about the construction, study, management and purpose of heritage in Colorado and beyond. The integration of PBT into living heritage research permits exploration of existing and potential relations among individuals, communities and heritage places. It also introduces an inclusive approach that engages both place users and place-keepers in considering the roles they and others do and might play in conserving, managing and constructing heritage and invites them into a process of assessing, defining and transforming their relations to and responsibilities for heritage places.

In addition to the evaluative, integrative and restorative approaches illustrated above, PBT also encourages other forms of engagement with place building relations. For example, PBT can be used to foster place building among emergent communities in relation to heritage places. The Roots Project (UNC 2013), a community-engaged heritage place building pilot project embedded, like the Meeker

Home Project, in an applied anthropology course, focuses on the role that local heritage can play in inviting movement from exploitive/contingent to transformational place building identities in members of Greeley's "newcomer" refugee and immigrant communities from Latin America, Africa and Southeast Asia. Preliminary results suggest that when newcomers actively discover intersections between their life histories and the stories and lifeways of past immigrants to the region through interaction with local heritage (in this case, Greeley's Centennial Village Museum), their levels of both place dependence and place identity tend to increase. Future research will aim to verify this phenomenon and assess the degree to which it helps newcomers transform space into place and place into "home" (Tuan 1977).

PBT also facilitates comparative approaches. For example, it might be possible to juxtapose Chapagain's (2013) Lomanthang Buddhist monastery case study with, say, the results of the Meeker Home Project. In both cases there are clear examples of placekeeper identities, but those associated with the Meeker Home correspond much better to those of the temple's conservators than to those of its core community. Likewise, there are divergent definitions with respect to traditionalist attitudes: along the social relations, ethical and material environment place building dimensions, the Lomanthang core community constructs, re-constructs and preserves heritage through direct physical and social interaction with it; in contrast, the Meeker Home's European American core community, in keeping with GOD and SPF, appears to relate to heritage through passive interaction with it and efforts to preserve its "authentic" physical attributes. A PBT lens can highlight differences and similarities such as these and thereby facilitate their assessment for and incorporation into heritage management and conservation planning.

Finally, PBT also allows for critical examination and improvement of the living heritage paradigm itself. For example, it offers inductively derived definitions of place agent identities, place users, placekeepers and even the construct we researchers, often uncritically, call "community." Waterton and Smith (2013: 5) warn that an essentialist notion of community (with Poulios [2010], we would also add "stakeholder" to this list) creates opportunities for oppression: "Community has ... emerged as a discomforting convenience we – and here 'we' includes professionals, policymakers and scholars – use to manage and make sense of 'others'." Rather than reifying these notions – such as those that might indeed be implicit in Poulios's (2010) "core" and "peripheral" community constructs – or imposing on people membership in groups based on rigid sets of criteria, PBT recognizes alternatives: evolution, within- and between-group variability, multivocality and shared systems of belief, practice, etc., that arise from life histories, social interaction and interaction with place, thus fostering a "local future" for place-keepers and their living heritage places.

REFERENCES CITED

Agnew, John
    1987 *Place and Politics*. Boston: Allen & Unwin.

Agnew, John and James S. Duncan
    1989 Introduction to *The Power of Place*. Edited by John A Agnew and James S Dunca. London: Unwin Hyman.

Brunswig, Robert
    2008 *Informing Federal Lands Managers and Educating the Public on Past, Present and Future Climate Change through Archaeology and Paleoclimate Studies: complimentary research programs on National Park Service and Bureau of Land Management Lands*. Paper presented in the Symposium "What's New at the Intersection of Natural and Cultural Research in the Rocky Mountains?", chaired by Dr. Robert Brunswig at the CESU-Rocky Mountain Region Science Day Symposium, October 16, 2008. Estes Park, CO.

    2012 *The UNC-BLM North Park Cultural Landscape Project: Partnerships in Heritage Research, Preservation, and Management*. Paper presented at the CESURocky Mountain Region Science Day Symposium and Federal Managers Meeting. October 4, 2012. Devner, CO.

Brunswig, Robert and Frederik Sellet
    2010 *Archaeology and Civic Engagement Partnerships on Public Lands*. Paper delivered at the 43rd Annual Chacmool Conference, University of Calgary, Alberta, Canada. Conference theme: "Archaeology in the Public Eye," November 11-14, 2010. Calgary, Alberta, Canada.

Brunswig, Robert, David Diggs, and C.C. Montgomery
    2009 *Native American Lives and Sacred Landscapes in Rocky Mountain National Park*. Report to Rocky Mountain National Park, National Park Service. Department of Anthropology, University of Northern Colorado, Greeley, CO.

Brunswig, Robert, McBeth, Sally, and Louise Elinoff
 2009 Re-Enfranchising Native Peoples in the Southern Rocky Mountains: Integrated Contributions of Archaeological and Ethnographic Studies on Federal Lands. In *Post-Colonial Perspectives in Archaeology*. Edited by Peter Bikoulis, d. Lacroix, and M. Pueramaki-Brown. Pages 55-69. Calgary, Canada, Chacmool Archaeological Association.

Bourdieu, Pierre
 1969 "Intellectual Field and Creative Project." *Social Science Information* 8 (April): 89-119.

Byrne, Denis
 2008 "Heritage as Social Action." In *The Heritage Reader*. Edited by Graham Fairclough Rodney Harrison, John Schofield, John H. Jameson, Jr. Pages 149173. New York: Routledge.

CESU
 2001 *Cooperative Ecosystems Study Units: An Introduction.* Cooperative Ecosystem Studies Units, U.S. Department of the Interior, Washington, DC. 2013 *Fact Sheet: Cooperative Ecosystem Studies Units.* Cooperative Ecosystem Studies Units, U.S. Department of the Interior, Washington, DC.On-line at http://www.cesu.psu.edu/materials/fs-cesus.pdf.

Chapagain, Neel Kamal
 2013 "Heritage Conservation in the Buddhist Context." In *Asian Heritage Management: Contexts, Concerns, and Prospects*. Edited by Kapila D. Silva and Neel Kamal Chapagain. Pages 49-64. New York: Routledge.

Chapoose, Betsy, Sally McBeth, Sally Crum, and Aline LaForge
 2012 "Planting a Seed: Ute Ethnobotany, A Collaborative Approach in Applied Anthropology." *The Applied Anthropologist* 32(1):2-11.

Clavir, Miriam
   2002 *Preserving What is Valued: Museums, Conservation, and First Nations.* University of British Columbia Press.

Clay, Tracey and Michael Kimball
   2013 Place Building Paradigms: Exploring Heritage Sites Through the Lens of Place Building Theory. Unpublished Summary Report for Greeley Assistant City Manager, University of Northern Colorado, February 25, 2013.

Clifford, James
   1988 *The Predicament of Culture.* Cambridge, MA: University of Harvard Press.

Davenport, Mae A. and Dorothy H. Anderson
   2005 "Getting from Sense of Place to Place-Based Management: An Interpretive Investigation of Place Meanings and Perceptions of Landscape Change." *Society & Natural Resources* 18:625-641.

Diggs, David and Robert Brunswig
   2013 The Use of GIS and Weights-of-Evidence in the Reconstruction of a Native American Sacred Landscape in Rocky Mountain National Park, Colorado. Chapter 2 from *Continuity and Change in Cultural Mountain Adaptations: From Prehisotry to Contemporary Threats.* Edited by Ludomir R. Lozny and Daniel Bates. Pages 207-228. Springer-Verlag Studies in Human Ecology and Adaptation Series. Springer-Verlag, New York.

Foucault, Michel
   1980. *Power/Knowledge: Selected Interviews and Other Writings 1972-1977.* Edited by Colin Gordon. Pantheon, New York.

Glaser, B. and A. L. Strauss
   1967 *The Discovery of Grounded Theory: Strategies for Qualitative Research.* New York: Aldine de Gruyter.

Eyles, John
   1985 *Senses of Place.* Silverbrook, N.J.: Silver Brook Press.

Gramsci, Antonio
  1971 *Selections from the Prison Notebooks.* Edited by Quintin Hoare and Geoffrey Nowell Smith. International Publishers, New York.

Gustafson, Per
  2001 Meanings of Place: Everyday Experience and Theoretical Conceptualizations. *Journal of Environmetnal Psychology* 21(1):5-16.

Hudson, Ray
  2001 *Producing Places.* New York: The Guilford Press.

ICCROM
  2012 "Promoting People Centered Approaches to Conservation: Living Heritage." International Centre for the Study of the Preservation and Restoration of Cultural Property (ICCROM). Accessed October 14, 2013. http://www.iccrom.org/eng/prog_en/4people-centered-appr_en.shtml

Ingold, Timothy
  2000 *The Perception of the Environment: Essays on Livelihood, Dwelling and Skill.* New York: Routledge.

Jones, Emrys and Ray Eyles
  1977 *Introduction to Social Geography.* Oxford: Oxford University Press.

Kimball, Michael and david Thomas
  2012 "Place-Building Theory: A Framework for Assessing and Advancing Community Engagement in Higher Education." *Michigan Journal of Community Service Learning* (Spring): 19-28.

King, Thomas
  2003 *Places that Count: Traditional Cultural Properties in Cultural Resource Management.* AltaMira Press.

  2005 "What are Traditional Cultural Properties?" *The Applied Anthropologist* 25(2):125-130.

Kyle, Gerard, J. D. Absher, and Alan Graefe
2003 "The Moderating Role of Place Attachment on the Relationship Between Attitudes Toward Fees and Spending Preferences." *Leisure Sciences* 25:3350.

Kyle, Gerard, Alan Graefe, Robert Manning, and James Bacon
2004 "Effects of Place Attachment on Users' Perceptions of Social and Environmental Conditions in a Natural Setting." *Journal of Environmental Psychology* 24:213-225.

LeCompte, M. D.
1999 *Essential ethnographic methods: Observations, interviews, and questionnaires.* Lanham, VA: Lanham.

Lofland, Lyn H.
1998 *The Public Realm.* New York: Aldine de Gruyter.

Lowenthal, David
2000 "Stwearding the past in a perplexing present." In *Values and Heritage Conservation Research Report.* The Getty Conservation Institute, Los Angeles. Pages 18-25. Accessed October 14, 2013. http://www.getty.edu/conservation/publications_resources/pdf_publications/pdf/valuesrpt.pdf

Lynch, Kevin
1960 *The Image of the City.* Cambridge: MIT Press.

McBeth, Sally
2008 Ute Ethnobotany Project.Summary Report of a Cooperative Project of the Grand Mesa, Uncompahgre, and Gunnison National Forests and the Grand Junction Field Office of the Bureau of Land Management. Grand Junction, Colorado.

Morgan, G.
1986 *Images of organization.* Thousand Oaks: Sage.

1997 *Images of organization. (2nd Ed)* Thousand Oaks: Sage.

National Park Service
2007 Director's Order #75A: Civic Engagement and Public

Involvement. Accessed October 13, 2013. On-line http://www.nps.gov/policy/DOrders/75A.htm

Parker, Patricia L. and Thomas F. King
1998 *Guidelines for the Evaluation of Documentation of Traditional cultural Properties.*Second revised edition of formerly National Register Bulletin Number 38. First published in 1990 and first revised in 1992. Washington, District of Columbia: National Register of Historic Places, National Park Service, United States Department of the Interior. http://www.cr.nps.gov/nr/publications/bulletins/nrb38/

Pouios, Ioannis
2010 "Moving Beyond a Values-Bsed Approach to Heritage Conservation." *Conservation and Management of Archeological Sites* 12(2):170-185.

Proshansky. HaroldM.
1978 "The City and Self-Identity." *Environment and Behavior* 10:147-169.

Relph, Edward
1976 *Place and Placelessness.* London: Pion Ltd.

Rodman, Margaret C.
1992 "Empowering Place: Multilocality and Multivocality." *American Anthropologist* 94(3):640-656.

Sack, Robert D.
1988 "The Consumer's World: Place as Context." *Annals of the Association of American Geographers* 78(4):642-664.

1997 *Homo Geographicus.*Baltimore, MD: The Johns Hopkins University Press.

Sauer, Carl O.
1925 "The Morphology of Landscape." *Berkeley: University of California Publications in Geography* 2: 19-54.

Schein, Edgar H.
1992 *Organizational Culture and Leadership*. San Francisco: Jossey-Bass.

Schoenberger, E.
1997 *The cultural crisis of the firm*. Cambridge: Blackwell.

Silbernagel, Robert
2011 *Troubled Trails: The Meeker Affair and the Expulsion of Utes from Colorado*. Salt Lake City: University of Utah Press.

Smircich, L.
1983 Concepts of culture and organizational analysis. *Administrative Science Quarterly* 28(3):339-54.

Smith Laurajane
2006 *Uses of Heritage*. New York: Routledge.

Stokowski, Patricia A.
2002 "Languages of Place and Discourses of Power: Constructing New Senses of Place." *Journal of Leisure Research* 34(4): 368-382.

Stolp, Annelies, Wim Groen, Jacqueline van Vliet, and Frank Vanclay
2002 "Citizen Values Assessmetn: Incorporating Citizens' Value Judgement in Environmental Impact Assessment. *Impact Assessment and Project Appraisal* 20(1):11-23.

Thomas, David
2004 *Toward an Understanding of Organization Place Building in Communities*. Unpublished Doctoral Dissertation. Colorado State University, Fort Collins, Colorado, USA.

Tuan, Yi-Fu
1977 *Space and Place: The Perspective of Experience*. Minneapolis, MN: University of Minnesota Press.

UNC (University of Northern Colorado)
2013 "'Roots Project' Partners UNC Students with Greeley's Refugee Communities." *University of Northern Colorado*.

Accessed October 11, 2013. http://www.unco.edu/news/releases.aspx?id=5883.

Waterton, Emma and Laurajane Smith
2013 "The Recognition and Misrecognition of community Heritage." *International Journal of Heritage Studies* 16(1-2):4-15.

Waterton, Emma and Steve Watson
2013 "Framing Theory: Towards a Critical Imagination in Heritage Studies." International Journal of Heritage Studies. http://dx.doi.org/10.1080/13527258.2013.779295

Weick, K.E.
1995 *Sensemaking in organizations.* Thousand Oaks:Sage.

Wright, Miranda
1994 Valuing cultural diversity and treasuring cultural differences.*Newsletter of Western Museums Association* 1 (Winter):1-2.

Wright, Susan
1994 *Anthropology of organizations.*New York: Routledge.

(Endnotes)

1 Byrne refers to here to James Clifford's (1988:5) critique of colonialist perspectives: "Swept up in a destiny dominated by the capitalist West and by various technologically advanced socialisms, these suddenly 'backward' peoples no longer invent local futures."

2 This paper is an expanded version of a talk we delivered at the 7th World Archaeological Congress, Dead Sea, Jordan, in January, 2013. Michael Kimball, Ph.D., is an Associate Professor of Anthropology; Robert Brunswig, Ph.D., is an Emeritus Professor and Research Fellow in Anthropology; Sally McBeth, Ph.D., is a Professor of Anthropology; and David Thomas is an Assistant Professor of Management at the University of Northern Colorado. Contact regarding this article can be made via Kimball, at: Michael.Kimball@unco.edu.

8

ENHANCING STUDENT ORGANIZATIONS AS AGENTS FOR COMMUNITY DEVELOPMENT AND CIVIC ENGAGEMENT

Linda Kuk, James H. Banning, and David Thomas

Colorado State University; Northern Colorado University

Abstract

The concept of community has become an important component of the learning process on most college campuses. However, campus-based student organizations have not been effectively integrated into these initiatives. This article presents a new typology to develop student organizations as agents for community development, civic engagement, and organizational development on college campuses. This typology presents a way of conceptualizing student organizations as agents that can promote student learning and civic engagement, and enhance relationships with the greater community in which they exist. The authors utilized a focus group approach to explore the application of this new typology to student affairs practitioners' work with student organizations as the first step in the application of this model.

The concept of community has become a focus for student engagement and student learning within colleges and universities (Baxter Magolda & King, 2004; Blimling, Whitt & Associates, 1999;

Boyer, 1990; Cheng, 2004). The establishment of residential and learning communities, the focus on service learning based curriculum, and civic engagement and leadership development activities have been central to the effort to create community within higher education institutions (Baxter Magolda & King, 2004; Cheng, 2004; Jacoby, 2003; Komives, Longerbeam, Owens, Mainella, & Osteen, 2006). These efforts have redirected educational efforts toward student learning and have re-energized the concept of social and community development.

However, campus-based student organizations have not been effectively integrated in the surge of activity to build communities in residence halls, create learning communities inside and outside of the classroom, and develop service-learning and civic-engagement efforts in the greater community. There is almost no mention of students organizations in most of the writing and research related to these efforts, and little research related to student organizations over the past two decades. While student organizations function at the core of student life, collegiate institutions generally have not viewed or developed these organizations as effective agents for building community and civic responsibility (Cheng, 2004; Kuk, Thomas & Banning, 2008). Student organizations as components of student involvement have great potential for more extensive integration into community-building and civic-engagement efforts within collegiate institutions. (Kuk, Thomas & Banning, 2008; Rowan-Kenyon, Soldner & Inkelas, 2007).

This article presents a place/agent typology model for student organizations that was initially developed by Thomas (2004) and Thomas and Cross (2007) for use with business organizations, and advanced for application with student organizations by Kuk, Thomas, and Banning (2008). The article briefly explains the typology, and through the use of a professional focus group, provides a discussion of potential uses of the conceptual model in the development of community within student organizations. This model has the potential to serve as an effective tool in promoting community building, civic responsibility and student engagement among collegiate student organizations.

Background for the Importance of the Model

Three established findings from student organization literature serve as background for the introduction and discussion of the place/agent typology model. First, there has been considerable research regarding student involvement with peers and with the broadly defined co-curriculur experience. Much of this research has focused on the concept of Involvement, as fostered by the work of Astin (1977, 1984, 1993, & 1996). In his work, What matters in college? Four critical years revisited, Astin (1993) states that "the student peer group is the single most potent source of influence on growth and development during the undergraduate years" (p.398).

The second finding serving as background for this study is that over the years, student affairs professionals who work with student groups have not provided significant attention to the development of student organizations as organizations (Delve & Rice, 1990; Shertzer & Schuh, 2004). They have, however, focused extensively on the leadership development of individual students and this has served as a means of interacting with student groups and fostering student involvement (Delve & Rice, 1990; Shertzer & Schuh, 2004). Although student leadership development is an important aspect of student life, so is the development of student organizations into effective, sustainable organizations (Cooper, Healy, & Simpson, 1994; Shertzer & Schuh, 2004).

Third, student organizations exert a powerful influence on their members and may serve as a primary connection with campus life and the noncurricular aspects of the collegiate experience (Pavela, 1995; Whipple & Associates, 1998). The place/agency model builds on these three foundational considerations: student involvement is important to student success, student organizations need to be viewed from an organizational perspective, not just from a leadership perspective, and student organizations have powerful influences on individual student behavior.

A New Typology for Creating Community Development within Student Organizations

This place/agency model is built on the foundation of the organizational/place model and typology presented by Thomas (2004) and Thomas and Cross (2007). It is offered as a model to help foster a way of understanding and enhancing community development, social responsibility and connections within the greater community in which student organizations exist.

Thomas and Cross (2007) framed their initial organizational typology within the context of two key concepts. First, the idea that organizations act as place builders, where place building is defined as constructing a relationship between themselves and the community, within the context of both the physical and social environment of the community in which they exist. Second that organizations act as agents, where agent is defined as the constructor of the meaning of the relationship that is given to place and community. The combination of these two sets of characteristics influence the organization's goals, contributions to place as a form of social responsibility, and also contribute to their varied organizational behaviors.

Within this typology, organizations are construed as place builders based on how they value place and community, and as a result, how they contribute to or detract from the social construction of place. This model considers the dimension of place and community in the context of three environments: the natural environment, the material environment, and the social environment. Each of these environments can be used to understand how the organization values place from the perspective of how the organization interacts and engages with each of these environments.

An organization's agent perspective distinguishes between two distinctive viewpoints held by the organization, one that conceptualizes its success as interdependent with the well-being of place, and another that conceptualizes its success as independent of place. Organizations with an interdependent perspective view themselves as integral members of the larger community in which they exist and view their relationship to place and community as interdependent. Organizations that are viewed from an independent perspective view themselves as occupants of place and view the realms of plae as resources to satisfy the organizations' internal needs with little regard to the broader community in which they exist (Thomas & Cross, p.10).

Briefly stated, the model presents four organizational constructs/typologies, based on the interaction of these perspectives along a continuum. These typologies focus on creating and/or moving student organizations developmentally toward transformational functioning and building community within the context of place. The following modified descriptions related to the four place-related organizational constructs are taken from Kuk, Thomas, and Bannign (2008).

Organizational Place/Agent Typology

Four distinct place/agent typologies have been identified; transformational, contributive, contingent, and exploitative (Thomas, 2004).

Transformational organizations. Transformational organizations view themselves as critical agents for change in a community. They hold an interdependent perspective regarding their organization and its relationship to the greater community. They have organizational missions which focus on improving life and creating positive change for both the organization and the greater community in which they are located. The organizational culture is highly focused on team learning, collaboration with other organizations, openness to change, and building partnerships and developing community across and among student groups and with the leadership of the institution. Members of a transformational organization have developed the skills and mindsets that embrace the organization's philosophy and attitudes related to learning, teaching and outreach beyond their organization. The organization collectively views itself as a member of the place and central to the concept of community, not separate from it.

A student organization at this level of development would exhibit qualities of campus leadership that transcend the organization and be viewed as a role model and leader among other student organizations. These organizations would model exceptional teamwork, cross organizational collaboration, organizational learning, and community-centered values. Their members would model campus leadership in both academic and community engagement and publicly reflect the organization's integrated connection to the institution and the greater community.

Contributive organizations. Contributive organizations view themselves as a contributing member of a network of campus organizations and leaders who share a common ideology about he campus and the community. In contrast to transformational organizations that view themselves as responsible for the well-being of place and central to the development of community, a contributive organization views itself as a contributor to the well-being of place.

Contributive student organizations are truly engaged in the greater community and serve as active participants in both academic and co-curricular involvements, but the organizational focus is clearly internal. They view the greater community as a place to be engaged, to socialize, and to secure members, but they do not view themselves as being integrated into the community.

Contingent organizations. Contingent organizations view themselves as disassociated and autonomous organizations. These groups narrowly define social and community responsibility as obeying existing laws, campus policies, and ethical codes, and they make a concerted effort to act accordingly. Rather than view themselves as interdependent with place (transformational) or key members of place (contributive) they view themselves as control and compliance agents, not external community developers. The organizatin's culture appears structured and internally focused.

These types of student organizations essentially exist as independent student groups with little connection to, and focus on, the greater community. They pride themselves on their unique characteristics. Their leadership focus is internal and they often act in a competitive manner toward other groups. Although they are willing to engage in volunteer and community activities they do so as a means of self-promotion and competition. Their view of community engagement is focused on obeying rules and regulations and not on enhancing or building community. They would prefer to be left alone and do not value collaboration with other student organizations. They seek to exist as independent entities and have little real connection with community other than to exist within it.

Exploitative organizations. Exploitative organizations view themselves as occupants of place. They are isolated with respect to the traditions and values of the campus community. These organizations plan and organize their control over place with little if any regard for the greater community. Organizational success and/or the gains of individual members trump any campus or community needs (Thomas, 2004). Exploitative organizations value place as a commodity where each of the three environments of place is valued for what that environment can provide the organizations.

Exploitative organizations practice a separatist strategy. Their missions focus on maximizing the personal gains of individuals from within the organizations, and that determines the exploitative organizations' strategy. They deliberately target certain places without regard for the risk or harm to the campus or greater community, or the potential to extract resources without accountability. While some exploitative organizations may, at times, appear to contribute to the campus, these organizations are not invested in ways that contribute consistently to place or community well-being. Exploitative organizations are likely to leave a place or disaffiliate if they determine they do not fit, or if they are asked to change their behavior to comport with institutional or the greater community's expectations or policies. In some cases, they may act contrary to existing norms and values as acts of defiance or to exhibit their independent and unique characteristics.

The Application of the Student Organization Place/Agent Typology

The student organizations place/agent typology can be used in a variety of ways to foster student organizational development regardless of the nature and purpose of the group. As a first step to applying the typology model to student organization development and community building, the authors convened a focus group of student affairs practitioners. The authors wanted to understand the potential utility of this model in the development of student organizations and to secure feedback on the development of tools that could be utilized in the training and assessment process. Grounding the typology in the actual workings of student organizations was a necessary step to maximizing the full use of the typology.

The focus group consisted of 12 student affairs practitioners who provided feedback regarding the typology, its application to student organization development, and community building. The professional practitioners who contributed to this review were from a variety of student affairs offices at a research university. These offices included: student activities and student organizations, student recreation and club sports, student leadership and civic engagement, and Greek life. Most of the participants had worked with student organizations at a number of collegiate institutions during their professional careers.

The typology model was presented to the focus group was discussed, with responses recorded and later analyzed by the authors. The practitioner-participants provided a number of insights and suggestions on the use of the typology/agent model in the development of student organizations. The authors organized the results of these discussions into themes and recommendations for use. These ideas will be used to further develop the typology for use with student groups and to foster the development of tools for its use in organizational assessment and development.

Viewing student organizations within a new paradigm, as agents for community development

The focus group provided a new way of thinking about the participants' work with student organizations. A number of the professionals commented that the typology helped them to recognize the possibility of a new way of thinking about and working with student organizations. One practitioner stated, "we've never really talked about or thought about organizations this way" (focus group participant, personal communication, December 6, 2007). A director-level practitioner acknowledged that most of the work with student organizations was done through the development of organizational leaders and in working with the organization's advisor. She acknowledged that they had no idea of how much of their office's leadership development efforts reached into the organization itself. Collectively, the group acknowledged their frustration with the "roller coaster" lives of student organizations as they struggled from year to year to be effective, to find continuity, and to realize organizational goals.

The group discussed how student organizations varied in their ability to be successful based on how much they knew and how developed their skills were in accessing the institutional processes and resources. They presented examples of student organizations that were largely successful because they had leaders who knew how to "get things done" within the institution, or who were persistent in accessing advisors and student affairs staff who could provide them with answers on how to accomplish their goals. They shared a concern that the depth of leadership within an organization was generally unknown and had not been a major focus within leadership development activities.

Throughout the discussion, the conversation focused largely on skill-building and not on instilling organizational or institutional values within organizations or their members. The participants generally indicated that they had not done much work in developing the members of the organization or in approaching organizations from the perspectives presented in the model. They acknowledged that the model had a number of potential uses in working with student organizations across a broad spectrum of student groups. They generally thought the new approach could be developmental for a number of student groups, as well as for their leaders.

Organizations can be viewed developmentally along a continuum regarding their values and identification with place/community

The participants recognized and provided examples of how this typology could be useful in the development of student organizations. They envisioned the typology's continuum of organizational attributes and values as being valuable indices for engaging students in discussions and serving as the bases for goal-setting, planning, and organizational assessment. They expressed concern about boxing groups into categories or using labels to name their organizations. They felt the typology could be valuable in stimulating discussion, but the categories should not be attached as organizational labels in an administrative sense.

The focus group participants expressed concern that almost no student organizations were at the transformational level, however a few organizations had the potential to achieve this level. They were not certain that all student organizations could become transformational and they also were not certain that all organizations would have the ability to do so. They thought some organizations did exist for the sole purpose of providing benefits to their members, and that this was not necessarily a bad mission. An example was given of a ski club that existed solely to provide low-cost skiing opportunities to its members. This could be viewed as exploitative behavior. At the same time, they thought the basic concepts and the continuum of organizational development along the values and behaviors expressed by the model would be beneficial in discussions with most student organizations. The model could be used as a framework of advancing organizational development within a new paradigm that went beyond exclusive leadership development.

Initial implementation. Participants spent considerable time discussing the role of an organization's advisor and the critical nature of this role in providing for organizational success and ongoing continuity. They discussed the lack of sufficient resources available for organizational development and how they, as practitioners, relied on an organization's advisor as the key person who provided continuity within the organization's structure and culture. They readily acknowledged the large disparity that often occurred among organizational advisors and their individual ability to positively influence organizations. They expressed how difficult it was to ensure that advisors were providing the level of involvement needed to effectively serve the organization. The participants repeatedly stressed the lack of institutional support for appropriately rewarding faculty and staff who served in these roles. They indicated that training of practitioner staff and faculty advisors regarding the use of the new model with student organizations would be a critical first step in utilizing it effectively. They emphasized helping staff and faculty advisors understand how to help organizations develop along the model's values and behavior continuum. For example, although the ski club might organize for the purpose of obtaining discount tickets for its members, the model suggests that through discussion and awareness they could decide to move up the developmental typology by starting a ski lesson program for kids in campus family housing or organizing ski opportunities for members of the greater community. The model holds that every organization, no matter what its purpose or mission, could decide to enhance its connection with place and its social responsibility to the community in which it exists. The group also suggested its use as a formative and nonlabeling process for growth and community building would be critical for its effectiveness.

Help individual members explore their relationship to the organization. Participants suggested that within organizations the members see their relationship to their organizations very differently. Individual members never may have thought about their role and responsibility to promote community development within their group. Focus group participants shared a belief that it had been the role of the organizational leadership to promote such understanding. They acknowledged that many organizational leaders do not have the skills or maturity needed to effectively manage this process, especially in the face of membership resistance. The group concurred that the model could help frame a more intentional consciousness regarding students' roles within the organization and help student members understand how they as individuals either contribute to, or detract from the organization's success. One participant of the focus group expressed that "few people want to be viewed as exploitive, but individually members may not fully comprehend the relationship between their individual behaviors and the collective actions that are associated with their organizations" (focus group participant, personal communication, November 15, 2007).

Organizational perceptions. Participants discussed their belief that many organizations do not understand how they are perceived in the larger community. The group expressed strong agreement that having this knowledge might assist members in their desire to change negative perceptions and develop more positive perceptions about their group. Using the model to promote reflective discussions can demonstrate how an organization, through its collective behavior, might act more intentionally to present and integrate a desired image. These types of discussions might help leaders gain a stronger hand in utilizing peer pressure to convert the resistors in the group to become more community-focused.

Building collaboration across student organizations. The group discussed viewing the model as a tool for building collaboration and community between student organizations and increasing organizations' connections to the institutions. They expressed excitement for the possibility of the model serving as a means of increasing collaboration and organizational commitment to activities that might not be initially apparent to students or their advisors. Participants saw the model as creating windows for discussion around organizational beliefs and/or perspectives that may have served as wedges and/or sources of antagonism in the past. The group provided examples of how collaborations and understanding between organizations such as Campus Crusade for Christ and the GLBT organization of politically divergent international organizations, might be fostered through the use of the perspectives and values promoted within the model. For example, fostering dialogues between such groups using the model and focusing on their joint commitment to commonly held values about place could help each group develop a understanding and greater appreciation of the "other" and foster a means for finding common ground and possible community-centered collaboration.

The Typology Model as a Tool for Developing Student Organizations and Building Community

Participants of the focus group acknowledged that the organizational typology presented a new way of viewing student organizations and their work with them. They saw the new typology as a developmental framework that could foster greater collaboration within and among student organizations. From the advisor perspective, participants thought the model provided a way of initiating discussions regarding the role and purpose of student groups in relation to place and community and their own organizations' development.

The focus group confirmed the assumption held by the authors that there were a number of possible and varied applications for the typology with student organizations. The participants were in strong agreement that the typology provided a conceptual framework and the language to view student organizations' relationship to the community. The typology also showed promise for use across a wide spectrum of organizational types. Although it was stipulated that use of the typology might differ depending on the nature and goals of an organization, its potential uses as training, planning, and assessment tools within organizations were the central and unanimous finding of the group's contributions.

The following potential applications for the use of this conceptual framework were developed from the results of the focus group discussion:

1. The typology has great potential to serve as a training tool for student affairs practitioners in their work in advising student organizations. The tool could assist advisors and peer trainers in fostering student organizations as community builders within the campus environment. It could set the foundation for extending a current focus on student leadership development to a new role of helping develop the organization's members as well as the organization itself. The model should not be used for administrative purposes or for labeling or categorizing organizations. The model has great potential as an awareness and thought-provoking tool. Utilizing the model as a discussion tool could promote a less rule-oriented, less authoritative, role for advisors and organizational leaders within their organizations.

2. The typology could serve as the basis for student organizational development within student organizations. The model provides a new set of paradigms for viewing the roles of student groups as agents of organizational development, as well as member development. The typology model can foster organizational development by proving a conceptual framework and language from which to view different levels of student organization relationships to the community. It presents the idea that organizations can grow and change developmentally along a continuum of agency that fosters organizational development by connecting individual members and the group to the idea of community and their connection to it. Based on their experience in working with student organizations, the professional participants and the authors believe that most student groups want to ensure their organizational leadership into the future. While every student organizations' goals and purpose may not necessitate their aspiring to become transformational organizations, most student groups want to sustain themselves over time and to foster the development of their organization. This model can serve as a means of fostering organizational sustainability and helping organizations understand that one aspect of sustainability is related to their connection to place and community. Enhancing

awareness of their connection to place can help organizational members understand how their individual and collective behavior contributes to both the well-being of their organization, as well as the greater community in which they exist. As an assessment and planning tool, the model can be used to enhance the organizations' collective understanding of how to obtain their goals and how to enable the members to make informed choices about the future of their organizations.

3. The typology can serve as a means of promoting discussion among individual members regarding their individual and collective values and perceptions related to community, social responsibility, and commitment. As an assessment and training tool, the model can serve as a vehicle for helping promote an understanding of the value of social responsibility and commitment to the greater community. It can serve as a vehicle for organizations to understand their image within the greater community and to work more intentionally to change this image when such change is called for. It can provide organizational leaders with a tool to help convert resistor members to more active, positive engagement within the organization. Most importantly, this model provides a vehicle for helping students understand how they can contribute to community engagement by promoting the mission and purpose of their student organizations. Through exploring the model in relation to the purpose, goals and values of the organization the members can determine how they want to intentionally relate to each other and to be engaged with the greater community in which it exists.

4. The typology shows great promise as a basis for organizational assessment and as a means of promoting organizational growth and change. Most student organizations exist in a vacuum of understanding regarding their relationship to place and community. For many, it is not an issue that they have contemplated or intentionally addressed. Through the use of this developmental model, an organization can assess the congruence

between their organizational values, mission, and purpose. They can intentionally decide where they want their organization to be in relationship to place and determine to what extent they want to move their organization toward growth and sustainability. This model provides a powerful lens for viewing and discussing critical community-related issues.

5. The typology can be used to foster greater collaboration and understanding among various student organizations, especially among those that may have experienced disagreement or antagonism related to beliefs or past behaviors. It can help promote organizational networks across student groups that can foster greater understanding and a stronger sense of community among all students. By using the model in joint discussions across various organizations, especially those where conflict may exist, the model can be used to explore common interests and concerns, shared values and ways the groups can seek to collaborate in spite of their differences.

Summary and Future Considerations

Community development and a focus on service, leadership and civic responsibility, have become strong tools for fostering student learning and student success within higher education institutions. Student organizations have not been readily included in these initiatives despite their significant role in student involvement and their potential to foster individual and community development. The future holds much promise for the use of the organizational place/agency typology in the development of student organizations. It provides a framework for viewing and developing student organizations as agents of community building and organizational development within the greater collegiate community.

The practitioner focus group provided a first step in assessing the usefulness of this typology model for working with student organizations as agents of community and member development on college campuses. The next step in the use of this typology will require the development of specific strategies and tools for its application to student organizational development. These tools might include a survey instrument for assessing organizational status along the typology's organizational continuum, and training tools for its use in leader and member organizational development training. It will also be necessary to pilot assessment instruments and training tools and to gauge their effectiveness.

These initial steps in the model's application development process have provided a critical link to the development of this new typology in working with student organizations. It has introduced a new way of viewing student organizations within the context of community, social, and civic engagement and has the potential to serve as an effective new tool for advancing community development within campus life.

Linda Kuk is an Associate Professor of Education at Colorado State University where she is program chair of the Educational Leadership, College, and University distance doctoral program.

James H. Banning is an environmental psychologist and is a professor in the School of Education at Colorado State University.

David Thomas is an Associate Professor of Business at the University of Northern Colorado.

References

Astin, A. (1997). *Four critical years: Effects of college on beliefs, attitudes, and knowledge.* San Francisco: Jossey Bass.

Astin, A. (1984). Student Involvement: A developmental theory for higher education. *Journal of College Student Personnel, 25,* 297-308.

Astin, A. (1993). *What matters in college? Four critical years revisited.* San Francisco: Jossey Bass.

Astin, A. (1996). "Involvement in learning" revisited: Lessons we have learned. *Journal of College Student Development, 37,* 123-134.

Baxter Magolda, M. & King, P. M. (2004). Learning Partnerships: Theories and models of practice to educate for self-authorship. Sterling Virginia: Stylus Publishing.

Blimling, G. S., Whitt, E. J., & Associates (1999). *Good Practice in Student Affairs: Principles to Foster Student Learning.* San Francisco: Jossey Bass.

Boyer, E. L. (1990). *Campus life: In search of community.* Lawrenceville, New Jersey: The Carnegie Foundation for the Advancement of Teaching.

Cheng, D. X. (2004). Students' sense of campus community: What it means, and what to do about it. *NASPA Journal, 41,* 2, 216-234.

Cooper, D. L., Healey, M. A., & Simpson, J. (1994). Student development through involvement: Specific changes over time. *Journal of College Student Development, 35,* 98-102.

Delve, C. I. & Rice, K. (1990, Summer) The Integration of Service Learning into Leadership and Campus Activities. In C. I. Delve and K. Rice, *Community Services as Values Education.* New Direction for Student Services, 50, San Francisco: Jossey Bass.

Jacoby, B. & Associates (2003). *Building partnerships for service learning.* San Francisco: Jossey Bass.

Komives, S. R., Longerbeam, S. D., Owens, J. E., Mainella, F.C. & Osteen, L. (2006). A leadership identity development model: Applications for a grounded theory. *Journal of College Student Development, 47,* 4, 401-418.

Kuk, L., Thomas, D. & Banning, J. (2008). Student organizations and their relationship to the institution: A dynamic framework. *Journal of Student Affairs, 17,* 9-20.

Pavela, G. (1995). *The power of association: Defining our relationship with students in the 21st century.* Washington, D.C.: NASPA.

Rowan-Kenyon, H., Soldner, M. & Inkelas, K. K. (2007). The contributions of living-learning programs on developing sense of civic engagement in undergraduate students. *NASPA Journal, 44,* 4, 750-778.

Schneider, B., Brief, A. P., & Guzzo, R. A. (1996, Spring). Creating a climate and culture for sustainable organizational change. *Organizational Dynamics,* 7-18.

Shertzer, J. E., & Schuh, J. H. (2004). College student perceptions of leadership; Empowering and constraining beliefs. *NASPA Journal, 42,* 1, 111-131.

Thomas, D. F. (2004). *Toward an understanding of organizational place building in communities.* Unpublished doctoral dissertation, Colorado State University, Fort Collins, Colorado.

Thomas, D. F., & Cross, J. E. (2007, September). Organizations as place builders. *Journal of Behavioral and Applied Management.*

Whipple, E. G., & Associates (1998). *New challenges for Greek letter organizations: Transforming fraternities and sororities into learning communities.* San Francisco: Jossey Bass.

9

PLACE-BUILDING THEORY: A FRAMEWORK FOR ASSESSING AND ADVANCING COMMUNITY ENGAGEMENT IN HIGHER EDUCATION

Michael J. Kimball and David F. Thomas
University of Northern Colorado

Place-building theory, originally developed to assess corporate social responsibility, explains to what degree an organization values and invests in its geographical and social location. Different lines of inquiry—descriptive, evaluative, and prescriptive—elucidate how the organization values place, which in turn suggests its type, its strategies for building place, and recommendations for how it might move in a desired direction between the ends of a place-building continuum that includes four organizational prototypes—exploitive, contingent, contributive, and transformational. In this paper, we introduce place-building theory, the notion of the placekeeper (place-based stakeholder), and apply the theory to assessing a university's community engagement. We then demonstrate how a university course can use the place-building method to discover perceptions of the university's place-building role held by students, staff, administrators, faculty, and community partners as a way to engage students and other placekeepers in assessing, advancing, and critically examining community engagement in institutions of higher education.

What begins as undifferentiated space becomes place as we get to know it better and endow it with value. Architects talk about the spatial qualities of place; they can equally well speak of the locational (place) qualities of space. The ideas "space" and "place" require each other for definition. From the security and stability of place we are aware of the openness, freedom, and threat of space, and vice versa. Furthermore, if we think of space as that which allows movement, then place is pause; each pause in movement makes it possible for location to be transformed into place. (Tuan, 1977, p. 6)

Place-building theory, originally developed to assess corporate social responsibility (Thomas, 2004), explains the degree to which an organization values and invests in its social and geographical location, its "local community"—i.e., how it actively creates place from space (Tuan, 1977). In a sense, all community engagement, whether it be participatory and reciprocal or technocratic and linear, represents a kind of place-building practice whose outcomes—economic and social relation, ethical conduct, construction and treatment of built and natural environments—embody a set of intrinsic beliefs and values motivating engagement strategies.

Discovering these motivating factors affords opportunities to clarify, debate, and transform them as well as to assess, enhance, and realign their concomitant strategies. Place-building theory's origins are situated in the desire not only to identify and define motivating factors and strategies, but also to engage *placekeepers* (place-based stakeholders) as participants in an evaluative and proactive process. It is with this in mind that we have applied place-building theory to community engagement in higher education.

In this paper, we show how we have expanded place-building's focus on corporate social responsibility to include a broader scope of institutional social responsibility through a new orientation that explores how universities build place and how place-building researchers, including student researchers, in partnership with other placekeepers (i.e., community partners, staff, faculty, students, and administrators) can initiate and facilitate intentional and potentially transformative place-building work.

In the following pages, we introduce place-building theory by discussing its interdisciplinary origins; two perspectives on place held by organizations; and Thomas's research defining a continuum of place-building by organizations ranging from exploitive to transformational. Further, we describe how the place-building framework possesses *descriptive, prescriptive,* and *evaluative* lines of inquiry for assessing and improving higher education institutions' community engagement work. Next we briefly discuss relations between place-building and corporate social responsibility and how these two concepts speak to a new focus for place-building research and application—the university. We describe how we incorporated the place-building framework into Kimball's applied anthropology course as a community-engaged research project and we offer a general discussion of the university as a context, and community-engaged research as a vehicle, for place-building and place-building research. We conclude with recommendations for how place-building theory, combined with community-engaged research, might be employed as a useful framework for assessing and advancing place-based community engagement in institutions of higher education.

Place-Building Theory

"Place-building" as a concept has been referenced by sociologists, geographers, and other social scientists interested in matters such as enterprise movement, community and systems sustainability (Schneider, Brief, & Guzzo, 1996), sustainable development, and enterprise attributes of communities (Hudson, 2001; Jacobs, 1984; Sagoff, 1996; Schoenberger, 1997; Wright, 1994). Sense of place, community development, corporate culture, and organizational behavior have been investigated by sociologists (Gans, 2002; Gieryn, 2000), geographers (Agnew, 1987; Entrikin, 2000; Seamon & Buttimer, 1980; Tuan, 1977; Werlen, 1993), anthropologists (Geertz, 1983; Wright, 1994), environmentalists (Gustafson, 2005; Snyder,

1995), and business researchers (Delheim, 1986; Hatch, 1993; Thomas, 2004; Thomas & Cross, 2007).

Place is defined as both geographical and social, and is organized around the meanings individuals and groups give to a place in its setting (Rodman, 1992). Places take on the meaning of events that occur there, and their descriptions are fused with human goals, values, and intentions. These "shared meanings," held in common by the collective, are historically generated and tend to be durable (Alvesson & Berg, 1991). Geographers refer to place as "context," explaining how social relations attach to space and place and only secondarily to people (Staeheli, 2007). Place, therefore, is described in this sense as a setting for social action. An organization can impact a given place in ways that influence social action, often on its own terms and seeking a certain outcome. As Entrikin (2000) states, "Place shares meanings or interpretive frames of events for different actions, and second it provides resources for action" (p. 6). Thus, place as a platform can mediate between individuals, social groups, organizations, and broader political structures (Thomas & Cross, 2007).

Therefore, place is not merely a phenomenon that exists in the minds of individuals but also a social construct that develops from and becomes part of everyday life and experiences. The ordinary routines of life produce places that are meaningful, sacred, and special to individuals, organizations, and communities (Williams, 1989). Thus place is not "discrete" or merely local. Place is seen as an intricately binding locale with broad processes and, with other locales, binding processes and constructs that are themselves constantly in flux (Massey & Jess, 1995).

Using a grounded theory approach (Glaser & Strauss 1967), Thomas (2004) and Thomas and Cross (2007) derived place-building theory from the work of organizational researchers such as Morgan (1997).

Enhancing Student Organizations as Agents for Community Development and Civic Engagement

Two Organization Perspectives on Place

All organizations have an agent perspective which connotes the viewpoints they have about how they conceptualize themselves in relation to place as well as the meaning they give to place, which then influences their goals, contributions to place, and all variety of their behavior. There are two types of agent perspectives—one conceptualizes organizations and their success as interdependent with the well-being of place and the other conceptualizes organizations and their success as independent of place.

Organizations with the *interdependent* perspective view themselves as members of a community and recognize that organizations and places are mutually dependent on each other. Interdependent organizations consider themselves responsible for the well-being of a place, view their success as intimately tied with the greater well-being of the place, and actively seek a variety of opportunities to invest and contribute to the multiple aspects of a place. In contrast, organizations with an *independent* perspective view themselves merely as occupants of place and economic agents of place rather than integral members of place. Organizations seeing themselves as independent agents focus their activities on satisfying internal organizational goals while viewing the realms of place as resources to satisfy their needs. In other words, an independent perspective views a place as serving the organization and not vice versa. These organizations view their primary responsibility to their shareholders, not to the places in which they do business. They consider generating jobs and tax revenues as their primary, if not only, contribution to place. Independent organizations are not committed to the well-being of place and will only maintain the relationship as long as it benefits their organizational goals (Thomas, 2004; Thomas & Cross, 2007).

Place Building Dimensions

Place-building theory explains how an organization values place on five dimensions: nature, social relationships, material environment, ethics, and economic relationships.

Nature. This dimension includes the natural, as opposed to human-made, elements, forces, and spaces, such as the landscape, earth, geography, and natural resources. How does an organization relate and contribute to nature and the environment?

Social relationships. This dimension includes the full spectrum of interactions between an organization's employees and stakeholders and among and between other organizations. How does an organization encourage the development of social capital? How is certain space treated that reflects the culture and values of the organization?

Material environment. This dimension includes human-made buildings, roads, and other structures such as the buildings an organization occupies and how that space is treated, including interior office spaces. This also reflects the value placed on the building's architecture, landscaping, and historical significance (if any).

Ethics. This dimension includes the organization's practices and its implicit and explicit contract with the community. How are an organization's practices modeled in its industry, its culture, and with all its placekeepers?

Economic relationships. This dimension includes the organization's level of investment in the fiscal well-being of the community. How does the organization attract skilled labor to the community? How does it seek to improve the economic viability of the community? How does the organization create new opportunities for economic growth?

Four Types of Place-Builders

How the organization values place suggests its type, its strategies for building place, and recommendations for how it might move in a desired direction between the ends of a place-building continuum. Thomas (2004) has subjected this continuum, with four benchmarks representing types of place-building organizations, to both quantitative modeling and continuous empirical testing.

Four distinct *place agent identities*—transformational, contributive, contingent, and exploitive—further elucidate the interdependent and dependent agent perspectives described above. Place agent identities reveal how organizations conceptualize themselves as social actors in relation to the places in which they are located. The four types differ in how they conceptualize themselves as agents, the value they assign to the realms of place, their corporate culture, and their strategies and behaviors. *Transformational* organizations conceptualize themselves as change agents acting to improve the lives of individuals and groups in a place. *Contributive* organizations conceptualize themselves as investors and contributors to the well-being of places in which they operate. *Contingent* organizations view themselves simply as participants in places. And *exploitive* organizations view themselves as independent agents with little to no obligation to the places in which they are located.

Each of the four types of organizations create institutional missions which demonstrate different levels of commitment to place well-being. Organizations with the same agent perspective, but different agent identities, develop similar although not identical missions and strategies, which include similar commitments to place well-being. Organizations with an interdependent agent perspective strive for a relatively equal balance between place well-being and their own success, whereas organizations with an independent agent perspective put much more emphasis and weight on their own success with little or no concern for place well-being.

Transformational organizations. Transformational organizations view themselves as critical agents with a mission and focus on improving life and creating positive change for both the organization and the place (Thomas, 2004; Thomas & Cross, 2007). The transformational organizational culture is highly focused on team learning, collaboration, openness to change, and building partnerships. They view themselves as *interdependent* members of a place, rather than independent members, and their success contributes to advantage beyond that of the organization (Thomas).

Transformational place-builders demonstrate an *integrative* strategy that focuses on building a shared vision with the community and holding itself accountable to the community for the quality of its contribution to place. Their behaviors are not solely for public relations advantage but an effort to surpass trends and regulations, perhaps even at a cost to the organization (Thomas & Cross, 2007). Their strategies include initiating new policies and business practices for protecting the natural environment, neighborhoods, cultural heritage, local economy, and other local resources (Thomas & Cross).

Contributive organizations. Contributive organizations view themselves as being contributing members of a network of community leaders who share a common ideology. Their identity as a local contributor is affirmed by engaging with local organizations, fundraising, and by philanthropy that builds place (Chaskin, Brown, Venkatesh & Vidal, 2001; Schneider, Brief, & Guzzo, 1996). In contrast to transformational organizations that view themselves as responsible for the well-being of place, contributive organizations view themselves as contributors to the well-being of place. The organizational culture is focused on "giving back" and conforming to local norms and values (Thomas, 2004).

Contributive organizations value place first for its social relationships and second for its economic opportunities and potential for business growth. These organizations need a place that needs them, where they can simultaneously prosper and give back. They practice an *integrative* strategy that cultivates their role as a key contributor in their community through the network of organizations that facilitate social and philanthropic activity (Thomas, 2004; Thomas & Cross, 2007).

Contingent organizations. Contingent organizations view themselves as disassociated and autonomous agents. They narrowly define "organizational social responsibility" as obeying existing laws, regulations, and ethical codes, and make a concerted effort to act accordingly. Rather than viewing themselves as interdependent with place (transformational), or key members of place (contributive), they view themselves as control agents.

Contingent organizations practice a *separatist strategy* that centers on a plan that distinguishes the organization in terms of its economic power. Contingent organizations value place for what it provides for the organization, such as workers for its labor force. They practice philanthropy only as a method for advancing their own causes, not out of any intrinsic commitment to place, and their principle contribution is economic as well as adhering to laws and regulations (Thomas & Cross, 2007).

Exploitive organizations. Exploitive organizations view themselves as occupants of place and are isolated from the values of the community. They are active users of the local economic cultural social and political resources, valuing place as a commodity that they utilize to their greatest economic benefit (Entrikin, 2000; Rodman, 1992; Sagoff, 1996). They largely plan and organize to control space in which short term organizational goals trump local needs (Thomas, 2004), and their preference is to be granted the rights and legal protections typically afforded only to individual citizens (Vogel, 2005).

Exploitive organizations' mission to achieve their goals determines their organizational philosophy, and it is usually practiced by deliberately targeting certain places for the potential to extract resources without accountability for the risks posed to the local population. While these organizations may employ local people, they practice a *separatist* strategy in which they are not invested in ways that contribute to a sense of place. Exploitive organizations are likely to leave a place once they have determined they do not fit or the return is not as lucrative as originally anticipated (Thomas & Cross, 2007).

Each of the four types stands out from the others in their perspectives on place and the consequences of their actions. Transformational organizations orchestrate their contributions in ways that transform themselves and place. As agents of change, they are distinguished from other organizations in that they view place in a holistic manner in which all five dimensions are interactive and interdependent. Consequently, the practices of transformational organizations contributive to place well-being through learning and teaching in partnership with other organizations and community entities (Thomas, 2004; Thomas & Cross, 2007).

Place-Building Lines of Inquiry

A line of inquiry connotes a vantage point or point of departure from which to understand an organization's place-building identity. Place building has three lines of inquiry. The first is *descriptive* in the sense that the organization's place-building identity reveals how an organization values place (Thomas, 2004; Thomas and Cross, 2007). The organization's valuation of place informs its strategic actions and its interactions within the community, determining how the organization designates the use of space in ways that ascribe meaning and reflect the organization's culture. This means that place-building is also *evaluative* in the sense that it reveals how an organization determines the significance, worth, or condition of a place, and how that organization assesses or estimates the quality or condition of a place relative to its role. Finally, place-building is *prescriptive* to the extent that an organization specifies, generally through its mission statement, its intentions toward the wider community, i.e., how it will use resources and engage in activities that impact the community, and what social and ethical responsibilities it acknowledges and strives to meet. Below, we provide more detail on how these lines of inquiry articulate with the four organization place-building typology.

Descriptive Line of Inquiry

Place-building research operates in a descriptive mode when it identifies how an organization values place.

Transformative organizations. These organizations value place in terms of advocacy for investing its assets to build competitive advantages for both place and organization. They a leadership role as "place advocate" in advancing construction of new organizational competencies that improve community well-being.

Contributive organizations. These organizations value place in terms of its *social network* in which its contributions are intended to gain it recognition as a member of the community. They strategically move the organization into supporting roles in the community where the firm finds a suitable fit.

Contingent organizations. These organizations value place primarily in *measurable terms*, i.e., what contribution does place return on its economic and financial worth and/or what it can afford and negotiate. They negotiate contributions and value place for its economic and political advantage, provided they advance the organization's mission.

Exploitive organizations. These organizations devalue place in quantifiable terms that describe place as a product or commodity. The organization negotiates its position in the community without regard to the impact of its operations and operates outside acceptable practices—no local knowledge of the place and its historic or cultural history.

Evaluative Line of Inquiry

Place-building research operates in an evaluative mode when it identifies how an organization assesses and estimates the value(s) of what place offers, what it provides or furnishes in the way of resources to the community and the organization.

Transformative organizations. These organizations determine the value of place based on the shared qualities of all five place-building dimensions (economics, ethic, social, nature, and the built environment), each of which is viewed for its intrinsic values that gain prominence from an integrated and complex setting in which it operates interdependently or symbiotically

Contributive organizations. These organizations determine the value of place based on the their relationship to some propositional good, such as the "fit" or the "match" between the organization's goals and the place's contributions.

Contingent organizations. These organizations calculate the value of place in terms of its worth based on what it can contribute to the organization, i.e., what a place affords that can enhance the organization's market position and business model.

Exploitive organizations. These organizations assess the value of place primarily as an economic factor. They monetize place and spaces as resources for their own purposes.

Prescriptive Line of Inquiry

Place-building research operates in a prescriptive mode when it identifies, typically through an organization's mission statement and business model, how the organizations orders the use of its strategic resources and assets to, for example, restore or protect place (nature); attract new businesses and industries that build commerce (economic); create new opportunities to invest in community (social and economic relationships); or represent its social contract or responsibility to its stakeholders (ethical relations).

Transformative organizations. These organizations commit resources and assets to lead and create new opportunities for civic participation and economic partnerships and collaborations. They advocate for change and improvements consistent with their business mission and purposes.

Contributive organizations. These organizations commit resources and assets to help build place, and seek membership in similar organizations as a method for building business and enhancing its reputation as a contributor.

Contingent organizations. These organizations engage in the conditional development of resources and assets to attain some good or purpose for the organization's benefit.

Exploitive organizations. These organizations capture financial gains through aggressive and self-centered strategies that often de-value place. They perceive place as an acquisition or commodity.

Place-Building and Institutional Social Responsibility

Corporate Social Responsibility (CSR) as a concept and process has a deep and rich history, arguably extending back hundreds of years and encompassing much debate and diversification within the business community (Carroll, 1999). Among the varied definitions of CSR that have arisen over time, there have been emphases on everything from philanthropy to broader commitments to community wellbeing through business practices and corporate resources (Kotler & Lee, 2005), to establishing long-term commitments to social issues, initiatives, and forming strategic alliances (Smith, 1994).

Thomas and Cross (2007) draw a connection between the active and collective process of constructing place from space and the active role that organizations play in driving and facilitating this process. Using this perspective as a frame, they propose a new CSR definition, "one that defines corporations as agents, whose actions, values, behaviors, and strategies contribute in myriad ways to the social construction of places (p. 34)." Thus, with this definition—in effect, one for Place-Based CSR—they make explicit the implicit relations among place-building, collective entities (social groups, organizations, corporations), social responsibility, and agency.

Place-Based CSR and the University

Corporate Social Responsibility, despite its roots in the world of business (Carroll, 1999), offers a model that appears to be equally applicable to the world of higher education. For example, Wood (1991) defined a corporate social performance model whose components speak to higher education's recent trend toward engaged universities (Mayfield, 2001). Wood's model includes three principles of corporate social responsibility: (a) the Principle of Legitimacy, which says that society grants legitimacy and power to business, and in the long run, those who do not use power in a manner which society considers responsible will tend to lose it; (b) the Principle of Public Responsibility, which says that businesses are responsible for outcomes related to their primary and secondary areas of involvement with society; and (c) the Principle of Managerial Discretion, which says that managers are moral actors, and within every domain of corporate social responsibility, they are obliged to exercise such discretion as is available to them toward socially responsible outcomes (p. 696).

When this perspective is brought to bear on another trend, universities' increasing investments in "placemaking" strategies (Stout, 2008)—i.e., town or city planning initiatives to improve quality of life and enhance the university brand—it is possible to recognize the emergence of a place-based institutional social responsibility phenomenon. In this case, it might be appropriate to replace Wood's (1991) use of the term "society" in her Principle of Legitimacy with the word "community"—social grants legitimacy and power to business, and in the long run, those who do not use power in a manner which the community considers responsible will tend to lose it. For this purpose, we adopt Stoecker's (2003, p. 41) parsimonious definition of community as "the people living with the problem and those organizations that they democratically control." Therefore, we assert that the theory of organizational place-building can be applied to institutions of higher education. How do colleges and universities, through the eyes of their placekeepers, perceive and enact their relationship with their geographical and social location?

A University Example

The authors' collaboration began in 2008 as we discovered intriguing and potentially productive overlaps in our research and teaching interests. Kimball was asked by his Department of Anthropology to design and deliver an undergraduate applied anthropology course. Applied anthropology, arguably anthropology's fifth field or subdiscipline (Baba, 1994)—the traditional four being archaeology, cultural anthropology, physical or biological anthropology, and linguistics—is especially well-suited for community-engaged research because of its collaborative, solution-oriented mission and methods. Given his interests in service-learning and engaged scholarship, Kimball wanted the course experience to include engagement with the community and to contain typical service-learning components such as academic rigor, reciprocity, and reflection.

Place-building research, like anthropological research, uses a mixed-methods approach with a heavy emphasis on rigorous analysis of qualitative date for inquiry and theory-building. This, in addition to their respective fields' shared interests in the concept of place as it manifests individually and collectively, quickly made it clear to both authors that there was great potential for a collaboration that incorporated research methods training, community-engaged research, and place-building theory into an applied anthropology curriculum. To date, we have constructed four, interrelated projects over the last four years. Due to our own University's aspirations to develop a "University District" (University of Northern Colorado, 2012), we decided to construct our 2010 and 2011 community-engaged research around the identification and analysis of perceptions of our University as a place-builder.

In brief, the curricular component of our Institutional Review Board-approved research design consists of academic preparation (course work on the history and theory of applied anthropology, place, and place-building); methodological training in research design, semi-structured interviewing, transcription, and open-code transcript analysis (LeCompte, 1999); implementation of the research project (disclosure and discussion of study cohorts, formation and deployment of interview teams, transcription and data analysis); meaning-making of project results through mid-and end-of-semester reflection papers, in-class discussions, and group process interpretative work; and a final report and poster presentation at our University's annual engaged and applied research symposium.

The design for our 2010-11 community-engaged research consists of study cohorts and use of quantitative and qualitative data collection and analysis. Our cohorts thus far have been drawn, through convenience sampling, from populations we believe to be placekeepers in our community, i.e., representatives of community-based organizations engaged in partnerships with the University and the University's administrators, students, staff, and faculty.

In addition to being required to serve as student researchers, our students were also invited to participate as subjects of the place-building research by completing a pre- (during the first week of class) and post- (during the last week) administration of Thomas's *Place Building Survey* (PBS).[1] Researchers have used the PBS in previous years to explore differences in place-building characteristics between various organizations and groups. In each case, the survey responses from the organizations under study were judged to be highly reliable for respondents, with a reliability coefficient of 0.923. The PBS is presently used in various research settings involving organizations across industry, size, and national borders.

The PBS is composed of 29 Likert-type items represented in the four types of place-building organizations. The PBS uses a seven point response scale from "Strongly Agree" to "Strongly Disagree." The goal of the PBS analysis for our project was to focus on the differences within and between our cohorts' responses and pre/post test variation in student assessment of our University's place-building strategies.

In the 2010 fall semester, research teams of two to three students interviewed faculty members and representatives of community-based organizations. Their research protocol consisted of semi-structured interviews designed to elicit interviewees' perceptions of our university's place-building role. In addition, student participants and interviewees were invited to complete an online or paper version of the PBS whose results were incorporated into in-class, guided, and collaborative interpretations of qualitative data; an end-of-semester focus group with the students; and into the second author's own, broader place-building research.

During the fall 2011 semester, through a grant from our university's Provost Fund for Scholarship and Professional Development, we introduced a participatory research model by building iPad technology into our research design. Each team, again consisting of two to three student researchers, administered the PBS to an assigned interviewee who, this time, represented a faculty, staff, or University administrator. In addition, students taught their interviewee how to use the iPad device and Evernote®, a commercially available application, with which interviewees captured and annotated images that visually summarized their perceptions of the university's place-building role along each of the five place-building dimensions. After processing the surveys, students shared the results with their interviewees and conducted a semi-structured interview around the images and annotations they had gathered. Data analysis, interpretation, and incorporation proceeded in a way similar to the 2010 protocol.

Products from our research include PBS results for students (pre/post) and interviewees; coded interview transcripts; focus group transcripts; charts depicting the location of interviewee perceptions and survey results along the place-building continuum; images and annotations (2011); student memos on their observations; and final reports presenting students' interpretations and syntheses of results. At the end of each semester, we conducted a focus group with students, which explored the meaning they were making from their interviews after considering key quantitative results from both their own and their interviewees' Place-Building Surveys. We asked the students to reflect on the interview results and discuss their insights, motivations, and experiences with respect to the research process and results.

Based on the focus group data, we have realized that in addition to engaging placekeeper groups in the process of participatory research, the curriculum appears to have had a noticeable impact on students' awareness of variation in placekeeper perceptions (e.g., they report having been previously unaware of faculty perspectives and how they can differ from those arising from other placekeeper groups); awareness of how the University values and enacts place; and perceptions of themselves as transformative place-building agents.

Community-Engaged Place-Building Research in the Curriculum:

Implications and Prospects

The place-building framework not only offers a method for describing, evaluating, and prescribing a university's location on the place-building continuum; it also offers a *process* for identifying tension for change among placekeepers and a *structure* for defining, debating, and envisioning a university's commitment to institutional social responsibility. The participatory nature of the design—the opportunity for students to serve both as researchers and study participants and for interviewees to interact with place-building perspectives and data through their interviews, PBS results, and the images they captured with the incorporation of iPad devices—initiates a dialogue between students and their interviewees, between interviewees and place-building researchers, potentially among placekeepers and between placekeeper groups (community partners, staff, administrators, faculty, students) that allows the community to unpack its perceptions of and define its vision for the university's place-based community engagement mission.

An applied anthropology curriculum is just one context in which place-building research can be embedded. It could be adapted with relative ease to a variety of courses, disciplines, and educational levels, including geography capstones, sociological research methods, environmental studies, organizational psychology, communication, business, higher education, and student affairs leadership courses—in other words, wherever there is room for an interdisciplinary, participatory, mixed methods, and community-engaged approach to assessing and negotiating place-based institutional social responsibility.

Of course, the place-building framework is efficacious outside of a community-engaged curriculum as well. Indeed, Thomas's place-building research in business and municipal organizations is conducted exclusively outside of this context. Thus, the place-building method could be employed in a variety of other ways in higher education, such as strategic planning initiatives; unit- or university-level self studies; and assessments of community-university relations and partnerships. Participating in place-building research offers the potential for any place-keeper to gain insight into their role in institutional, organizational, and individual place-building, which reflects on the institution's perceived level of community engagement.

In addition to its utility in applied and participatory research, it is useful to simultaneously see place-building as a theoretical paradigm for reflexive inquiry into community engagement itself. Butin's (2007) perspective (see also Chupp & Joseph, 2010) on status quo service-learning and social justice education sheds some light on this perspective. As part of his critique, Butin argues that both of these movements have been slowed by a kind of dilution:

> The top-down nature of such knowledge production and dissemination supports a perspective of service-learning first and foremost as a "technical" practice of (simply) an effective pedagogical practice without the attendant complexity or controversy. Likewise, social justice education—through the less-threatening discourses of "diversity," "multiculturalism," and "fairness"—has come to signify a stance available to all concerned with education…. Dilution thus serves, within both service-learning and social justice education, as a way to make initially difficult practices amenable to all with the consequence of undercutting and avoiding the very difficulty originally meant to be engaged (p. 178).

Arguably the same critique may be levied against community engagement, especially at the level of the institution. In their pursuit of a competitive advantage, e.g., with help from the Carnegie Foundation's Community Engagement classification (Carnegie Foundation, 2012), institutions of higher education can inadvertently dilute the complexity and controversy inherent in the construction and practice of community engagement by reducing it to a set of inventories (e.g., How many service-learning courses do we offer? How many of our students are engaged in service?), tag lines, and compelling human interest stories without critically examining the core values and strategies that undergird community engagement itself.

As we show in our university example above, place-building theory offers a lens through which this practice can be assessed and potentially transformed within the context of a participatory research framework. In addition to this evaluative approach, which recognizes the interdependence of organizations, placekeepers, and place itself, we also advocate using place-building theory to identify and address contested perceptions and values.

Through the act of gathering, validating, and interpreting placekeeper perceptions and experience, researchers and their collaborators intentionally identify and address structural inequalities, dissonances, hidden curricula, etc. We can evoke and communicate the polyvocality of placekeepers; we can uncover, illuminate, and engage with tensions that exist among competing narratives and meta-narratives. This approach, in concert with a participatory process, allows us to embrace the contingent nature of engagement and continue to transform community engagement from a technical practice to a deliberative, reflexive, and transparent institutional place-building paradigm.

Notes

The authors thank the fall 2010 and 2011 applied anthropology students for their enthusiastic involvement, engagement, and investment as students, researchers, collaborators, and citizens on this project. We also thank Sarah Wyscaver for her help with preparing our Institutional Review Board application; Tracey Lancaster for developing an online version of the PBS and compiling survey results; and Michaela Frank for her creative and industrious investments as a teaching and research assistant for our fall 2011 class. In addition, we thank the University of Northern Colorado's Provost Fund for Scholarship and Professional Development for its support of our 2011 community-engaged research.

References

Agnew, J. A. (1987). *Place and politics.* Boston: Allen & Unwin.

Alvesson, M., & Berg, P. O. (1991).*Corporate culture and organizational symbolism: An overview.* New York: W. de Gruyter.

Baba, M. 1994. The fifth subdiscipline: Anthropological practice and the future of Anthropology. *Human Organization, 53*(2), 174-186.

Carnegie Foundation (2012, February 4).*Community Engagement Elective Classification.* Retrieved February 4, 2012 from: http://classifications.carnegiefoundation.org/descriptions/community_engagement.php

Carroll, A. (1999). Corporate social responsibility: Evolution of a definitional construct. *Business and Society, 38*(3), 268-295.

Chaskin, R. J., Brown, P., Venkatesh, S. & Vidal, A. (2001). *Building community capacity.* New York: Aldine de Gruyter.

Chupp, M. G., & Joseph, J. L. (2010). Getting the most out of service learning: Maximizing student, university and community impact. *Journal of Community Practice, 18*(2), 190-212.

Dellheim, C. (1986). Business in time: The historian and corporate culture. *The Public Historian, 8,* 9-22.

Entrikin, J. N. (2000). *The betweenness of place: Towards a geography of modernity.* New York: Routledge.

Gans, H. J. (2002). The sociology of space: A use-centered view. *City and Community, 1(4),* 329-339.

Geertz, C. (1983). *Local knowledge.* New York: Basic Books.

Gieryn, T. F. (2000).A space for place in Sociology.*Annual Review of Sociology, 26,* 463-496.

Glaser, B., & Strauss, A. L. (1967). *The discovery of grounded theory: Strategies for qualitative research.* New York: Aldine de Gruyter.

Gustafson, P. (2005). Meanings of place: Everyday experience and theoretical conceptualizations. *Journal of Environmental Psychology, 21,* 5-16.

Harper, K. (2009). New directions in participatory visual ethnography: Possibilities for Public Anthropology. *98th meeting of the American Anthropological Association,* November 17-21, 2009, Philadelphia, PA.

Hatch, M. J. (1993).The dynamics of organizational culture.*The Academy of Management Review, 18(4),* 657-693.

Hudson, R. (2001). *Producing places.* New York: The Guilford Press.

Jacobs, J. (1984). *Cities and the wealth of nations.*New York: Random House.

Kotler, P. & Lee, N. (2005). *Corporate social responsibility: Doing the most good for your company and your cause.* Hoboken, N.J.: Wiley.

LeCompte, M. D. 1999.*Essential ethnographic methods: Observations, interviews, and questionnaires.* Lanham, VA: Alta Mira Press.

Massey, D., & Jess, P. (1995). *A place in the world?Places, cultures and globalization.*New York: Oxford Press.

Mayfield, L. (2001). Town and gown in America: Some historical and institutional issues of the engaged university. *Education for Health, 14(2),* 231-240.

Morgan, G. (1997). *Images of organizations.*(2nd Ed.). Thousand Oaks, CA: Sage.

Rodman, M. C. (1992). Empowering place: Multilocality and multivocality. *American Anthropologist, 94(3)* 640-656.

Sagoff, M. (1986). Values and preferences.*Ethics, 96(2),* 301-316.

Schneider, B., Brief, A. P., & Guzzo, R. A. (1996). Creating a climate and culture for sustainable organizational change. *Organizational Dynamics, Spring,* 7-18.

Schoenberger, E. (1997). *The cultural crisis of the firm*.Cambridge, MA: Blackwell.

Seamon, D. and Buttimer, A. (1980). *The human experience of space and place*.London: Croom Helm.

Smith, C. (1994). The new corporate philanthropy.*Harvard Business Review, 72*(3), 105-116.

Snyder, G. (1995). *A place in space: Ethics, aesthetics, and watersheds.* Washington, D.C.: Publishers Group West.

Staeheli, L. A. (2007) Place.In J. Agenew, K. Mitchell, & G. Toal (Eds.), *A companion to Political Geography* (pp. 157-169). New York: Blackwell Publishing.

Stoecker, R. (2003). Community-based research: From practice to theory and back again. *Michigan Journal of Community Service Learning, 10*(2), 35-46.

Stout, A. C. (2008). *New towns from gowns: Urban form and placemaking at college campuses.* (Masters thesis.) Retrieved March 28, 2011 from: http://hdl.handle.net/1721.1/44345.

Thomas, D. F. (2004). *Toward an understanding of organization place building in communities*.Unpublished doctoral dissertation, Colorado State University, Fort Collins, Colorado.

Thomas, D. F. & Cross, J. (2007). Organizations as place builders. *Journal of Behavioral and Applied Management, 9*(1), 33-61.

Tuan, Yi-Fu. (1977). *Space and place: The perspective of experience.* Minneapolis, MN: University of Minnesota Press. University of Northern Colorado.*University District*. Retrieved February 4, 2012 from http://www.unco.edu/universitydistrict

Vogel, D. (2005). The low value of virtue. *Harvard Business Review, 83*(6), 26.

Werlen, B. (1993). *Society, action, and space: An alternative human geography.* London: Routledge.

Williams, R. (1989) *Resources of hope: Culture, democracy, socialism.* New York: Verso Publishers.

Wood, D. (1991). Corporate social performance revisited. *The Academy of Management Review, 16*(4), 691-718.

Wright, S. (1994). (Ed.). *Anthropology of organizations.* New York: Routledge.

Authors

MICHAEL J. KIMBALL (Michael.kimball@unco.edu) is an associate professor of Anthropology and directs the University of Northern Colorado's Center for Honors, Scholars & Leadership. A 2006 winner of Maine Campus Compact's Donald Harward Faculty Award for Service Learning Excellence and 2007/08 Robert O. Schulze Chair in Interdisciplinary Studies, Kimball collaborates with Thomas on place-building research, teaches community-engaged and local and international service-learning courses, and co-leads university strategic planning and initiatives for engaged scholarship and learning.

DAVID F. THOMAS (david.thomas@unco.edu) is an assistant professor of Management. He is responsible for the program development of the University of Northern Colorado's Entrepreneurship program. This innovative program concentrates on the applied aspects of entrepreneurship with an emphasis on supporting student start-up opportunities and collaboration with the Northern Colorado business community. University of Northern Colorado has recognized his contributions to students and faculty as both advisor of the year and professor of the year in the Monfort College of Business. His research has produced a new model for describing and evaluating how organizations contribute to their communities. His models have been instrumental in helping communities recruit and retain best fitting firms. Thomas serves as a board member on the Rocky Mountain Initiative Institute and is actively involved in community development initiatives in the region.

(Endnotes)

1. Readers wishing to review or complete the Place-Building Survey may contact David Thomas at David.Thomas@unco.edu.

10

FUTURE OF ORGANIZATIONAL PLACE BUILDING: CONCEPTUAL AND RESEARCH POTENTIAL

In this chapter, we present four key developments we see as emerging in future work with organizational place building: expansion of application, pursuing the notion of levels of application, exploring the role of placelessness and authenticity, and the importance of organizational symbols and artifacts in understanding organizational place building. Following the developments, we present a taxonomy for organizational place building and give illustrations of its utility. We believe if attention is given to these developments and the taxonomy, then future efforts in application and research of organizational place building will be enhanced.

Expansion of Application

One, the place building model has been primarily focused on business organizations with a few looking at the organizational aspect of education. In the future, we see the model making significant contributions to a wider range of organizations, particularly those that have a unique relationship to the community, such as non-profit service organizations, churches, and other unique organizations. For example, a unique organizational relationship between organization and community can be found in professional sports organizations. The combination of consumer and fan presents unique challenges and responsibilities to both community and the sports organization (Alonso & O'Shea, 2012), and a study of this relationship from a building organizational place perspective could be instructive. From a community and organizational perspective, place building can guide a community in recruiting and retaining best fitting organizations. Recruiting best fitting organizations can save a community from the costs, both economic and social, from recruiting organization's whose values are not aligned with the community.

Organizational Place Building: Levels of Application

Behavioral concepts are often employed at different levels. In a very common way to use behavioral concepts, for example, we can talk about a person being angry, or an organization or group of persons being angry, or larger entities like nations being angry. Concepts like "place building" imply implementation of a process, and this type of activity is often presented in terms of levels. For example, Banning and Kaiser (1974), in their work regarding implementing campus designs to better serve the mental health needs of community, suggest three levels of implementation. Level one is termed "macrodesign" where the focus is on the entire campus environment. Level two is "macrodesign" and represents efforts of implementing programs targeted at specific campus groups. The third level is referred to as "life space design" and is concerned with the individual. Bronfenbrenner (1979), in his presentation of human development from an ecological perspective, also included levels of settings that influence the individual. He used the term "microsystems" to refer to the immediate environmental setting, like the home. The concept of "mesosystem" is used to refer to the influences outside the home, for example, schools and peer groups. More distant influences like legal systems and media are termed "exosystems." Finally, Bronfenbrenner uses the term "macrosystems" to denote the level of influence represented by values and traditions of a society that impact all of the other systems.

This second area for development of the organizational place building model follows the above work regarding levels of implementation and influence. Most, but not all studies to date, have looked at organizational place building as occurring between organizations and the community. This level of place building can be referred to as "macro organizational/community" level. Chapter 8 looked at the relationship between a higher education organization and the sub organizations of student organizations, but there are many other rich opportunities for exploration within many additional types of organizations and the sub-units within, both in terms of how the units build place with the "main" organization, and how the sub-units build place with each other. The level of place building assessment and implementation can be denoted as a "micro sub-organizational" level. Finally, the building place model can also be extended to individuals within the organization. Clearly, some employees take on an exploitive or contingent relationship while others build more of a contributive/transformational relationship to the organization. The concept of "life place building" would capture place building at the individual level. Exploration of the levels concept holds interesting promise for the future.

Placelessness and inauthenticity

The concepts of placelessness and authentic place comprise the third area of exploration. Placelessness (Relph, 1976) is defined by an uncritical acceptance of mass values and efficiency techniques that lead to sameness and the lack of community or sense of place uniqueness. The issue of placelessness becomes important to place building, especially when place is being designed and built between a local community and a nationally branded organization where brand protection often includes processes of mass communication, mass values, and corporate control that tend to override local conditions. These processes can produce the conditions that relate to Relph's concepts of authenticity and inauthenticity. Relph (1976) notes the following:

An authentic sense of place is "a direct and genuine experience of the entire complex of the identity of places" (p. 64). He describes inauthentic sense of place as being mediated and distorted through a series of quite arbitrary social and intellectual fashions about how that experience should be, following stereotyped conventions. Key to organizational place building that produces a transformational relationship between the organization and the community is full appreciation of all conditions of the sense of place for the community without the conditions of placelessness and inauthenticity being imposed from outside the community. How these conditions related to all aspects of the organizational place building typology and its components call for future exploration of the interface between organizational place building and organizational symbols/artifacts.

Symbols/Artifacts and Organizations

A symbol can be defined as "any object, figure, or image that represents something else, such as a flag, a logo, a pictogram. A written or spoken word can be regarded as a particular symbol . . ." (VandenBos, 2007). Organizations use and can be described by a number of different symbols—logos, mission statements, physical structures (nature of the design of the building, for example). Penn (N.D.) defines the use of symbols in corporate culture:

> Symbols can shape how individuals in a corporation think about their organization. The culture is expressed in terms of public symbols and the use of these symbols creates a sense of solidarity between individuals. Corporate symbols express the ideology of the organization in a simple way so that the ideas they express can be reinforced easily. Symbols used to express corporate culture can be verbal stories, ritualized events, and physical artifacts. (Retrieved from http://smallbusiness.chron.com/symbolic-approach-corporate-culture-16076.html)

Rafaeli and Worline (2000) summarize the importance of symbols in organizational culture and point to the four functions they serve: symbol as reflection of organizational culture, symbol as a trigger of internalized values and norms, symbol as a frame for conversation about experiences, and symbol as an integrator of organizational systems of meaning.

Relationship of Organizational Place to Organizational Artifacts

A major source for understanding organizational place is provided by viewing organizational artifacts as symbols of place communication. Organizational place includes the social and physical aspects the organization's functioning, and it also can include the member/people made objects or artifacts (Strange & Banning, 2015). These artifacts can include art, adornments, modifications of structures, the landscape, furnishing, and other organizational objects (Prown, 1982). The importance of the organization's material artifacts is underscored by Hetherington's observation that "At the very least, the story of place cannot make sense without them" (1997, p. 183). Banning, Middleton, and Deniston (2008) developed a taxonomy for the multicultural messages sent by educational artifacts of artwork and posters, signs, graffiti, and other person made objects.

Using a similar approach, organizational artifacts can be classified by the taxonomy of organizational place building. (See figure 1.) For example, Whole Foods often provides a waste disposal kiosk with explicit instructions and physical examples of which items are for recycling and which items are for waste. This material artifact (kiosk) signals a prescriptive stance to have its customers participate in valuing the dimensions of nature/sustainability of resources and suggest a contributive if not transformative (customer may transfer the learning at Whole foods and change their own home disposal practices) place identity. But, is this symbol a public relations trick, or is it consistent with its mission? A look at its mission statement indicates an alignment of mission and place values. For example, in concert with the Whole Foods Market mission statement, eight core values are listed including one that reflects the kiosk: "We Practice and Advance Environmental Stewardship." (Retrieved from www.wholdfoodsmarket.com.) In contrast, many "fast-food" establishments only provide one waste disposal unit (without single stream capabilities) for customers to return every item except the large serving trays. The results of these actions would suggest a place identity of exploitive where little obligation to the local nature is present and little value is given to place within the community and responsibility to environmental stewardship. As noted in this example, a taxonomy for understanding organizational place building is useful.

A Taxonomy for Organizational Place Building: A Visual for Connections and Intersections

The concept of taxonomy is typically noted as stemming from Greek concepts of denoting a method of arranging and is used today to describe a method to group things together. The purpose of a taxonomy (Milgram & Kishino, 1994) is to present an ordered classification system that allows and promotes discussions that are focused, developments that are evaluated, research that is conducted, and data that is meaningfully compared. Figure 1 represents a taxonomy for place building *concepts* and provides a visual for understanding the connections and intersection possibilities. It is designed around three dimensions with each dimension containing sub-categories. The dimensions of Principles of Place Building contain the categories of evaluative, descriptive, and prescriptive. The Relationship Type dimension holds the categories of exploitive, contingent, contributive and transformational. The third category of the cube pertains to the dimensions of Place Building: ethics, social, economics, nature, and material. The cells of the taxonomy provide the placement of organizational concepts that are described by the three dimensions of the cube. These "cells for concepts" could contain the various actions and symbols that an organization employs intentionally or unintentionally to communicate its place in the community. For example, the expansion of an organization's physical structure into a neighboring treed area used informally by the community causing the trees to be removed could be seen as falling into the cell described by evaluative, exploitive, and nature. Categories and cells of the taxonomy are not crisp, but fuzzy, so boundaries are often blurred and items may not be rendered with a clear placement within categories. Multiple interpretations may be available.

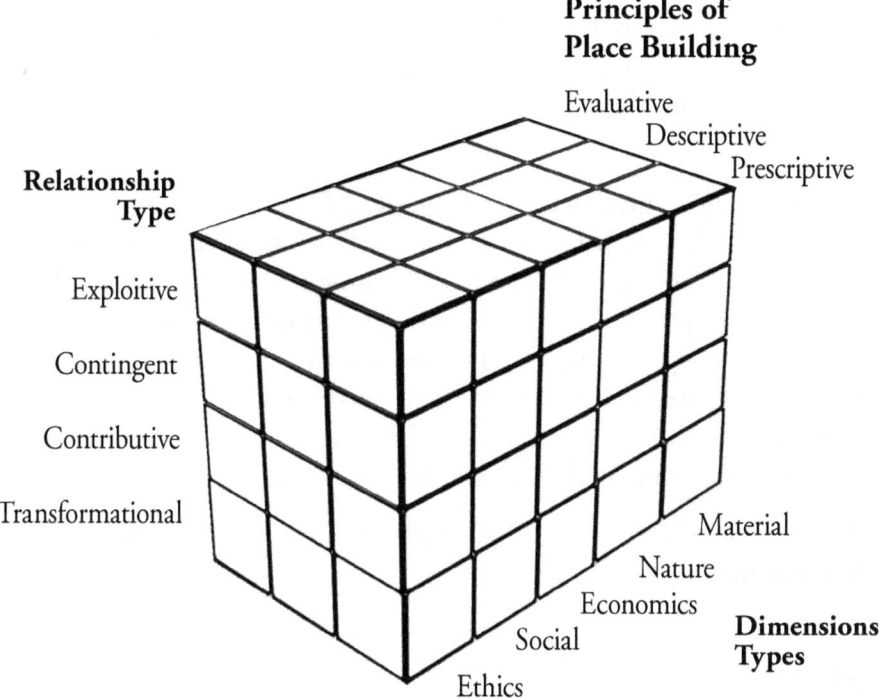

Figure 1: A Taxonomy for Place Building

How to use the Taxonomy for Place Building

To use the place building taxonomy for classification of organizational behavior and symbols/artifacts, a series of questions can be asked to guide the process. First, the behavior/artifact can be observed/questioned from the principle's perspective. Is there evidence that the behavior/artifact gives an indication that organizational place is going to be intentionally (prescriptive) used within the wider community? Does the behavior/artifact give an indication of the significance or worth (evaluative) of the organization's notion of place? Or, does the behavior/artifact only describe (descriptive) the status of place within the organization?

Next in the process of using the template are a series of questions regarding the dimensions of place: nature, social, material, ethics, and economic. Are these concepts reflected in the behavior/artifact that is being examined for classification? For example, do the items reflect any notion regarding the landscape or natural resources (nature)? A similar question, then, is asked regarding the remaining dimensions of place.

Finally, by examining the principles and dimensions of the behavior or artifact, the organization's place building can then be judged to be transformational, contributive, contingent, or exploitive. The results of the process of classifying organizational behavioral/artifact symbols allows the purpose of taxonomy to utilized. It allows and promotes focused discussions on the evaluation of new developments, the implementation of research, and the opportunity for data to be meaningfully compared (Milgram & Kishino, 1994).

Illustrations: The Taxonomy for Place Building and Mission Statements

We share several illustrations or examples for the use of the Taxonomy for Place Building involving mission statements as symbols and conclude with a detailed guide on how to use the principles of place building dimension of the cube to explore and identify the type of place builder (Relationship Type dimension of the cube).

Mission Statements as Symbols

Mission statements are often used to symbolize organizations and are typically brief statements that speak to the questions such as who are we, what is our purpose, where are we going, how are we going to accomplish it, and why do we exist? (Bart, 2001). In essence, they stand for the culture and purpose of the organization. Pearce and David (1987) identified three major categories that capture the common characteristics of most mission statements. The first category includes the organization's primary services or products. The second category includes the goals of the organization. The third category comprises the organization's philosophy. We add a fourth category: the role of a mission statement as a symbol of organizational place (see Chapter 5). The Taxonomy for Place Building Symbols, then, can be used to deepen the understanding of what the mission statement communicates and what it does not. For example, we present the *two* mission statements associated with the coffee house sector and place each statement within a cell of the taxonomy. (http://www.missionstatements.com/coffee_house_mission_statements.html)

Starbucks:

Mission Statement: To inspire and nurture the human spirit—one person, one cup and one neighborhood at a time.

This mission statement would fall within the prescriptive principle (to inspire and nurture), speaks most directly to the social dimension (human spirit), and is focused on contributing as an identity for its place.

City on a Hill Coffee:

Mission Statement: Our mission is to operate a sustainable retail specialty coffee shop and wholesale coffee roasting business to serve people and positively contribute to our local community and our partner coffee-growing communities.

This mission statement would fall within the evaluative principle (to serve and positively contribute), focuses on the economic dimension (contribute to our local community and our partner coffee-growing communities), and would give support to a contributive place identity. By suggesting interest in the "partner coffee-growing communities," the mission statement moves toward the transformational; again, cells are fuzzy not crisp. Fuzzy cells are preferred as they encourage reflection and exploration. The latter is the hallmark of advancing a business model that illustrates how an organization competes, often using local resources and other raw materials to fashion some competitive advantage. It may be that an organization's strategic resources and assets can be utilized to advance policies that favor both the organization and the community. The utilization of strategic resources, or how they are employed, is a key indicator of how place is valued.

Vail and Associates:

Mission Statement: Our mission is simple: Experience of a Lifetime. At Vail Resorts, our mission is simply to create the experience of a life time.

They espouse the values of serving others, doing right, driving value, doing good, being safe, and having fun. Their mission statement would fall within two principles: the evaluative and the descriptive. The evaluative principle (to serve and positively contribute) focuses on the relationship to its employees and customers. The "fun" or recreational aspect would seem to fit within the tourism and hospitality industries. The descriptive principles (describe the status of place within the organization) focus on the social network in which it lives. The organization's contributions are intended to gain recognition and favorably position the firm as an important player in the community.

Fort Collins Chamber of Commerce:

Mission statement: The Fort Collins Area Chamber of Commerce champions our community and region's quality of life and economic vitality through strong business advocacy and collaborative leadership.

This mission statement would fall within the evaluative principle (to serve and positively contribute), focuses on the economic dimension (contribute to our local community and our business community), and would give support to contributive place identity. The mission statement positions the Chamber as the city's advocate for economic growth and inaugurating a quality of life.

Illustrations: The Taxonomy and the Principles of Place Building

The three principles of place building, as described in the taxonomy *(descriptive, prescriptive, and evaluative)* can be used as a guide to identify the type of place builder. A brief explanation of each principle as it relates to the type of place builder is included here as a guide in matching a place principle in identifying the place building organization.

The first principle is descriptive (see Figure 2) in the sense of strategies that reveal how an organization values or de-values place (Thomas, 2004; Thomas & Cross, 2007; Kimball & Thomas, 2012). The organization's valuation of place informs how the organization *designates the use of space* in ways that ascribe meaning and reflect the organization's culture.

The second principle of evaluative (see Figure 3) reveals how an organization *determines the significance, worth, or condition of a place* and how that organization assesses or estimates the quality or condition of a place relative to its role. Each organization determines the significance of place across five dimensions (see Figure 1). This can be apparent in terms of the words and intentions of its Mission Statement.

The third principle of prescriptive (see Figure 4) specifies, generally through its mission statement, its intentions toward the wider community: how it will *use resources and engage in activities that impact the community* and what social and ethical responsibilities it acknowledges and strives to meet.

These three principles of the essential values of place building we contend are evident in the organization's business model, especially in its strategic intentions, and are illustrative of its mission statement.

Descriptive. Place building is described in terms of how the organization value(s) place, which is informative rather than normative, i.e., place building is discussed as expressing the quality, kind, or condition (or strategy employed) of place building in each of the five place dimensions.

Place Builder Identity	Description
Exploitive	Organization values place in quantifiable terms that describe place as a product or commodity. The organization negotiates its position in the community without regard to the impact of its operations and operates outside acceptable practices – no local knowledge of the place and its historic or cultural history.
Contingent	Values place primarily in measurable terms. What is the return on its contributions to place (i.e. how does the organization gauge its investments and estimates of the economic and financial worth to the organization)? What economic and political advantages can be gained that advance its mission?
Contributive	Values place in terms of its social network. The organization's contributions are intended to gain recognition and favorably position the owner or leader as an important player in the community.
Transformational	Values place equally on all five place dimensions. The organization invests its assets to build competitive advantages for both place and organization. Assumes a leadership role in advancing new community capacities and competencies that improve community well-being.

Figure 2. Descriptive

Prescriptive. The organization specifies, generally identified by an organization's mission statement and its business model, *how it orders the use of its strategic resources and assets* to restore or protect place, e.g., restoring natural forest conditions (in the case of nature), attracting new businesses and industries that build commerce (economic), creating new opportunities to invest in community (social and ethic relationships), and how it views its social contract or responsibility (ethics) to its stakeholders.

Type of place builder	Designates the use of strategic resources and assets that value and/or de-value place.
Exploitive	To capture financial gains through aggressive and organization-centric strategies that often value place as an acquisition or commodity.
Contingent	Conditional development of resources and assets to attain some good or purpose for the firm's benefit.
Contributive	Commits resources and assets to help build place, seek membership community organizations as a way of enhancing its reputation as a contributor.
Transformational	Commits resources and assets to lead and create new opportunities for civic participation and economic partnerships. An advocate for change and improvements consistent with its and the community's business mission and purposes.

Figure 3. Prescriptive

Evaluative. The evaluative aspect of place building details how an organization assesses and appraises the significance, worth, or condition of a place. How the organization assesses or estimates the value(s) of place (in terms of social, economic, ethical, architecture, and nature) to the organization and its stakeholders. How the organization assesses or estimates the value(s) of place is conducted in terms of what place offers, what it provides or furnishes in the way of resources to the community and the organization. To an organization, it means those natural and human resources that are accessible and provide unique opportunities to the organization that can create a competitive advantage.

Type of place builder	Description
Exploitive	Assesses value of place primarily as an economic factor. It monetizes place and spaces as resources for its own purposes.
Contingent	Calculates the value of place in terms of its worth based on what it can contribute to the organization. What place affords that can enhance its market position and business model.
Contributive	Determine values based on the organization's relationship to some propositional good, such as the owners "fit" in the community.
Transformational	Determines the value of place based on the shared qualities of all five dimensions (economics, ethic, social, nature and the built environment). Each of which are viewed for their intrinsic values that gain prominence from an integrated and complex setting in which it operates. Transformational organizations can help revive the long dormant assets in a community by changing their business structure(s) to facilitate new investments in community capacity and or adopting new policies that value place on all five dimensions.

Figure 4. Evaluative

In summary, how an organization aligns its business operation, evident in its Mission Statement and business model, can predict its likely behavior as one of the four types of place builders. Thus, in recruiting best fitting organizations as co-place builders, it is important to partner with its community in creating a new rigor to economic development that stretches beyond a single focused approach. A detailed exploration of organizational/community place decisions and activities will be enhanced by the use of an organizational place building taxonomy. It promotes the asking of deeper questions in both application and research endeavors to understand the connections and intersections of organizational place building. The future research efforts will continue to employ qualitative methods (Thomas & Banning, 2014), as well as the development of quantitative surveys (Thomas, Kimball, & Suhr, 2016), along with the use of a mixed methods approach that *can* strengthen future research by combining quantitative and qualitative methods.

The use of the Organizational Place Building Inventory (OPBI) (see Chapter 6), in concert with a qualitative method, is an effective tool in advancing a different and richer discussion on the reasons for being responsible in and for a community. We suggest that the OPBI can provide a participatory and deliberative process through which organizations can describe and explain how they build place via their business model and possibly predict the likely contributions they will make based on their place building profiles. The place building research takes a more comprehensive view of the contributions the organizations make in defining place and will assist organizations and communities in leveraging their assets that can lead to a sustainable competitive advantage for both organizations and their community.

References

Alonso, A. D., & O'Shea, M. (2012). "You only get back what you put in": Perceptions of professional sport organizations as community anchors. *Community Development,* 43(5), 656-676.

Banning, J. H., Middleton, V., & Deniston, T. (2008). Using photographs to assess equity climate: A taxonomy. *Multicultural Perspectives,* 10(1), 1-6.

Bart, C. K. (2001). Exploring the application of mission statement on the World Wide Web. *Internet Research: Electronic Networking Applications and Policy,* 11, 360–368.

Hetherington, K. (1997). In place of geometry: The materiality of place. *The Sociological Review,* 45(S-1), 183-199.

Milgram, P., & Kishino, F. (1994). A taxonomy of mixed reality visual displays. *IEICE Transactions on Information Systems, E77-D* (12). Retrieved from http://vered.rose.utoronto.ca/people/paul_dir?IEICE94/ieice.html

Penn, S. (2016.) *The symbolic approach in corporate culture.* Houston, TX: Houston Chronicle. Retrieved from: http://smallbusiness.chron.com/symbolic-approach-corporate-culture-16076.html

Pearce, J. A. & David, F. (1987). Corporate mission statements: The bottom line. *Academy of Management Executives,* 1, 109-115.

Prown, J. D. (1982). Mind in matter: An introduction to culture theory and method. *Winterthur Portfolio,* 17(1), 1-19.

Rafaeli, A., & Worline, M. (2000). Symbols in organizational culture. In N. M. Ashkanasy, C. P.

M. Wilderson, & M. F. Peterson. (Eds). *Handbook of organizational culture and climate.* (71-84). Thousand Oaks: CA. Sage Publications.

Relph, E. (1976). Place and Placelessness. London: Pion.

Strange, C. C., & Banning, J. H. (2015). *Designing for learning: Creating campus environments for student success.* San Francisco, CA: Jossey-Bass.

Thomas, D. F, & Banning, J. H. (2014). Place building and mission statements: A match or misfit? *Journal of Contemporary Issues in Business Research, 3*(2), 52-74.

Thomas, D. F., Kimball, M., & Suhr, D. (2016). The organizational place building inventory. *The Journal of Corporate Citizenship Issues, 63*, 17-41. DOI: 10.9774/GLEAF.4700.2016.SE.00004

VandenBos, G. R. (Ed.). (2007). *APA dictionary of psychology.* Washington, D.C.: American Psychological Association.

ABOUT THE EDITORS:

David F. Thomas

David Thomas is an Adjunct Professor of Business at Regis University and President & CEO of the Stove Prairie Group. He has held various senior level positions in the travel and tourism industry. In addition, he has managed corporate start-up enterprises and small business turn around operations. After receiving his Ph.D. from Colorado State University in organizational development, his career focused on exploring new models for describing and evaluating how an organization contributes to their community. His research models have been instrumental in developing economic programs that advance a community's recruit and retain best fitting firms.

During his career, David has authored and co-authored several journal articles on organization place building. Both the University of Northern Colorado and Regis University have recognized his contributions to students and faculty as both advisor and teaching at the graduate and undergraduate level.

James H. Banning

Jim Banning is professor emeritus in the School of Education at Colorado State University. After receiving his Ph.D. in clinical psychology from the University of Colorado-Boulder, his career has focused on student services administration, ecological/environmental psychology, and the application of environmental psychology to educational settings. He has particularly focused on the application of the ecological perspective and the development of the campus ecology model and has taught a course in campus ecology in the Student Affairs in Higher Education Program at Colorado State University for more than 30 years and continues to teach an online version. In addition to teaching, Jim's administrative leadership experience has included Director of Counseling and Testing, University of Colorado, Vice Chancellor for Student Affairs, University of Missouri-Columbia, and Vice President for Student Affairs, Colorado State University. During his career, Jim has authored and co-authored several books, book chapters, and journal articles on the ecological perspective of student services, including the recent publications of *Designing for Learning: Creating Campus Environments for Student Success*, *Student Affairs Leadership: Defining the Role Through an Ecological Framework* and *Campus Ecology and University Affairs: History, Applications, and Future.*

www.ingramcontent.com/pod-product-compliance
Lightning Source LLC
Chambersburg PA
CBHW060457090426
42735CB00011B/2015